A WORLD OF CONFLICT/1987

Canada Among Nations

A WORLD OF CONFLICT/1987

Canada Among Nations

EDITED BY MAUREEN APPEL MOLOT AND BRIAN W. TOMLIN
THE NORMAN PATERSON SCHOOL OF INTERNATIONAL AFFAIRS, CARLETON UNIVERSITY

James Lorimer & Company, Publishers
Toronto, 1988

ISBN
1-55028-045-7 paper
1-55028-046-5 cloth

ISSN 0832-0683

Cover Design: Falcom Design & Communications
Cover Photo: Canapress Photo Service

James Lorimer & Company, Publishers
Egerton Ryerson Memorial Building
35 Britain Street
Toronto, Ontario M5A 1R7

Printed and bound in Canada

6 5 4 3 2 1   88 89 90 91 92 93

Contents

Tables and Figures   vii

The Authors   ix

Preface   xi

Part I: Canada's International Policies   1

1   A World of Conflict
    Maureen Appel Molot and Brian W. Tomlin   3
2   Managing Global Conflict: Canada and International
    Summitry
    John Kirton   22

Part II: International Security   41

3   Regional Conflict: De-escalation and Prospects
    for Resolution
    Brian S. Mandell   43
4   Call to Arms: Canadian National Security Policy
    Fen Osler Hampson   68

Part III: International Political Economy   93

5   The World Economy: Consultation Without Performance
    John M. Curtis   95
6   Weathering the Storm: North America in the Global
    Economy
    Murray G. Smith   106

Part IV: International Development   117

7   The Environment and North-South Conflict
    John T. O'Manique   119
8   Canada and North-South Conflict
    David R. Morrison   136

Part V: Canada-U.S. Relations   159

9   Canada-U.S. Trade Disputes and the Free Trade Deal
    David Leyton-Brown   161
10 Conflict over Common Property: Canada-U.S.
    Environmental Issues
    Don Munton   178

Part VI: The Year in Review   199

11 1987: Chronology and Statistical Profile
    D. Keith Heintzman   201

Notes and References   227

Tables and Figures

Table 2-1	Prime Minister Mulroney's Summit Meetings by Partner, September 1984 to March 1987	*35*
Table 5-1	Annual Changes in Real Output, 1982-87	*98*
Table 5-2	Unemployment Rates in the OECD Area, 1982-87	*98*
Table 5-3	Interest Rate and Consumer Price Index Movements in 1987	*99*
Table 5-4	General Government Financial Balances, Surplus or Deficit as a Percentage of GNP/GDP	*101*
Figure 5-1	Current Account Balance of OECD Countries as a Percentage of GNP/GDP	*102*
Figure 11-1	Economic Performance of Ten OECD Countries: Percentage Change in GDP from the Previous Year, 1982-86	*219*
Figure 11-2	Trade Balance of Ten OECD Countries, 1982-86	*220*
Figure 11-3	Growth in Exports of Ten OECD Countries: Percentage Change from the Previous Year, 1982-86	*221*
Figure 11-4	Share of World Exports of Ten OECD Countries,1982-86	*222*
Figure 11-5	Military Expenditures of Ten OECD Countries, 1982-86	*223*
Figure 11-6	Relative Military Expenditures of Ten OECD Countries, 1982-86	*224*
Figure 11-7	Public Expenditures for Development Assistance of Ten OECD Countries, 1982-86	*225*
Figure 11-8	Relative Expenditures for Development Assistance of Ten OECD Countries, 1982-86	*226*

The Authors

John M. Curtis is an adjunct professor in The Norman Paterson School of International Affairs, Carleton University, and senior policy advisor, Trade Negotiations Office.

Fen Osler Hampson is an assistant professor in The Norman Paterson School of International Affairs, Carleton University, and research associate at the Canadian Institute for International Peace and Security.

D. Keith Heintzman is a doctoral candidate in the Department of Political Science, Carleton University.

John Kirton is an associate professor in the Department of Political Science, University of Toronto.

David Leyton-Brown is an associate professor of political science and deputy director of the Centre for International and Strategic Studies, York University.

Brian S. Mandell is an assistant professor in The Norman Paterson School of International Affairs, Carleton University.

Maureen Appel Molot is an associate professor and associate director of The Norman Paterson School of International Affairs, Carleton University.

David R. Morrison is professor of comparative development and political studies and dean of arts and science at Trent University.

Don Munton is an associate professor in the Department of Political Science, University of British Columbia.

John T. O'Manique is a professor in The Norman Paterson School of International Affairs, Carleton University.

Murray G. Smith is director of the International Economics Program, Institute for Research on Public Policy, Ottawa.

Brian W. Tomlin is a professor and director of The Norman Paterson School of International Affairs, Carleton University.

Preface

This is the fourth in a series of annual volumes on Canada in international affairs produced by The Norman Paterson School of International Affairs at Carleton University. Organized around the just-completed calendar year, each publication presents an analysis and assessment of Canada's foreign policies as well as significant developments in the domestic and external environments that shape policy.

The annual does not simply review international events and Canadian international behaviour in the preceding year; nor is it our intention to offer an alternative package of priorities and policies for Canada. Rather, we hope to provide a better understanding of important developments in Canadian policies and the environments that influence them and, thereby, to contribute to the ongoing debate about appropriate policies and priorities for this country. Selection of the calendar year as an organizing focus for the book admittedly imposes constraints on authors because policies and issues, both domestic and international, are not in themselves discontinuous from one year to the next. Some demarcation principle is necessary to our enterprise, however, and the calendar year offers a convenient time frame for analysis, while the series itself provides continuity across the years.

This fourth volume has as its theme conflict in the global system and the way in which the wide spectrum of international conflicts affects Canada, and the way Canada responds to them. Many of the chapters focus on conflict — regional, military, economic, North-South and Canada-U.S. — while others address opportunities for, and examples of, conflict resolution. As in other volumes in this series, each chapter in the present collection addresses either the international environment or aspects of Canada's situation in that environment, as well as the prospects for and implications of continuity or change in those areas selected for inclusion: the structures of policy making; international security, political economy and development; and relations with the United States.

Financial support for this project was provided by The Norman Paterson School of International Affairs and the Social Sciences and Humanities Research Council of Canada. The editors are grateful to the contributors for their willingness to participate in the endeavour, and to the faculty and staff of The Norman Paterson School of International Affairs who provided valuable advice and assistance. Special thanks are due to the school's administrator, Brenda Sutherland, for her role in preparing the manuscript and to Tracey Goodman for her research assistance.

MAUREEN APPEL MOLOT
BRIAN W. TOMLIN
Ottawa
January 1988

Canada's International Policies

1 | A World of Conflict

MAUREEN APPEL MOLOT and
BRIAN W. TOMLIN

Nineteen hundred and eighty-seven was a year of conflict and instability among nations. Leaders of the world's foremost nations, including Canada, grappled with a series of seemingly intractable issues on economic, military and political fronts. The world economy appeared headed towards a return to the volatility that had prevailed during the first half of the decade. And despite significant progress by the superpowers on arms control, a number of protracted regional conflicts continued unabated, with their attendant risks of superpower involvement and escalation.

The articles in this volume discuss a variety of international conflicts — economic, environmental, military, political, global and regional — many of which appear to be difficult to resolve, others for which solutions, short or longer term, were proferred during 1987. Common to many of these conflicts was the fact that existing mechanisms for conflict management or resolution were insufficient to address the fundamental problems that generated deep-seated disputes. Our aim here is to examine these various conflicts — their causes and consequences, and their implications for Canada — and identify the role that Canada has played, as a protagonist, a mediator or even simply as observer.

As Canada continued the consideration of its proper role in the world through a series of Green and White Papers, parliamentary studies and reports, and government responses, the international conditions that would, in the end, do most to shape the Canadian role changed with a speed that frustrated efforts to make policy congruent with the changing global environment. Even as the decision to put Canada's economic eggs in the American basket was being implemented through bilateral trade negotiations, the U.S. economy was faltering; and the deterrence rhetoric used to justify increased Canadian defence spending was being undermined by Soviet-American rapprochement.

The conflict and instability that marked international affairs during 1987 posed difficult choices for Canada. In a world badly needing

conciliators, and one offering new opportunities for mediation, Canada
had to choose its initiatives in this regard carefully. Canadian resources
and capacity to influence outcomes are not limitless, and a government
response to all of the demands for involvement and action would severely
tax capabilities. Furthermore, in many of the disputes, Canada was more
protagonist than potential mediator, with only limited opportunities to
ameliorate conflicts. Here too, choice was necessary, as the government
had to stake out its position through policy statements and actions,
choosing sides in an effort to shape international events.

These assessments and conclusions about Canada's international
policies and the forces influencing them emerge from the analyses
contained in this volume. Among additional arguments made are the
following:

- As seen through the eyes of foreign policy planners, Canadians
  confront a world of conflict and limited options where scarce
  resources and domestic priorities circumscribe the role that Canada
  may play. From the perspective of Canadian parliamentarians, on the
  other hand, Canada should extend its participation in a world that
  requires Canada's constructive internationalism more than ever.
- Through its contribution to the seven-power, francophone, and Commonwealth summits of 1987, Canada has assumed a central role in
  the principal conflicts that confront the nations of the Western
  community in their relations with one another, and in their relationships with the nations of the impoverished and strife-torn South.
- Movement towards greater stability in Soviet-American relations in
  1987 did not produce any positive spillover to the various regions of
  the world, where numerous conflicts continued unabated without
  any prospect for resolution in sight.
- The Mulroney government's defence White Paper charted a dramatic new course for Canadian defence policy, one intended to
  catapult Canada into the ranks of a great maritime power.
- Notwithstanding the efforts at international consultation during
  1987, the market, rather than policy makers, forced much of the
  international economy policy coordination that occurred during the
  year.
- Although the political momentum behind the U.S. omnibus trade bill
  had waned in late 1987, the glowing embers of American protectionism could be re-ignited by continued high trade deficits, and the
  Canada-U.S. free trade agreement could be caught up in manoeu-

vring between the Congress and president over the trade bill.

• There is a growing prospect of North-South conflict arising out of different perceptions of development and its environmental consequences, as a new dimension of ecological threat increases international tensions and shifts them more to a North-South axis.

• The government strengthened its commitment to infuse Canada's external relations with a central concern for human rights, yet proposed legislation to control refugee abuses that may contravene both the Charter of Rights and Freedoms and international law.

• The attempt to manage bilateral conflict with the United States through the free trade negotiations paradoxically created conflict within Canada.

• Canada has become increasingly dependent on the United States with respect to the quality of its environment, and continues to be frustrated by the refusal of the Reagan administration to respond to the acid rain issue with policy proposals.

Canada Among Nations: 1987

Each of the chapters in *Canada Among Nations 1987* addresses a particular dimension of international conflict during the last calendar year, as well as Canada's role in a world of conflict and the characteristics of the global system that constrain or shape Canadian foreign policy priorities and alternatives. The remainder of this chapter examines Canada's position with respect to a number of international conflicts. Of central concern here are the various government statements that set out official policy, as well as public assessments of Canada's international policies and the record of Canadian behaviour during 1987 in a number of different settings. Chapter 2 focuses on international summitry as a means of conflict resolution and explores Canada's participation in a number of international summits held in the last year. Summitry has assumed an important role in the efforts of world leaders to manage an unstable international environment, and Canada has made summit participation a key feature of its foreign policy.

The second section of the volume addresses the international politico-security system. In contrast to the improvement in superpower relations, which was highlighted by the December signing of a U.S.-U.S.S.R. arms control treaty, chapter 3 discusses the continuation of three important regional conflicts — the Iran-Iraq War, Central America and Southern Africa — all of which have the potential for superpower intervention.

This chapter also reviews the prospects for resolving these conflicts and the role Canada might play in conflict resolution. Chapter 4 examines the government's defence White Paper, *Challenge and Security*, in light of changing superpower relations and domestic economic and political constraints. It suggests that the new role projected for Canada as a maritime power may flounder on the shoals of fiscal restraint.

The volume next turns to the global political economy and the implications of developments for Canada and other actors in the international system. Chapter 5 reviews the performance of the world economy in 1987, noting that the consequences of the unsustainable trends and patterns that had been developing for a half-decade began to have a significant negative impact during the year. And despite efforts by governments to offset these negative effects through coordination of monetary and fiscal policies, global imbalances persisted. Chapter 6 examines the implications of a stabilization of global trade and payments imbalances for Canada. It points out that although the result is likely to be a decline in bilateral conflict with the U.S. over trade issues, new strains will result in Canada's global economic relations.

The fourth section of the book focuses on the developing world. The Brundtland Commission report on environment and development, the subject of chapter 7, spells out the strain that growth places on the environment. The chapter suggests that differences over the appropriate rate and kind of growth and its environmental impact could generate serious North-South conflict in the future. Chapter 8 examines Canada's role in various dimensions of North-South relations, including aid, trade and debt, human rights, and military conflict. The chapter also presents an assessment of the parliamentary committee report on Canadian development assistance policy, as well as the government's response to the report.

The Canada-U.S. relationship is discussed in the fifth section of the volume. Chapter 9 examines trade-based Canada-U.S. economic conflict and the free trade agreement as a means of preventing such conflict. The dispute avoidance and settlement mechanisms embodied in the agreement are analyzed to determine the extent to which they will contribute to bilateral conflict management. This chapter also considers domestic opposition to the free trade agreement and the tensions this has created in both countries. Chapter 10 examines Canada-U.S. conflict over environmental issues, notably acid rain and Great Lakes pollution. In contrast to the efforts to resolve bilateral disputes over trade, environmental questions have been laden with conflict that will not easily be defused given the different understanding of the problem on both sides of the border. Finally, chapter 11 presents a chronology of important events during 1987 in Canada's international policies and environments, as well as a five-year statistical profile of Canada among nations.

No attempt has been made in the volume to express a collective view of Canada in international affairs during 1987, nor have we attempted to reconcile the differences of opinion that emerge, preferring instead to encourage the contributors to enunciate their positions in the interest of stimulating debate on important public policy issues. Within this diversity, global conflict and its impact on Canada form the predominant focus, as all authors address their specific topics from that perspective. To provide a context for the studies that follow, we devote the balance of this first chapter to an overview and assessment of Canada in a world of conflict, contrasting Canadian behaviour in various conflict situations during 1987 with the way in which the government projects a role for Canada in international conflicts.

Canada's Role in a World of Conflict

The forces that gave rise to international conflicts in 1987 also created opportunities for Canada to play a more influential role both as a participant (protagonist) in the conflicts and, in some cases, as a conciliator in the resolution of conflict. In the face of deepening Soviet-American rapprochement, the principal arena for East-West competition shifted to various regional conflicts where there existed greater potential for a Canadian role. In addition, the reduction in bipolarity that resulted from Soviet-American detente and the diffusion of power that accompanied the continued decline in U.S. hegemony in the international political economy both contributed to the development of an increasingly multipolar world. Whereas Canada's options had been limited in a system characterized by dominant American leadership and intense bipolar divisions, the spread of multipolarity offered a greater range of options and possibilities for Canadian policies, and in the process rendered the task of choosing among them more complex.

Following a period in which the dominant axis of international conflict had once again centred on strategic competition between the superpowers, 1987 saw a resurgence of conflict among the advanced industrial countries of the North over trade and monetary issues, and increased divergence between the interests of these countries and those of the South. The locus of the predominant international security conflicts was to be found in various regions of the South as well, and these threatened to engage the superpowers despite the resumption of detente at the system level. The dramatic turn in superpower relations was manifested in the Soviet-American summit held in Washington at the end of the year to sign the breakthrough arms control agreement eliminating intermediate-range nuclear forces from Europe. Canadians could breathe more easily with the strategic dimension of East-West relations being managed firmly once more by the superpowers, for it was an area in which Canada could do little to influence or ameliorate the course of events.

Perhaps partly as a reaction against the whirlwind peace initiative of former prime minister Pierre Trudeau in 1983-84 (von Riekhoff and Sigler 1985), the Conservative government has largely eschewed an independent Canadian effort on arms control. Acknowledging that in East-West arms control relations Canada sides with the United States, the government opted to exercise influence through allied councils and in direct dealings with the U.S. (Sokolsky 1986). This decision to return to the fold was reflected generally in Canada's international security policies, which became much more firmly centred on the collective security foundation of its traditional Western alliance relationships. There was, however, some irony in the fact that in a year of unprecedented Soviet-American rapprochement Canada unveiled a national defence policy that was seen by many as a Reagan-style "call to arms," peppered with the rhetoric of deterrence. The reaffirmation of the salience of East-West rivalry and the consequent importance of collective security obligations was adroitly linked with a new emphasis on northern defence and sovereignty, to be pursued through significant new expenditures on nuclear-powered submarines to patrol the Arctic.

Canada's involvement in international security conflicts was not confined to the role it played in East-West competition resulting from its alliance relationships. Beyond this, the government was engaged to varying degrees in the various regional security conflicts that preoccupied the world during the year. Foremost among these for Canada was the conflict in Southern Africa over the threat posed by apartheid. The year 1987 saw an escalation of Canadian efforts to mobilize a concerted response to continued South African aggression, which the government felt threatened the peace and security of the entire region. Aimed at securing agreement for economic sanctions and support for the Front-Line States, these efforts were played out in a variety of multilateral arenas, including the Commonwealth and francophone summits held in

Canada and at the Western economic summit in Venice.

Canada did not seek the same active role with respect to the conflicts in Central America and the Middle East. In the former, Canada voiced its support for efforts to facilitate the peace process and its disapproval of military intervention by third parties. Although these positions put Canada at odds with the Reagan administration, nevertheless Canadian policy was more cautious and ambivalent than was the case for Southern Africa. As for the Middle East, the various conflicts received little attention beyond routine Canadian participation in the various supervisory and observer groups in the region.

Canada's role in the developing areas of the globe has been more prominent on development issues than on those of international security. Nonetheless, on the principal issue dividing North and South — the global distribution of resources — Canada has done little to ameliorate the conflict. On the issue of trade, Canadian policy has been among the most protectionist. Although the government has accepted the principle of making the promotion of imports from aid recipients and the reduction of barriers to such imports an objective of development assistance, it is not at all certain that Canadian practices will change appreciably. For domestic reasons Canada has been very slow to liberalize its policies on imports from the Third World. It was one of the key supporters of the 1986 renewal of the Multi-Fibre Agreement, which discriminates against textile and garment exports from those countries.

The issue of international debt has also produced conflict between North and South. Here, the United States has been the leading industrialized protagonist, while Canada has not played a major role, its policies largely mirroring those of the U.S. In a number of areas, however, the government took steps to shift a portion of the debt burden from those poorest countries least able to afford it. Canada forgave the official development assistance (ODA) debt of several of the poorest African countries, and the government took a leading role in promoting debt relief for these countries at the Western economic summit. In addition, Canada supported initiatives to provide additional loans to debtor nations, carrying its proportionate share of increased funding to the International Monetary Fund (IMF) and the World Bank and pledging a full share to the IMF Structural Adjustment Facility.

Official development assistance continued to be used as an instrument of foreign and commercial policy, even at the expense of effective development in the recipient country. Canada has one of the highest proportions of tied aid among donors. Moreover, Canadian aid was distributed in over 100 countries, many of them middle-income nations, often as a means to augment diplomatic relations or open the door for trade. In addition, the government accepted the principle of making bilateral aid more directly conditional upon the performance of recipient governments in respecting human rights.

While relations with the developing world on the issues of aid, debt and trade played a role in Canada's international economic policies, it was the conflict in the dominant economic system of the industrialized nations that preoccupied Canadian policy makers during the year. Massive imbalances in global trade and payments created serious instabilities in the international political economy in 1987. The major industrial countries, including Canada through its membership in the annual Western economic summit and the Group of Seven (G-7) finance ministers, attempted to achieve coordinated monetary and fiscal policies in order to reduce the imbalances and maintain economic growth, but with little success. The persistent American trade deficit heightened protectionist pressures in the United States and generated intense conflict among the dominant parties in the international trade system.

In the presence of this increasing disorder, the new round of multilateral trade negotiations (MTN) that began in Geneva early in the year was judged to be essential, but an unlikely prospect for international economic tension reduction. Faced with intense conflicts among the major traders in the system — the European Community (EC), Japan and the United States — Canada played a significant role in the preparatory meetings that agreed on an agenda for the new MTN round. Acting as a member of an informal grouping of countries from North and South (the Cairns Group) concerned about the injurious effects of agricultural export subsidies by the EC and the U.S., Canada promoted a consensus that would permit negotiations to begin. Prime Minister Mulroney spoke for the Cairns Group at the Western economic summit as well, in the process serving the enormous Canadian stake in orderly agricultural trade.

Although Canada played an active role, both as protagonist and conciliator, in these wide-ranging global politico-security and economic conflicts during 1987, the year proved once again that Canada's principal arena of international conflict is North America. Here were centred two prominent territorial disputes that captured the attention of the most senior Canadian policy makers. The first centred on a dispute with France over fishing rights in the Gulf of St. Lawrence, a conflict that resulted from differing definitions of appropriate territorial zones around the

French islands of St. Pierre and Miquelon. Although the parties agreed to international arbitration to settle the dispute, the conflict escalated during the year when Canadian ports in the region were closed to French vessels in response to alleged overfishing by France in the area, an action termed hostile and unjust by the French president. The second territorial dispute centred on conflict with the United States over the recognition of Canadian sovereignty in the Arctic, more specifically with respect to the Northwest Passage. This had been a subject of Canada-U.S. contention since the 1985 journey of the U.S. icebreaker *Polar Sea* through Canadian Arctic waters, and in 1987 the government not only staked out its position again, but also underlined it with a commitment to acquire nuclear-powered submarines to patrol the area, thereby actively asserting Canadian sovereignty.

North America also served as the stage for Canada's most dramatic effort at conflict resolution during 1987, the negotiation of a free trade agreement with the United States. In the previous year, Canadian foreign policy had been dominated by a flurry of protectionist initiatives unleashed by the United States in the midst of the free trade negotiations. In 1987 the negotiating arena provided a less public forum in which to play out the fundamental conflict in the approaches of the two countries, as Canada attempted to persuade the U.S. to accept the concept of a code of conduct on subsidies as an underlying principle for the agreement, thus regulating the types of subsidy practices that would be subject to the application of American contingency protection remedies. When it proved impossible to agree to an acceptable code of conduct that would apply to both countries, the negotiations went to the eleventh hour in an effort to discover a dispute settlement mechanism that would be acceptable to the American side while providing Canada with some protection against arbitrary applications of the countervail, anti-dumping and safeguard provisions of U.S. trade law.

Coming to terms with the United States on procedures for settling conflict over trade issues, thus ensuring secure access to the American market, was to be one important product of the Mulroney government's North American gambit, designed to restore the special relationship that Canada had enjoyed with the U.S. in an earlier era. The second result was to be a bilateral agreement to reduce emissions causing acid rain. Here the government did not achieve the same success that it had on the trade issue, and 1987 reinforced the fundamentally conflictual nature of Canada-U.S. relations on environmental issues.

In addition to positions taken and policies adopted in 1987, Canada's actual and potential role in a world of conflict may be assessed through the various statements and studies put forward during the term of the Mulroney government. The government was prolific in the statements it issued on international affairs, and in those it stimulated. Since the publication of the Department of External Affairs (DEA) Green Paper *Competitiveness and Security* in May 1985 (Government of Canada 1985), the government released three other documents on Canada's external policies, ranging from the specific — the defence White Paper *Challenge and Commitment* in June 1987 (Government of Canada 1987b) — to the more broadly focused — *Canada's International Relations* (Government of Canada 1986b), a reply to the Special Joint Committee report *Independence and Internationalism* (Government of Canada 1986a). These documents provide us with considerable insight into the way in which Canadian policy makers view the changing global environment and Canada's place in it and, from the perspective of this chapter, Canada's role as a protagonist or conciliator in international conflict.

A Search for Roles: The Foreign Policy Reviews

What we see from the government's perspective is a world in which some features appear immutable — East-West conflict, for example — and others, such as the global economy and Canada's place in it, that have changed considerably. In this view, Canada has a contribution to make to the amelioration of international problems, but its ability to do so is limited by its resources and domestic priorities. The reports of parliamentary committees, on the other hand, reflect a rather different view of the world and Canada's abilities and responsibilities, one which argues for an active Canadian presence internationally and which emphasizes the need for continuing, if not increasing, Canadian contributions to improving the lot of many in the world. From the perspective of those evaluating policy, Canada can and should make a difference internationally.

There is some divergence between the government's agenda for foreign policy and that which emerges in the wider public arena of parliamentary assessment and recommendation, on the one hand, and between these desiderata and actual Canadian behaviour, on the other. In the pages that follow, we will explore these positions and draw some comparisons with Canada's role in international conflict during 1987.

We begin with the two government "coloured" papers, then discuss the two parliamentary reports and finally the two Department of External Affairs responses to these reports.

Government "Coloured" Papers. The Mulroney government's most general foreign policy statement, *Competitiveness and Security* (Government of Canada 1985),[1] focused primarily on the two major international systems within which Canada was seen as operating, the international economic system and the international politico-security system. In the former, the Green Paper emphasized Canada's declining international competitiveness, the rise of protectionism and the importance of secure market access — particularly in the United States — for Canadian goods. Other trading partners received nary a mention, save for the acknowledgment of the rapid growth of Pacific Rim countries.

Under the rubric of the international economic system, the Green Paper addressed North-South economic problems and questions of development assistance. Although recognizing the enormous problems of the less developed world — debt, population growth, health — the document did no more than pose questions about Canada's international development assistance policies. In a report that focused heavily on the realities of the Canadian economic situation, the problems of the Third World were less significant.

Security considerations constituted the second major thrust of the Green Paper and were phrased almost totally in terms of East-West conflict. The Soviet Union and its allies were depicted as implacably hostile to Canadian interests. In East-West conflict, there was no question that Canada would remain committed to membership in collective security organizations such as the North Atlantic Treaty Organization (NATO) and the North American Aerospace Defence Command (NORAD). Canada would support superpower arms control negotiations and was prepared to offer whatever assistance it could to advance common security interests (p. 40). Included in security concerns was attention to protection of Canadian territory, including airspace and coastal waters. The latter issue would become more significant in the Department of National Defence (DND) White Paper (Government of Canada 1987b).

Regional conflicts were noted as engaging Canadian humanitarian, and possibly economic, interests but were of very limited importance to Canada's security concerns. Reflecting the general philosophy that

Canada must make choices among the international issues it can pursue, the report suggested that "Canadian interests in regional conflicts need careful scrutiny before we commit scarce resources" (p. 42).

The Green Paper, in sum, presented a view of the world as rapidly changing and as not necessarily hospitable to Canadian interests. Canada was a protagonist in East-West conflict, though its role was limited, and also in the global economic system as it protected its own interests to secure its future. From this vantage point, the Green Paper gave the impression that Canada was a country that had to make choices: particularly in terms of security, Canada had to determine priorities among the needs of domestic sovereignty and surveillance, alliance commitments and participation in peacekeeping.

The Mulroney government's second paper addressing Canada's place in the world was the DND White Paper, *Challenge and Commitment: A Defence Policy for Canada,* released in June 1987. It too was important in terms of the image it presented of Canada as a protagonist or a mediator in international conflict.[2]

The DND White Paper conceived East-West conflict in the same *realpolitik* way as did *Competitiveness and Security*: "Canadian security policy must respond to an international environment dominated by the rivalry between East and West" (Government of Canada 1987b: 5). The combination of ideological differences and Soviet military power "cannot help but make everyone else decidedly insecure" (p. 5). The White Paper underlined Canada's commitment to the collective security framework provided by NATO (p. 17). It suggested that one result of its recommended defence procurement would be an enhanced capacity to meet alliance undertakings, although the commitment to acquire nuclear-powered submarines would also serve Canada's sovereignty claims in the Arctic. While concerned to strengthen its defence capability, the government saw arms control as "one of the pillars of Canadian security" (p. 26). In its discussion of East-West conflict, however, the White Paper implicitly acknowledged that Canada was not, nor would it become, a major player.

In contrast to the emphasis in *Challenge and Commitment* on Canada's position in East-West conflict and the need therefore to buttress Canadian defences, there was dramatically less attention paid to armed disputes elsewhere in the world. Like the DEA paper, DND's suggested that such disputes "seldom directly involve the security of Canada" (p. 24). Although the White Paper noted that regional conflict might engage the superpowers, these conflicts were discussed only in terms of Canada's traditional role as a peacekeeper. From a DND perspective, regional conflicts constituted a foreign policy rather than a defence problem.[3]

Parliamentary Reports. The two parliamentary reports, one by the Special Joint Committee on Canada's International Relations, *Independence and Internationalism* (Government of Canada 1986a), the other by the House of Commons Standing Committee on External Affairs and International Trade, *For Whose Benefit?* (Government of Canada 1987a), suggested a rather different view of where Canada stands among nations than the two departmental papers discussed above. The parliamentary reports painted an optimistic scenario with regard to what Canada could and should do: there are, to be sure, many intractable situations, but "Canada has the capacity as well as the inclination to work actively to promote international peace and well-being" (Government of Canada 1986a: 26). This viewpoint reflected the attitudes of the many Canadians who submitted briefs to, or appeared before, these parliamentary committees: Canada is a country of consequence, particularly in economic terms, and therefore has a responsibility to participate across a variety of issues in the search for solutions to global conflicts.

Interdependence and Internationalism was a product of the foreign policy review process that began with the Green Paper. The parliamentary committee held extensive hearings, at which Canadians not only expressed their concerns about a wide range of global issues, but they also promoted active Canadian involvement to ameliorate international tensions. This perspective on Canada as an activist member of the international community was captured in the committee's recommendation that "Canada's activities abroad should be guided by an approach based on constructive internationalism" (p. 137). Whether on its own or in concert with other countries, Canada has the capability to "sustain a substantial involvement in international affairs and should accept a considerable degree of responsibility for finding solutions to many international problems" (p. 30).

For Whose Benefit?, the report of the Standing Committee on External Affairs and International Trade (SCEAIT) on Canada's official development assistance policies and programs (Government of Canada 1987a), is reviewed in detail in chapter 8 of this volume. Over 350 Canadian organizations and individuals made written or oral presentations to SCEAIT supportive of Canada's concern for development but pressing for, among other things, a larger aid budget, a review of aid priorities, less tied aid and more attention to the relationship between human-rights abuses and development assistance. What came through, once again, was not only the extraordinary commitment of Canadians to ameliorating conditions in the Third World but also the responsibility their country was perceived as having. To many, Canada's aid program had reached the point where its goals and methods had to be re-examined to ensure that the program accomplished its primary objective, that "of helping the world's poorest to achieve self-reliance" (p. 3). The committee, critical of many aspects of Canada's ODA, hoped that its report would give the Canadian aid program the "fresh jolt of political energy [it needed] to keep it on course and be able to adapt to the realities of the 1990s and beyond" (p. 3).

Government Responses. The government responded to the parliamentary reports in two papers of its own, *Canada's International Relations* (Government of Canada 1986b) and *Canadian International Development Assistance: To Benefit a Better World* (Government of Canada 1987c). In the former, the Mulroney government accepted "with enthusiasm the theme of active internationalism" that shaped the Special Joint Committee report (Government of Canada 1986b: 1). In contrast to the 1985 Green Paper, however, *Canada's International Relations* resembled earlier statements on Canadian foreign policy, which were characterized by a commitment to the active pursuit of goals through a variety of multilateral and bilateral institutions. Thus, the emphasis in 1986 was more on the positive than on the negative, on influence and activism rather than on the need for priorities and the realities of constraints. In effect, the DEA response, seen by some as a White Paper in all but name, reaffirmed the eternal verities of Canada's international policies.[4]

Canada's International Relations recognized Canadian vulnerabilities arising from an international system that is frought with economic, military and political uncertainties. From the perspective of politico-security concerns, the DEA statement viewed the world in largely, though not totally, bipolar terms. Acknowledging the continuing rivalry of the superpowers, the report also noted that new centres of power were emerging, both military and economic, and that much of the instability in the world had its genesis in regional conflicts. With this analysis, which distinguished it from the more narrow superpower focus of both *Competitiveness and Security* and *Challenge and Commitment*, the report was able to put forward a role for Canada that recognized Canadian membership in the Western alliance but also endorsed a role for this country in the search for settlements to regional disputes. Finally, the DEA document highlighted Canadian contributions to arms control and the control of international terrorism (pp. 11-14).

In terms of international trade and economic policy, *Canada's International Relations* placed considerable emphasis on Canadian participation in a variety of international forums "to deal with present challenges to the international economic system" (p. 15). Rather than an emphasis on Canada's economic weakness and the need to restore Canadian competitiveness, the 1986 DEA paper noted with some satisfaction the recognition of Canadian global economic weight that inclusion in the Group of Seven finance ministers implied.

With respect to international development, the government acknowledged the consensus that exists in Canada on development assistance, noting that "we should not only continue but increase our efforts" (p. 19). Anticipating SCEAIT's *For Whose Benefit?*, the DEA report raised questions about the effectiveness of Canadian aid programs and ways in which these might be improved. While promising continued Canadian commitment to alleviating problems of the Third World — most notably debt, the particular difficulties of the very poorest of the less developed countries, and human-resource development — the government was not prepared to restore the goal of achieving the 0.7 per cent foreign aid/gross national product ratio by 1990.

The government's response, *To Benefit a Better World* (Government of Canada 1987c), welcomed the SCEAIT report, noting that it offered "a valuable set of recommendations about the future objectives and conduct of our development cooperation" (p. 1). As a statement on Canada's international policies, the government's paper was simply a "response" to the SCEAIT rather than a comprehensive aid strategy; this would be forthcoming. That the government felt it necessary to respond to the committee within a few months of the submission of its report suggests its awareness of the importance of development issues in the minds of Canadians. Recognition of interest notwithstanding, however, it is clear that the government did not share all of the perspectives on Canadian ODA put forward in *For Whose Benefit?* As outlined in chapter 8, the government was hesitant to adopt a number of the committee's recommendations: for example, with respect to human-resource development (pp. 44-45), the linking of aid to human rights (pp. 50-56) and tied aid (pp. 57-59), among others. In both its responses to the aid issues in the parliamentary reports, the government made it clear that changes in its development policies were dependent on domestic commercial and fiscal realities.

Managing Global Conflict:
Opportunities and Constraints

The reduction in bipolarity accompanying Soviet-American detente and the diffusion of power resulting from the decline in U.S. hegemony have produced increasing multipolarity in the international system. In this multipolar system, the capacity of major powers other than the U.S. and U.S.S.R. to influence the course and outcomes of international conflict through their actions and policies becomes more important, in terms of both opportunity and need.

In a bipolar system, conflicts are intense but frequently unidimensional along the dominant line of division in the system. Bipolarity also imposes sharp constraints on the behaviour of other nations in the system, largely relegating them to support roles. In a multipolar system, on the other hand, conflicts are less likely to be subject to the escalating intensity that results from the mutually reinforcing divisions characteristic of bipolarity. The multidimensional conflicts in such a system are likely to be more numerous and cross-cutting, however, and thus difficult to manage by virtue of their complexity. Dominant system actors are also less able to control outcomes in a multipolar world, and consequently other major powers assume a more important role.

Under these circumstances, Canada has a much greater potential than in the past for influence in international affairs, both as a protagonist and conciliator in various global and regional conflicts. In terms of national capabilities, the Canadian profile of substantial economic power and international prestige is more similar to that of traditional great powers such as France, Germany and the United Kingdom than to such middle powers as Australia and Sweden. Wealth and reputation thus provide Canada with the opportunity to play a significant role in the emerging multipolar international system, and it is the nature of this role that lies at the heart of the incongruence between the parliamentary and government perspectives on foreign policy, discussed above. The parliamentary view is that of constructive internationalism, with Canada playing an active role in the amelioration of global and regional economic, military and political conflicts. The government view appears more concerned with national interests and constraints, with emphasis on the preservation of Canada's economic and military security in the face of threats from the international environment and a limited capacity for independent action.

As might be expected, the reality lies somewhere between these two extremes. The emerging multipolar system provides increased opportunities for influence for a country with Canada's substantial national capabilities. In addition, Canada has virtually unparalleled access to the various organized multilateral forums that could play a role in efforts to manage multidimensional economic and politico-security international conflicts, including the Commonwealth, la francophonie, the G-7 and the Summit Seven. The conditions are right, therefore, for an active Canadian role in the management of international conflict.

At the same time, however, the nature of that role will be shaped to a considerable extent by the reality of Canadian interests and conditions in the international environment. Canada is a developed Western power, interested in protecting and enhancing its wealth and security in the global system. Since conflict resolution may require sacrifice by all parties to a dispute, the government may be compelled to act more as protagonist than conciliator in situations where Canadian interests are at stake. Even where Canada has a desire to promote conflict management, limited resources may preclude an active role in one dimension of conflict in favour of concentration on another. Finally, constraints imposed by the international environment itself may limit the Canadian role as a conciliator.

The influence of these interests and constraints on Canada's role in the contemporary system of international conflict is evident from the foregoing review of Canadian international activities during 1987. In the continuing politico-security conflict between East and West, Canada defines only a limited role for itself, largely through participation in Western collective security systems. Furthermore, to the extent that East-West competition is a factor in regional security conflicts, Canadian efforts at conciliation are less intense. For example, Canada is most engaged in the regional conflict in Southern Africa, where direct superpower involvement is least, less in Central America where U.S. interests are directly at issue, and least engaged in the conflicts in the Middle East where Soviet-American competition is most intense.

In North-South relations as well, the Canadian performance has been uneven, despite the fact that the Mulroney government has shown a more consistent interest in North-South issues than previous governments. Within multilateral forums such as the United Nations, the Commonwealth and la francophonie, Canada has staked out a strong position on such issues as development, human rights, and regional conflict resolution; its bilateral policies on these issues have not demonstrated a similar commitment to action, however. Similarly, the Canadian position on international debt has been most creditable with respect to the least developed, but generally consistent with that of the rest of the North on other aspects of the issue. Finally, Canada's role as a supporter of the status quo has been most apparent on international trade issues, where the protection of domestic industries takes precedence over economic growth in developing countries.

Accepting the real limits that interests and the environment impose on both desire and capacity to act, what are the prospects for a more active role for Canada in the management of international conflict, and how might that role best be achieved? As a first principle, the *realpolitik* implications of limited resources appear inescapable: Canada must carefully choose those areas and issues of conflict in which it seeks to promote conciliation, because Canadian resources and its capacity to influence outcomes are limited. Canada enjoys some international reputation as an honest broker and could probably play a more active third-party consultative role in selected international conflicts where its interests, capabilities and expertise combine to enhance Canadian influence. That reputation could be undermined, however, if Canada sought the role of "helpful fixer to the world," attempting indiscriminately to mediate international disputes. "Ability to influence" ought to be a primary criterion for choosing areas of involvement.

As for means, Canadian membership in a number of the principal multilateral organizations concerned with contemporary international conflicts provides a natural channel for conciliation activities. The government has used these memberships effectively in its efforts to promote change in Southern Africa, for example, and could act in a similar fashion on the international debt issue, consulting the principals in various forums in an effort to identify an acceptable middle ground. Clearly, such initiatives would require considerable consultation and mediation skills, and steps would have to be taken to enhance Canadian expertise as a third party in these areas. In addition, care would have to be taken to coordinate conciliation efforts through the various regional and functional bureaus of the Department of External Affairs, since diverse departmental interests might intersect on any particular conflict issue, requiring some internal management.

While fundamentally important, these organizational issues are ultimately secondary to the question of Canada's willingness and commitment to play a conflict management role among nations. There is no doubt that the emerging multipolar world will require management, and the principal vehicle is likely to be some form of concert system to replace the condominium of the fading bipolar era. Canada already has a place in this system, and therefore has an opportunity to play a more active international role than ever before in the country's history. The questions that remain to be answered concern the type of role Canada should play and the portion of Canada's admittedly limited resources and influence that will be devoted to efforts to manage a world of conflict.

2 | Managing Global Conflict: Canada and International Summitry

JOHN KIRTON

If 1987 was a year of serious conflict, it was also a year of successful conflict management. In the face of severe threats to the established international order in virtually all regional and functional subsystems of the globe, world leaders displayed a considerable capacity for responding rapidly, creatively and usually effectively to the new challenges that arose. In doing so, they went well beyond the standard channels of diplomacy, international institutions and transgovernmental relations to rely with unprecedented emphasis on face-to-face contact at the highest political level, at international summits.

Thus, 1987 was a year of abnormally intense, widespread and successful summit diplomacy, whether measured by the number and importance of the countries involved, the regions they covered, the significance of the issues they addressed or the substance of the results they achieved. The unusually rich record of summitry in 1987 was well captured during the final six weeks. That brief period witnessed the Washington summit between the two superpowers, the Copenhagen summit of the European Community, the Amman summit of the Arab League, the Riyadh summit of the Gulf Cooperation Council, the Addis Ababa summit of the Organization of African Unity, the Acapulco summit of the eight leading Latin American states and a host of bilateral encounters.

It was not merely the feverish pace but also the formidable products of summit meetings that commanded attention. Despite the tendency of skeptical commentators to dismiss summits as elaborate exercises in domestic political pageantry and popularity enhancement, the summits of 1987 generated some genuine diplomatic accomplishments on some of the toughest issues of the day.[1] The Washington superpower summit brought the first arms control agreement ever to eliminate an entire class of weapons. A summit of the five Central American leaders in Guatemala in August produced for that troubled region a peace plan that still offered the best hope for regional stability as 1987 came to a close. The African and Latin American summits defined coordinated approaches to the debt question and forced the creditor countries of the North to respond. And even the summits that appeared to end in failure, such as that of the European Community, engendered a behind-the-scenes consensus that could lead to action later on.

The real significance of the 1987 summits, however, lay beyond their far-reaching diplomatic results. As valuable as the diplomatic products were, the processes that generated them as well as the underlying pattern they revealed pointed to a transformation in the very structure of the established international order that had prevailed since the end of the Second World War. The intensifying interdependence of nations, the need to reinforce, reform and replace the existing network of international institutions, and the demand to define those core values that united the global community called for international management of the highest degree. And just as the postwar order had been set and shaped by the great 1945 summits at Yalta and San Francisco, so its successor was being forged by summit diplomacy of unprecedented scale, scope and success.[2]

Although the defining characteristics of the new order remained quite indistinct, four features seemed to stand out. The first was the thaw in the Cold War through the historic Washington superpower summit in December 1987, and the first-ever summit between an East German and West German leader on West German soil three months before. The second was the declining global reach of the two superpowers — and the diminishing global relevance of their rivalry — in the face of rising regional powers and groupings, evident in the German, European, Arab, Persian Gulf, African, Latin American and Central American summits. The third was the reduced importance of United States global hegemony as a foundation for order, and thus of the 1945 generation of international institutions built on this foundation, accompanied by the growth of newly institutionalized summit forums that admitted a wider array of powers to the management clubs. The fourth, and most fragile, feature was the emergence through these institutionalized summit forums of an international order that better highlighted a sense of global community, as the diffusion of power in the system engendered a broadening of the values on which it was based.

Such a system afforded an enhanced international relevance for

countries such as Canada, which had been confined by the old configuration of bipolarity and U.S. hegemony to a place in the middlepower
realm. And Canada moved energetically to play a full part in the summit
processes that were bringing the new order about. In the first process of
ending the Cold War, the government of Brian Mulroney had little to
offer directly, at least in comparison with the vigorous East-West summit
diplomacy of Pierre Trudeau in his peace initiative of 1983-84 (von
Riekhoff and Sigler 1985). In the second process, that of building
regional management mechanisms, Canada's effort was far stronger,
although its major thrust — the development of an annual summit with
its North American partner — threatened to confine Canada more closely
within the U.S. sphere of influence. It was in the third process of
replacing the old U.S.-centred management system with that of a broader
and more equal concert of principal powers that Canada concentrated,
primarily through an enhanced role vis-à-vis the issues, institutions and
members of the annual summit of the seven major industrial democracies
of the world. In the final process of building the values of the global
community, Canada enjoyed its greatest success, through its privileged
summit relationship with the countries of Africa and the Caribbean and
its leading role in the summits of the Commonwealth and francophone
world.

Taken together, Canada's summit-level investment in North-South
and West-West rather than East-West relations may have weakened its
claim to be a fully global power. But in a world in which constraints
abounded and compromises were necessary, it was a choice well designed to address the central players and issues of the emerging rather
than fading international order.

In order to assess the larger significance and success of Brian
Mulroney's summit diplomacy, this analysis begins with an examination
of the functions of summitry and its role in shaping international order
in the postwar world. It continues with a review of the major summits of
1987 and identifies the new elements of world order they helped put into
place. It concludes with an assessment of Canada's contribution to this
global process by focusing on the summitry of Prime Minister Mulroney
himself.

Summitry, Instability and International Management

As befits their location at the pinnacle of the political hierarchy, summits are potent instruments for the leaders who employ them. They serve a wide variety of political functions throughout the domestic, diplomatic and international domains.[3] Domestically, summits bring a leader's person and issues to public attention, in a controlled environment that is almost guaranteed an ample audience. Moreover, they catalyze a sluggish and parochial bureaucracy to generate coherent policy and concrete results. And they often familiarize internationally inexperienced local leaders with the problems and perspectives of the wider world.

Diplomatically, summits are also multifunctional tools. Particularly for small states lacking extensive, well-developed diplomatic establishments and for leaders short of trusted colleagues to serve as emissaries, summitry is a preferred way of conducting international affairs. For all countries, summits can be an integral part of the regular diplomatic process, catalyzing and shaping discussions in regular channels, concluding the work done at lower levels, and creating the big trade-offs that bring deals out of thin air. Finally, even when agreements are absent, summitry serves the vital symbolic and structural function of assuring both participants and outsiders that one's access and influence at the highest levels in foreign capitals is intact, should it be needed at a future date.

Perhaps most importantly, summitry is an important instrument in the construction, management and extension of international order. Summit visits constitute an act of acceptance of countries into the international or regional states system, signify the status order of those systems by identifying who gets invited to major conferences and, through their patterns, reveal the bloc structure and hierarchy that prevails in the world. Summitry also represents a response to intensifying international interdependence by creating new international institutions, by embodying the interconnectedness of global forces, by providing opportunities for public diplomacy into the countries where such forces originate, and by giving beleaguered leaders the international support required to take difficult decisions back home. Most expansively, in their declarations and decisions, summits articulate, elaborate and help render effective the fragile sense of global community that is slowly emerging in the world.

In times of international stability, leaders are relatively free to employ the potent instrument of summitry for the domestic and diplomatic purposes that they, as politicians, seek to fulfil. But in times of intense instability, their summit investments tend to be devoted to their larger responsibilities, as statesmen, to respond to the assaults on the established international order and, if necessary, to put a new one in place.

In 1987 the international order-building functions, rather than the domestic or diplomatic functions, of summitry prevailed for Canada and most other major countries in the world. It was a time when the postwar order was rapidly coming to a close. Unlike 1945, 1987 emerged from no great system-wide war that had destroyed the old order and had no single great summit, such as Yalta or San Francisco, to define the new. Rather it had, as a stimulus, a sharp increase in political and economic instability generated by a major shift in power in the world. And there was, as a response, an intense effort at the highest political level among a broad set of countries to cope with the issues, create the institutions and define the principles on which the new order would be based.

The twin 1945 summits of Yalta and San Francisco had defined an international order centred on four characteristics. First, the central strategic systems, along with Germany, Vietnam and Korea, were sharply divided politically on an East-West basis along a line that provided the Soviet Union with a small buffer on its western and southeastern borders but left a pre-eminently powerful United States free to manage international security throughout the rest of the world. Second, the combination of a closed, war-ravaged Soviet economy and an open, vastly expanded American one also permitted the United States to dominate the world economy and the institutions through which it would be managed. Third, for their errors in causing and losing the last world war, Germany, Japan and Italy were removed as legitimate ranking powers in the system. This left the United States, with its nuclear monopoly, and the five veto powers of the United Nations Security Council to manage the security sphere, and the United States alone, through its singular position in the International Monetary Fund and World Bank, to govern the economic one. Finally, the ideals of the postwar order, well articulated in the charters of the United Nations and its component organizations, left ample room for an order highly compatible with American values, including the principle of state sovereignty, to prevail.

By the 1970s, this postwar order had unravelled to the point where it prompted several high-level attempts at repair, reform and, ultimately, redefinition.[4] America's conduct of, and collapse in, the war in Vietnam took it to strategic parity with the Soviet Union, a situation to which the United States responded with its summit-level opening to China and its several arms control summits with the Soviet Union. The excesses of Vietnam and the oil shocks of 1973 and 1979 brought economic weakness in America and acute financial, employment and inflationary problems throughout much of the Western world. Here, the response came through summit-level efforts to write a new charter for the Atlantic community, the emergence in 1975 of the annual Western Economic Summit, and the North-South dialogue that culminated in the Cancun summit of 1981. The new economic power, military responsibility and political relevance of Germany and Japan increased the significance and scope of the Western Summit discussions and strengthened the role of the European Community both within the Western Summit and in the regional summits it began to hold regularly on its own. And while the United Nations Charter continued to be invoked as a rhetorical weapon, increasingly it was the principles espoused in the communiqués, declarations and summaries of the seven-power summits that represented the consensus that had real political force in the world (de Menil and Solomon 1983; Putnam and Bayne 1984).

During the first half of the 1980s the United States, led by President Ronald Reagan and supported by conservative allies elsewhere, attempted a sharp shift back to an order based on U.S. predominance and the centrality of the bipolar struggle. The effort was significant, sustained and largely unsuccessful. President Reagan's refusal to meet with the Soviet leadership, for the longest interval in Soviet-American relations since the 1950s, helped fuel a new and very chilly Cold War, prompting other Western leaders to try their own hand at personally bridging the East-West divide. One of these was then Canadian prime minister Pierre Trudeau, whose six-month-long peace initiative in 1983-84 took him into meetings with the leaders of all the major powers and almost half of the countries in the world. The U.S. expensive military build-up helped generate a U.S. budget deficit, as well as a trade deficit, that transformed the United States from the world's largest creditor to largest debtor, drove the Third World debt problem to crisis proportions, and gave Europe, Japan and others an enhanced role in solving the pressing economic problems of international trade, finance and Third World debt. Despite President Reagan's lack of enthusiasm for the forum of the seven-power summit, his assault on the United Nations system and his failure at the General Agreement on Tariffs and Trade (GATT) ministerial meeting in 1982, it was he who helped broaden the seven-power summit into a forum for trade, arms control and exchange rate management, through the U.S. role in the creation of the quadrilateral trade ministers forum, a summit-level six-power arms control consultation, and the Group of Seven (G-7) ministers of finance. And while Reagan's personal foreign policy perspectives remained isolationist in inspiration, the declarations of the seven-power summits he attended, from Ottawa onward, all defined important new principles governing the West's relationship with the East and the South.

The Reagan interlude had exposed the difficulty and discredited the concept of returning to an international order based on pre-eminent U.S. capabilities, America's isolationist tendencies and a sharp bipolar confrontation between the United States and the Soviet Union. It did not, however, by itself determine whether the successor system would be based on a renewed system of Soviet-American dominance — a condominium (with or without a Chinese partner), on a retreat into self-contained regional blocs, or on the emergence of a concert of Western principal powers able to manage their own interdependence and willing to make serious accommodations across the East-West and North-South divides. It remained for the intense and serious summitry of 1987 to shape the response and set the balance among these three very different paths.

The Summits of 1987

In 1987 the leaders of the world confronted three central changes in the international system they had inherited. The first, from the East, was the advent, however tenuous, of genuine moves to a capitalist economy, open international exchange and a degree of political democracy in the Soviet Union and China. The second, within the West, was the decline of the United States and the rise of the United Kingdom, France, Germany and Japan as the countries that counted. The third, from the South, was the emergence of a Third World that finally had a real capacity to hurt the North — through debt moratoriums, refugee movements, illegal immigration, communicable diseases and even mass starvation in a television age.

In responding to these challenges, the world's leaders in their summits tried a variety of approaches. A superpower condominium seemed in sight, as American and Soviet leaders moved from the tentative starts of Geneva in 1985 and Reykjavik in 1986 to the success of Washington in

1987 (and perhaps Moscow in 1988). Regionalism abounded as well, as the Europeans, Latin Americans and Africans flirted with inward-looking solutions to their particular debt problems, while the Arabs and Central Americans moved to enhance their regional security on their own. But on the whole the principles of condominium and regionalism were secondary strands. The East-West summits of Margaret Thatcher and Helmut Kohl in 1987, together with the role of Europe, Japan and even China in the intermediate-range nuclear forces (INF) agreement that capped the Washington summit, gave Soviet-American summitry a decidedly multilateral tinge. European unwillingness to continue open-ended subsidies in the name of regionalism, Latin American reluctance to renounce its debt, the rapid response of the North to Africa's problems, the external support for the Central American peace process, and the Arab world's reinstatement of Egypt — the renegade of Camp David — all pointed to a regionalism very well connected to the world system as a whole. And the hub that connected the spokes of the various regional and functional systems was no longer located only in Washington, but ran through an embryonic concert of the principal powers of the indus-trialized, democratic world as well.

Certainly the most significant of the 1987 summits was that between the United States and Soviet Union in Washington on December 7-10. It was the eleventh Soviet-American summit since Yalta and marked the high point of the most recent Soviet-American detente. Following a thirteen-year absence of superpower summit contact following Yalta, Soviet and American leaders had come together in September 1959 and June 1961 for the first thaw in their Cold War. A second stab at detente began hesitantly in June 1967 and continued vigorously in May 1972, June 1973, June 1974, November 1974 and June 1979 through the summits that brought the great arms control achievements of the Anti-Ballistic Missile (ABM) and SALT I (Strategic Arms Limitation Talks) treaties, and the negotiation of SALT II.

There followed a gap of six years and five months with no superpower summit. President Reagan's long effort to manage U.S. foreign policy without a regular presidential-level dialogue with the Soviet Union finally ended in November 1985 when he met in Geneva for his first summit with Mikhail Gorbachev. The two leaders met again in Reykjavik in October 1986 and in Washington in December 1987 (and planned to meet again in Moscow in the spring of 1988). Should the Moscow meeting take place, the four Reagan-Gorbachev summits would represent the advent of an institutionalized, annual bilateral superpower summit for the first time in the Soviet-American relationship and the most intense period of Soviet-American summitry since General Secretary Brezhnev's four summits in just over two years in the early 1970s. The Reagan presidency thus began with the strongest effort since the 1950s to revive the Cold War and ended with a period of detente, now institutionalized at the summit level.

In this attempt to permanently bridge the East-West divide, the Americans were not alone. In March of 1987 Prime Minister Thatcher of the United Kingdom had flown to Moscow to meet with General Secretary Gorbachev. While there, she publicly praised nuclear deterrence, met with dissidents and lit a candle in a church. But she also foreshadowed the Washington breakthrough by declaring Gorbachev a "man I can do business with" (*Maclean's* 1987). It was thus not surprising that on his way to the Washington summit, Gorbachev first stopped off in London for a meeting with Thatcher. Nor was it surprising that as the year ended, Gorbachev announced his intention to visit Italy in the new year, and in doing so fuelled speculation over the possibility of the first meeting ever between a general secretary of the Communist Party of the Soviet Union and the Pope.

The most historic and dramatic of the 1987 East-West summits came in Germany, at the geographical core of the great divide. As the year opened, the atmosphere had seemed most unpromising. In January West German Chancellor Helmut Kohl had compared the recent Reykjavik summit to that of Munich in 1938, and in June Ronald Reagan had paid his second visit to West Berlin in two years to demand that the Soviets tear down the wall. But these Cold War instincts were cast aside in the second week of September when Erich Honecker made the first-ever visit by an East German Communist leader to West Germany. His five-day visit, during which time he visited both Bonn and his home town in the Federal Republic, suggested at a minimum that Moscow was loosening its grip on its East European satellites and at a maximum that the two Germanys might again be unified, at least in this narrow way.

The entry of additional players into the superpower sanctuary was accompanied by new summit-level efforts by the superpowers to control their respective and increasingly restive allies and by the foray of some of these allies into such critical superpower spheres as the Middle East. In April Gorbachev journeyed to Czechoslovakia in an effort to sell his economic reforms to his skeptical ally. And in December, on his return home from Washington, he held a summit of his Warsaw Pact allies to brief them on the INF accord he had just reached.

For President Reagan as well, the strains within America's partnerships required summit-level attention. May proved to be the critical month. Portuguese President Mario Soares came to Washington. Then Prime Minister Nakasone of Japan arrived, hoping to dampen the protectionist pressures from America that threatened the relationship between the two largest economic powers in the world and the political survival of the Japanese prime minister back home. And the United States for the first time in its history refused a head of state entry — the discredited Austrian President Kurt Waldheim. This blow to Austria's honour led to a recall of the Austrian ambassador from Washington.

Perhaps the most visible sign of the superpowers' diminished influence over their allies came from the Middle East. Here Israeli Foreign Minister Shimon Peres was determined to press ahead with his plan for an international peace conference on the Middle East, despite opposition from his own head of government and that of the United States. To give him support, King Hussein of Jordan in April travelled to the Netherlands and Brussels searching for European support. And later in the year, the president of the European Community, Leo Tindemans of Belgium, went on a tour of moderate Arab countries to enlist them in the international peace conference cause.

If the Euro-Arab summit showed the declining control of the superpowers, summits within both of these constituent regions displayed the new strength of regionalism in these two critical areas of the world. In June the regular summit of the European Community had ended in deadlock when Margaret Thatcher remained firm in her demand that the Community control its burgeoning deficit that was driven by proliferating agricultural subsidies. Two subsequent meetings of agricultural ministers and one of foreign ministers failed to find a solution. So the issue returned to the European Community's summit in Copenhagen on December 4-5, driving issues such as European economic and political cooperation and other global issues from the forefront of the agenda. The meeting ended with little apparent progress, although the looming bankruptcy of the Community meant that a solution remained necessary.

Achievements were far more visible in the Middle East, where the heads of state and government or representatives of the Arab League met in Amman on November 8 for their first emergency summit in over half a decade. The issues that dominated the meeting were the Persian Gulf War and the status of Egypt. The results exceeded expectations, as the summit issued a harsh condemnation of Iran's role in the Gulf war and agreed that members should re-establish diplomatic relations with

Egypt. Just hours after the summit, the United Arab Emirates announced it was complying with that agreement, and Iraq, Saudi Arabia, Kuwait, Bahrain, Abu Dhabi and North Yemen later followed suit. It was an appropriate conclusion to the first Arab League summit since the inaugural gathering in 1948 at which the central focus was not the issue of Palestine and Zionism. The Amman summit also set the stage for the late-December meeting of the Gulf Cooperation Council in Riyadh, during which Saudi Arabia, Kuwait, Oman, Qatar, Bahrain and the United Arab Emirates approved a pact to boost security cooperation in the face of threats from Iran.

Another theatre where regional leaders gathered together to advance the local peace process in an effective way was the second area of world politics previously dominated most closely by the United States alone — Central America. On August 5, five Central American leaders gathered in Guatemala City and at the end of two days of talks agreed on a plan to introduce a ceasefire in the region within ninety days. Under the ten-point peace plan, Nicaragua agreed for the first time to introduce democratic political reforms and the leaders agreed to ask for an end to aid from outside the region for rebel groups of both sides. By October the sponsor of the plan, Costa Rican President Oscar Arias Sanchez, was in Washington winning congressional converts to the cause; for its part, Nicaragua permitted the opposition media to reopen, ended censorship, released political prisoners and introduced a regional ceasefire on a unilateral basis. Despite Christmas ceasefire violations, the atmosphere was cautiously optimistic as the five presidents prepared to meet again in mid-January of 1988.

The new strength and success of regional summitry in managing conflict was apparent in the economic realm as well. Here Third World debt provided the catalyst for summit-level efforts to reform existing relationships between North and South. As the largest debtors in the world, the major countries of Latin America took the most dramatic initiative. At the end of November the leaders of Argentina, Brazil, Colombia, Mexico, Panama, Peru, Uruguay and Venezuela gathered in Acapulco to discuss foreign debt, related international problems and security in Central America. Although Latin American leaders had met previously in 1962 and 1967, this was the first time they had gathered on their own initiative and without the presence of the United States. Indeed, the meeting was designed to establish a new, ongoing Group of Eight that would counter the Group of Seven major countries of the industrialized North. The presidents, who represented 80 per cent of the population of

Latin America, did not take the dramatic step of repudiating their debt but did criticize protectionism in the United States and the North, issued a manifesto on debt, and developed plans for closer economic integration on a regional basis along the lines of the European Community. They also agreed that their summit would become an annual event, the next meeting to be held in 1988 in Uruguay.

In Africa the debt crisis also provided the focus for the summit of the Organization of African Unity (OAU), which met at the same time. Nine leaders of the fifty-member organization gathered in Addis Ababa to call for more help from the affluent North, a ten-year moratorium on repayments of Africa's $200-billion (U.S.) debt, and a North-South conference in 1988 to consider these claims. A move towards meeting the demands of the summit came within the week, when donor nations and international agencies in the North, in an unprecedented partnership, organized an $8.3-billion package of financial relief.

The Canadian Contribution

In this global movement towards intense, institutionalized, effective summitry, Canada was a major participant. In 1987 Prime Minister Mulroney not only continued the active summit diplomacy that he had begun upon entering office in September 1984 but aggressively sought to employ summit forums for a more ambitious set of purposes than ever before. His focus, however, shifted from the summit relationship he had first sought to develop in his annual meetings with the president of the United States. His extended summit diplomacy took on new dimensions as he employed it to deepen the ties among the principal powers of the industrialized world and to restore the North-South dialogue that had died in the 1980s. The culmination of his efforts came in the period beginning September 1987 as Canada prepared to serve as host for three of the world's major multilateral, institutionalized summits — those of la francophonie, the Commonwealth, and the seven-power gathering.

The scale and scope of Brian Mulroney's summit diplomacy was apparent to close observers from the start. His reputation as an avid summiteer was established within a week of his being sworn in to office when he flew to Washington for a meeting with President Reagan. Many commentators felt that the United States had been singled out as a focus for Canada's attention at the highest political levels, but those who forecasted, and feared, a continentally oriented Canada were soon forced to revise their judgments. In the following seven months, Mulroney followed with visits to the Commonwealth Caribbean, the Soviet Union, the United Kingdom and the seven-power summit in Bonn. Indeed, in his first two years in office, Mulroney made almost twice as many summit visits abroad as had Pierre Trudeau in the full four years of his first term. And while Trudeau's visits had been divided equally among the United States, the Commonwealth/United Nations and the Soviet Union/Japan/ Vatican clusters (Dewitt and Kirton 1983: 89-91), Mulroney's were far less focused on the United States and far more multilateral in character.

For Brian Mulroney, this active summit diplomacy was a matter of choice and a mechanism that had large consequences for the Canadian foreign policy that ensued. As the postwar Canadian prime minister least expert and experienced in international affairs upon entering office, Brian Mulroney learned about the world and about how Canada should relate to other countries primarily through summitry. As an individual who placed a premium on personal contact and as a professional in labour mediation, he was very much at home in the summit environment (Kirton 1985). And as a politician who liked associating with fellow conservatives and with those who looked to him for leadership, he was particularly happy in the forums of the seven-power summit, the Commonwealth and la francophonie. As a result, he was particularly well positioned to absorb the logic and consensus of these forums, define the direction in which they were able to go, and mobilize them for compatible purposes with considerable success. It is hardly surprising that these three forums, and the countries within them, were to quickly surpass the United States as the centrepiece of Canadian summitry abroad.

Table 2-1 summarizes the record of Prime Minister Mulroney's summit diplomacy in his first two and a half years in office. Several striking trends stand out. The United States ranked only second as a summit partner of Canada. It was superceded by the United Kingdom and rivalled by France, the two countries that share with Canada the distinction of belonging to both the seven-power summit and the Commonwealth or la francophonie. The top-six countries in Canada's summit partner list were its associates in the seven-power summit, a striking indication of the centrality of that forum to Canadian foreign policy as a whole. In the layer immediately following stood ten partners of Canada in the Commonwealth, including the other old middlepower dominion of Australia as well as the countries of the Caribbean and Africa. And in the third tier stood more African and Asian Commonwealth countries and African countries of la francophonie. It is only at this level that the two

Table 2-1
Prime Minister Mulroney's Summit Meetings by Partner, September 1984 to March 1987

	Country	Total	Bilateral	Summit 7	Cmwth/ France	NATO	UN
1	United Kingdom	9	3	3	2	1	
2	United States	7	3	3		1	
3	France	6	2	2	1	1	
4	Japan	6	3	3			
5	Italy	6	2	3		1	
6	Germany	4		3		1	
7	China	2	2				
8	Soviet Union	1	1				
9	Jamaica	3	1		2		
10	Australia	3	1		2		
11	Zimbabwe	3	1		2		
12	St. Kitts/Nevis	3	1		2		
13	Granada	3	1		2		
14	St. Vincent/Grenadines	3	1		2		
15	Dominica	3	1		2		
16	Bahamas	3			3		
17	Tanzania	3	1		1		
18	Congo	2	1		1		
19	Tonga	2	1		1		
20	Senegal	2	1		1		
21	Uganda	2	1		1		
22	India	2			2		
23	Zambia	2			2		
24	Sri Lanka	2	1		1		
25	Norway	2	1			1	

Notes:

1 Scoring is by head of state or government met with, whether in a bilateral or multilateral context. Each pair counts as a discrete meeting. Excludes seperate bilateral meetings during a multilateral visit, with the exception of funerals, and a seperate official visit immediately before or after to the host country.

2 Excludes the Pope and leaders of international organizations who are not also heads of state of government.

3 Includes Prime Minister Fabius of France and Li Xiannian of China.

4 The following countries had one bilateral summit meeting with Prime Minister Mulroney during this period: Romania, Ireland, Peru, Korea, Czechoslovakia, Israel and the Cameroons. As well, all other Commonwealth Caribbean countries not included on the above list had two summit meetings with the prime minister: the first at the meeting with the Commonwealth Caribbean states in February 1985, and the second at the Commonwealth meeting in Nassau in October 1985.

Communist powers of China and the Soviet Union entered, indicating Canada's lagging direct involvement in the major East-West issues of the day. And almost entirely absent were the traditional middlepowers of the North Atlantic Treaty Organization (NATO), Scandinavia and the non-affiliated Third World.

The record of Prime Minister Mulroney's summitry also suggests that the era of bilateralism in Canadian foreign policy has withered and that a new multilateralism has taken its place. Only in the case of the Soviet Union and China is Canada's summit relationship conducted primarily on a bilateral basis. Even Canada's "special" relationship with the United States is conducted not so much in continental isolation but, in the main, in multilateral forums. This is true for Canada's major partners in Europe and Japan as well. It is also quite clear that Canada's preference for multilateralism is not an indiscriminate lust for international affiliations but an emphasis very tightly focused on four particular organizations: the seven-power summit, NATO, the Commonwealth and la francophonie. Only two of the four join Canada with the United States. And while two of the four are the central economic and military clubs of the industrialized Northern democracies, the other two are overwhelmingly North-South forums.

For a prime minister whose foreign policy was founded on the bedrock of a restoration of the close relationship between Canada and the United States, the lack of centrality for the United States in Canada's summit relationships is a particular surprise. But the diminished global pre-eminence of the United States, together with the erosion of the bipolarity that made Washington the centre for the Western alliance, has forced a different pattern to prevail. Indeed, his reputation for pro-Americanism notwithstanding, Mulroney's face-to-face summit visits with the U.S. president have been less frequent than those of several other Canadian prime ministers during their peak years (Swanson 1975: 8-11; Swanson 1978).

Prime Minister Mulroney's one innovation in Canadian-American summit diplomacy has been the creation of a very public annual comprehensive bilateral summit on a set schedule, the so-called Shamrock Summits that take place in alternate countries in March or April of each year. This summit process was created at the first Mulroney-Reagan meeting in Washington in September 1984, when the two leaders agreed to meet at least once a year and when the president publicly invited the prime minister to telephone him at any time (Jockel 1985). The first

Shamrock Summit, which took place between the two leaders of Irish descent on St. Patrick's Day in Quebec City, was best remembered for its showmanship. But it generated a series of substantial accomplishments, notably agreements on halting trade protectionism, constructing a new north warning system, civilian space cooperation, and the appointment of two envoys to write a report on acid rain. At the second Shamrock Summit, in Washington on March 17-19, 1986, the two leaders signed a five-year extension of their joint North American Aerospace Defence Command and accepted the report of their acid rain envoys. President Reagan also promised to secure funding for the $5-billion research program set out in the report.

By the 1987 meeting, held in Ottawa on April 5-6, the mood of expectation had turned to disappointment on the Canadian side. The Americans had done little to implement their commitment on acid rain. And with Reagan having lost control of the Congress the previous November and under a cloud for his role in the Iran-Contra affair, the benefits of a visible personal association with the president seemed sharply reduced. Indeed, American objectives for the visit consisted primarily of having Reagan survive it with no major public relations errors, thus showing that he was still competent and in command of America's foreign affairs.

Yet despite the dismal Canadian mood and low American expectations, the efficacy of summitry as a decision-making process was amply illustrated by three public presidential commitments that Canada secured and was unlikely to have otherwise obtained. The first, and least consequential, was a promise to consider once again Mulroney's proposal for a joint North American acid rain accord. The second was a strong endorsement of the negotiations for a bilateral free trade agreement. And the third was a pledge to find a satisfactory solution to the dispute over the legal status of Canada's Arctic waters. As 1987 ended, the acid rain promise had generated little action, but the free trade agreement had been successfully negotiated and an Arctic waters agreement that appeared to strengthen Canada's jurisdictional claims was about to be realized.

The results of the prime minister's investment in institutionalized summitry in the multilateral arena were slower in coming but were ultimately more effective, especially in Canada's preferred forums of the seven-power summit, the Commonwealth and la francophonie. Despite the challenges posed in dealing with a multitude of veteran leaders of differing cultures, ideologies, economic systems and geopolitical situations, these forums expressed Canada's traditional dislike of a U.S.-dominated regionalism and its desire for building community on a global basis.

The leaders of the seven leading industrial democracies of the world had been meeting annually since 1975, and Canada had joined the group, through U.S. and Japanese sponsorship, in 1976 (Gotlieb 1987; Holmes and Kirton 1988). Since its precarious entry, Canada's position in the group had steadily strengthened. It used the first summit it hosted, in 1981, to highlight North-South issues, and Pierre Trudeau emerged in the 1980s as the most experienced seven-power summiteer in the club. Brian Mulroney had begun hesitantly at his first summit in Bonn in 1985 (Gratton 1987). His potential mediatory role as the only leader who could speak in the same terms, both ideologically and linguistically, as both Ronald Reagan and President Mitterand of France, respectively, yielded no visible results. But in Tokyo in 1986, Mulroney succeeded in getting Canada admitted, along with Italy, to the select group of formerly five and now seven finance ministers who played an important role in stabilizing and coordinating exchange rates in the Western world. He also introduced onto the summit agenda, for the first time, an issue as vital to the Canadian economy as it was difficult for foreign leaders to address individually back home — the need to discipline the massive national subsidies through which Western governments distorted at enormous expense the world's agricultural trade.

At the Venice summit in 1987, Canada again moved forward the issues of international finance and agricultural subsidies, along with the critical question of Third World debt. But the true test of Canada's ability to shape international order in a way commensurate with Canadian values came over the question of apartheid in South Africa. None of the other leaders particularly wanted the issue dealt with at the summit. Some, notably Margaret Thatcher of the United Kingdom and Helmut Kohl of West Germany, were strongly opposed to having the question raised at all. But Mulroney succeeded in having the issue placed on the agenda, and he reported out of the meeting in language that reflected in large measure the strong principles that the Commonwealth had just defined. To Western publics weary of struggling with the nuances of summit summaries, it seemed like a small gain. But to a South African regime banking on the major Western powers to once again grow tired of the apartheid issue, the message was clear.

Canada's influence in this key forum of the North was accompanied by, indeed tightly interconnected with, its much greater weight in the two critical North-South forums of the Commonwealth and la francophonie (Kirton 1987). The biennial Commonwealth Heads of Government Meeting (CHOGM) was an old institution to which the Mulroney government and the South African issue gave new life. Prime Minister Mulroney's visit to the Commonwealth Caribbean regional summit in February 1985 was his second visit abroad. His first full-scale CHOGM, in the Bahamas in October 1985, was his first experience in a large North-South forum in which Canada ranked as a major power. He emerged from his meetings with the heads of the forty-nine countries present as the real leader of the organization owing to his strong denunciation of apartheid in South Africa and his firm declaration of support for active measures against its racist regime. At a special Commonwealth summit in the United Kingdom in August 1986 he continued the crusade. And in Vancouver in October 1987, at the regular CHOGM, he used his prerogatives as host to highlight the issues of Southern Africa, Third World debt and the need for liberalized world trade.

These issues were also prominent in the francophone summit. Canada not only enjoyed a position of leadership in this institution, but had taken the lead in its creation. La francophonie was born in Paris in February 1986 when representatives from forty-one countries that shared French as a common language gathered for the first time. The first francophone summit was a particular triumph for Canada, as its federal representatives were joined at the meeting by those from the provinces of Quebec and New Brunswick under an imaginative but somewhat controversial formula that enhanced the role of the provinces in foreign affairs. The francophone summit also represented a major advance for Canada's image and character as a francophone as well as an anglophone country, and for the issues of technical cooperation and economic redistribution that the world's francophone countries needed to address. The presence of a representative of Vietnam at the summit also gave Canada an unusual point of entry into the issue of East-West security, which formed a priority part of the summit's agenda. Canada's priorities, investments and status in the new organization were markedly strengthened in September 1987 in Quebec City when Brian Mulroney hosted the second summit of the francophone world.

Creating Global Community

Taken together, the Commonwealth and francophone summits give Canada privileged access to, and a position of leadership in, at the highest level, groupings that do not include the United States, that span the North-South divide, that embrace countries from all regions, and that include a majority of the countries in the world. The seven-power summit offers Canada a position as an equal in an exclusive club of the industrial world's major powers, where the United States' presence and power are available to be mobilized but can be balanced by Canada's family partners, the United Kingdom and France, and the economically indispensable countries of Japan, Germany and Italy as well. As the only country that is a member of all the Commonwealth, francophone and seven-power summits, Canada is positioned at the pivot of the political networks that extend across the North Atlantic and North Pacific and through the equator to all the regions of the South as well.

In the superpower-centred postwar international order, Canada was not given a seat on the United Nations Security Council but was free to assume an important role in the functional agencies of the United Nations' galaxy and to press in the General Assembly for an organization whose membership was both universal and committed to UN Charter ideals. By 1975 that historic imperative was largely realized, just as the configuration of world power on which it was premised was being fundamentally revised. As a more important actor in the new system, Canada has played an enhanced role in the summit-level processes that are, however clumsily and slowly, defining a new order in the world. In this effort Canada remains a marginal player in the ongoing management of major East-West conflict, although its peace initiatives, North-South diplomacy, and presence at certain regional security negotiations occasionally provide it with a role. But in the central conflicts that confront the Western nations in their relations with one another and their relationship with the impoverished South, Canada has acquired a place in the first rank. Canada has used this new position to press with renewed vigour for its historic conception of an integrated global community united by common values, rather than one divided into geographic regions and ordered by the superior power of the United States and the Soviet Union. Through its contribution to the seven-power, francophone and Commonwealth summits of 1987, Canada has achieved some modest but meaningful success in this endeavour. Through its role in hosting the next seven-power summit, which meets in Toronto on June 19-22, 1988, it has an opportunity to accomplish considerably more.

International Security

3 Regional Conflict: De-escalation and Prospects for Resolution

BRIAN S. MANDELL

On December 8, 1987, Moscow and Washington signed their first significant arms control treaty since 1979. Beyond its direct military significance, the treaty limiting intermediate-range nuclear forces (INF) in Europe symbolized a partial thaw in superpower relations. As the Washington summit drew to a close, it was apparent that the strident Cold War rhetoric of the earlier years of the Reagan administration had subsided markedly. Guided by Gorbachev's new diplomatic activism, the Soviet Union appeared to be inching towards the view that more-restrained superpower arms competition, together with efforts to contain regional conflicts, offered the best prospects for easing East-West tensions and undertaking significant economic and social reform at home.

Unfortunately, movement towards greater stability and predictability in U.S.-Soviet relations in 1987 did not produce any positive spillover at the regional level where numerous conflicts continued unabated. Neither great power was able to impose order and stability on regional conflicts deemed inimical to their respective interests. Nor did they fare any better at prompting local actors to manage their conflicts in less costly ways than armed violence. This lack of great power control proved especially problematic in the Iran-Iraq War — a conflict characterized by open-ended escalation with real potential for superpower confrontation. In contrast, the potential for greater U.S.-Soviet meddling in the affairs of regional states engendered an indigenous peace process in Central America where, in 1987, a number of states under the leadership of Costa Rica sought to manage their conflict without external assistance. In Southern Africa over the last year, the numerous conflicts seemed to stymie both local states and external parties in their efforts to reduce tensions throughout the region.

The prospects for a distinctly Canadian contribution to conflict resolution are greater in Central America than they are in the Middle East or South Africa. This chapter has three principal objectives: to highlight the major developments in these three regional conflicts, including superpower involvement; to explore current efforts at, and prospects for, regional conflict resolution; and to suggest why Canadian conflict-resolution initiatives are most likely to succeed in Canada's own hemisphere.

War in the Persian Gulf

Early in 1987 the shift of focus in the Iran-Iraq War to attacks on Gulf shipping, together with the growing involvement of the superpowers, carried the seven-year-old war to a new phase. The surge in Iranian attacks on commercial ships is best explained by Teheran's calculation that an Iranian victory was not possible as long as Iraq enjoyed the strong financial and military support of its Arab neighbours, especially Kuwait and Saudi Arabia. The military stalemate on land had caused the two belligerents to take their war to sea and attempt to injure each other by attacking the flow of oil. In late 1986 Iraq opened this phase of the war because of its superior air power and because most of Iran's oil is exported through the Gulf. For its part, Iran retaliated by attacking tankers carrying oil from Kuwait. While not a declared belligerent in the war, Kuwait gives financial aid to Iraq.

Between January and May 1987, Iran attacked sixteen ships leaving or entering Kuwaiti ports. Leaving no state with ships in the Gulf immune, Iranian gunboats attacked a Soviet cargo ship headed for Kuwait on May 6, 1987. This increase in attacks on Gulf shipping in May led to a Kuwaiti agreement with the Soviet Union to lease three ships that would be given Soviet naval protection. Not to be outdone, Washington initiated discussions with Kuwait to place eleven Kuwaiti ships under the U.S. flag and provide them protection by U.S. warships. Until early 1987, Iraq had carried out more attacks on ships than Iran, but these were largely confined to vessels moving to and from Iran's Kharg Island oil facilities.

The attacks on shipping assumed dangerous proportions on May 17 with an Iraqi air strike on the U.S.S. *Stark* navy frigate in the Gulf. Apologies from Baghdad aside, the attack on the *Stark* had immediate repercussions in both Washington and the Arab world. Though the U.S. Navy quickly sharpened the rules of engagement for its warships remaining in the Gulf, the broader role and objectives of the U.S. Navy task force in the Gulf — including the appropriateness of efforts undertaken to end the Iran-Iraq War — suddenly became a matter of extensive congressional and public debate. Did the United States have a responsibility to keep international shipping lanes open? Could the burdens and risks of maintaining a presence in the Gulf be shared with other Western nations more dependent on Middle Eastern oil?

In defending the U.S. naval presence in the Gulf in the wake of the *Stark* attack, the Reagan administration argued that this incident served as a clear test case of America's commitment to the Gulf Arab states, especially Saudi Arabia and Kuwait. U.S. abdication of its naval role in the region would incur long-term costs — the disruption of navigation, which would threaten the oil lifeline to the West; the heightened possibility of an Iranian victory in the war, which would put another squeeze on Middle Eastern oil at a time when the West's dependence on Middle East supplies was growing; unconstrained Islamic fundamentalism, which would breed more terrorism and threaten the stability of Gulf governments; and finally, the U.S.S.R., now playing a conspicuously active role in the area, would benefit from a decline of American influence and resolve (*Christian Science Monitor* 1987a). Seen from this perspective, Kuwait's request for protection of its shipping provided a tangible way for the United States to strengthen its commitment to stability in the region. Such resolve was particularly important in light of the administration's efforts to construct a reinvigorated and coherent post-"Irangate" Middle East policy and to show support for United Nations Security Council efforts to negotiate a ceasefire in the Iran-Iraq War.

Responding to criticism that Washington was bearing an unmanageable burden in the Gulf, President Reagan sought broad diplomatic and military backing for U.S. Gulf policy at the June economic summit in Venice. There, the summit leaders, including Prime Minister Mulroney, reaffirmed the principle of freedom of navigation in the Gulf and pledged support for a UN Security Council initiative to end the Iran-Iraq War. Additional support for U.S. policy was received from the Gulf Cooperation Council (GCC), which publicly endorsed Kuwait's efforts to safeguard its oil shipments from Iranian attack by appealing to the U.S. and the Soviet Union for protection.

Trying for a Ceasefire

On July 21 the UN Security Council's five permanent members issued an unprecedented unanimous call for a ceasefire in the Iran-Iraq War. Even China, a major supplier of arms to Iran, supported the initiative. UN Resolution 598 called for an immediate ceasefire on land, at sea and in the air, the withdrawal of forces to internationally recognized borders and the release and repatriation of prisoners of war. "Other" states were to exercise restraint and refrain from acts that could escalate or widen the conflict. As a concession to Iran, the resolution asked the UN secretary-general to inquire into responsibility for the conflict and to examine measures that would enhance regional stability and security.[1] Ambiguous in their response to Resolution 598, Iranian officials argued for a limited rather than comprehensive ceasefire in Gulf waters only. Iraq, on the other hand, insisted that any ceasefire arrangement be comprehensive to avoid giving an advantage in the war to one side over the other. Canada gave its full support to the resolution.

While satisfied with the UN resolution, Washington had hoped to couple the ceasefire resolution with a second measure calling for mandatory sanctions, including an arms embargo against any belligerent refusing to comply with the ceasefire. Aimed specifically at Iran, this additional measure has not received support from Japan and West Germany who depend heavily on Gulf oil and are unlikely to risk Iranian retaliation. Anxious to raise its diplomatic profile in the region, the Soviet Union supported the UN resolution. More importantly, Moscow also proposed talks with Washington about the mutual protection of shipping in the Gulf — an idea which some in Washington saw as entailing potential geopolitical costs.

The UN resolution prompted Britain and France to adopt a higher profile in the Gulf. Both London and Paris became embroiled in controversies with Iran over the activities of embassy personnel, and as a consequence the British sharply reduced, and the French severed, diplomatic ties with Iran. While these actions and the expansion of British and French naval forces in the Gulf buttressed the American position, European leaders made clear the limits of their support and expressed their concern that the Americans might provoke Iran to attack the various fleets in the Gulf. With these dangers in mind, after the July 24 mining of the *Bridgeton*, a U.S.-escorted reflagged Kuwaiti tanker, Britain and France agreed to send their respective minesweeping forces to the Gulf.

Other European nations proved to be more cautious in involving themselves in the Gulf, especially following the Mecca massacre in which 402
Muslim pilgrims and security men were killed (*Christian Science Monitor* 1987d).

The Mines of August: High-Tech Weapons and a Low-Intensity Conflict

Beyond the mining of the *Bridgeton*, the successful passage of another
reflagged Kuwaiti tanker, the *Gas Prince*, marked a triumph for the
troubled U.S. Navy escort mission. Even with this limited success for the
reflagging operation, it was unlikely that Washington would be able to
regain its low profile in the Gulf. In fact, the U.S. escort operation
increasingly offered Iran a convenient and symbolic target upon which
to vent its frustrations. Throughout the summer of 1987 the question
remained, could the United States carry out purely defensive escort
missions in the Persian Gulf, retaliate credibly if required, and sustain a
sizable presence in the area for an undetermined period? This question
weighed heavily on the minds of U.S. policy makers, as the Ayatollah
Khomeini warned that Iran would not be intimidated by the presence of
U.S. Navy warships in the Gulf. More troublesome still from a Western
strategic perspective was the early-August Soviet-Iranian oil accord
whereby Iran agreed to ship its oil exports through the Soviet city of Baku
and then have the oil pumped to one of the Soviet terminals on the Black
Sea (*Christian Science Monitor* 1987c).

Angered by Washington's decision to reflag and escort Kuwaiti
tankers through the Gulf, Iran announced in early August that it would
stage four days of war games in the Strait of Hormuz, the entry to the
Gulf. By mid-August, it was clear that if the American aim was to place
a military presence in the Gulf to deter Iranian actions, it was entirely
misplaced. Reagan administration officials believed the Iranians intended to harass the U.S. fleet rather than confront it head on. As one State
Department official put it: "Lebanon is the Iranian model....They believe
that Americans have a low threshold for pain and that eventually
American public opinion will force us out" (*Newsweek* 1987a). As if
repeating the nightmare that befell the U.S. marines in Beirut in October
1983, the U.S. Navy as peacekeeper in the Gulf was finding it increasingly difficult to anticipate the other side's intentions or to predict
whether the violence would escalate in this "guerrilla-style" war.

Conflict Escalation and Improved Prospects for Conflict Resolution

If military solutions to this protracted conflict were not working, diplomatic pressure on Iran to comply with UN Resolution 598 was proving equally futile. An emergency meeting of the Arab League in Tunis on August 25 — including Iran's supporters, Libya and Syria — called on Iran to obey the UN ceasefire demand by September 20 or face possible sanctions. But this call for a ceasefire from states within the region fell on deaf ears. With Iran's continued negative response to the UN ceasefire resolution, Iraq warned that it could no longer hold off its raids on Gulf shipping. To prevent Iraq from claiming the diplomatic high ground on the ceasefire, however, Iranian officials invited the UN secretary-general to Teheran to discuss ways in which the ceasefire might be implemented. Fearing that Iran would use the UN leader's visit as a respite in its war effort, Iraq revived the tanker war on August 29, after a forty-five-day lull, with attacks on Iran's Kharg Island terminal. Tankers off Iran's coast were also attacked at month's end, with Washington calling the timing of Iraqi attacks deplorable.

While the tanker war in the Gulf was renewed with a vengeance in early September, there was new activity on the diplomatic front. During the last week of August, Iran offered positive signs of interest in negotiating an end to war. Iran's Deputy Foreign Minister Muhammed Javed Lavijani spoke with members of the Security Council and expressed interest in consolidating and extending what he believed was already a de facto ceasefire in the Gulf, at least at sea (*Christian Science Monitor* 1987d). At the invitation of the parties, UN Secretary-General Javier Pérez de Cuéllar agreed to visit Baghdad and Teheran to seek Iranian compliance with Resolution 598 and bring an overall end to hostilities. The UN leader hoped to use the idea of a partial ceasefire in Gulf waters only — already agreed to in principle by Iran — as leverage to gain Iranian acceptance of a broader peace accord. The initiative was well timed given Washington's threat to press vigorously for an arms embargo if Iran failed to comply with the ceasefire resolution. Confronting the UN secretary-general was the challenge of whether a ceasefire in place could be converted into a ceasefire with forces withdrawn to the original Iran-Iraq border. And, if so, could the UN leader, backed by an uncertain consensus of the five veto-wielding powers of the Security Council, persuade Iran to give up territorial gains made in the war?

The Limits of UN Mediation

On the eve of the secretary-general's talks in Teheran, Iran indicated it would accept Resolution 598 provided the international investigation into who was responsible for the outbreak of the war was carried out *before* the ceasefire became operative. The Security Council resolution noted that the ceasefire was to be the *first* step agreed to by the combatants. In fact, the Security Council approved Pérez de Cuéllar's trip to both capitals only to "implement" the resolution as a whole and to get a firm acceptance or rejection from Iran (*New York Times* 1987a).

Despite four days of talks with the UN leader, Iran and Iraq remained far apart. In his private report to the Security Council, the secretary-general noted that Iran secretly proposed a de facto or undeclared cessation of hostilities with Iraq (*Newsweek* 1987b). Iranian officials maintained: "There must be a linkage between establishing the impartial body [investigating the issue of blame for the war] and observing a ceasefire; during that body's work Iran will, without saying so, observe a de facto ceasefire; after that body completes its work, the official ceasefire may begin" (*Christian Science Monitor* 1987e). Iraq rejected any notion of a de facto ceasefire and insisted on a declared and official ceasefire. With these inconclusive results and the fear that China and the Soviet Union were not prepared to accept sanctions, the Security Council appeared at year's end to be moving in the direction of a two-track policy: stepping up pressure by beginning work on sanctions and, at the same time, authorizing the secretary-general to pursue his diplomatic initiative.

Superpower Competition in the Gulf

The U.S. helicopter attack on the Iranian vessel *Ajr* on September 21 prompted a new round of diplomatic developments, as both superpowers again sought ways to end or at least contain the war. While the United States sought to strong-arm the Security Council into imposing an arms embargo on Iran, Soviet Foreign Minister Eduard Shevardnadze adopted a more low-key approach. He suggested that an international naval force under UN command take over responsibility for ensuring the safety of shipping in the Gulf. How was such new thinking in Soviet Middle Eastern policy to be explained?

Two factors dominated Soviet policy towards the Gulf in 1987: concern over the escalation of the war and a desire to make the most of Washington's post-Irangate problems in the Arab world. Throughout the year Moscow strengthened relations with the Arab Gulf states, maintained a close military relationship with Iraq and launched a tenuous rapproachement with Iran. Much to Washington's chagrin, by the end of 1987 the Soviets proved to be the only major power capable of sustaining a dialogue with both combatants. The Kremlin saw this dialogue as crucial, since, in Soviet eyes, the war could provide the United States with an opportunity to rebuild relations with Iran or at least convince the Arab Gulf states of the necessity for U.S. military bases in the region. Thus, throughout 1987 Moscow sought to expand its role in the region while seeking to curtail Western influence and, in the process, strengthen its claim to a role in any overall regional settlement.

Cognizant of the new aggressive Soviet approach in the Middle East, during the latter half of 1987 the United States attempted to reconcile a number of contending objectives in its Gulf policy. First, the U.S. remained determined to maintain its long-term commitment to defend the Arab states in the Gulf and rein in strident Iranian behaviour. The second U.S. objective was to ensure the safe flow of oil through the Persian Gulf. Third, the U.S. hoped to prevent the Soviet Union from further increasing its influence and presence in the region. And finally, it wanted to lay the groundwork for the restoration of a constructive relationship with Iran. By year's end, fulfilment of these goals remained elusive. The Arab Gulf states gave only lukewarm endorsement to U.S. efforts in the region at the November Arab summit meeting, with no concrete promises of additional base rights for U.S. forces (*Christian Science Monitor* 1987f).

While the U.S. and its European allies did, with some minor setbacks, keep the supply of Persian Gulf oil flowing, the highly sophisticated U.S. Navy task force was often caught off guard and thwarted by the low-intensity guerrilla-style warfare tactics used so effectively by the Iranians. Nor did the growing U.S. presence in the Gulf stem the growth of Soviet influence — especially in a situation where the United States was viewed as being the more belligerent of the two superpowers. In light of the Iran-Contra Affair, Washington was undermined by its own deeds and thereby unable to establish more credible relations with the government in Teheran.

Potential for Superpower Collaboration

As 1987 drew to a close, the solution to the escalation mentality in the Gulf seemed to lie with greater superpower collaboration to manage the conflict. The foundations for such collaboration had been developing incrementally. Both Moscow and Washington moved to protect Kuwaiti tankers from Iranian attack. The U.S. reflagging operation and its associated risks offered Washington a unique opportunity to engage the Soviets in a damage-limitation strategy in the Gulf that had heretofore been perceived as unwise and too costly. Traditionally, the primary objection to allowing greater Soviet influence in the Middle East was that the Soviets would use it to inflame further an already turbulent region. The Soviets did, however, indicate a new sense of commitment to regional conflict management and the principle of freedom of navigation as evidenced by their support for the Security Council ceasefire resolution. Pressure for greater superpower collaboration came from America's European allies, who feared that additional unilateral military moves by the U.S. could drag them increasingly into the Gulf conflict in 1988. Possible U.S.-Soviet cooperation under UN auspices, rather than continued open-ended military involvement, looked more plausible.

Canadian Reaction to Developments in the Gulf

Canadian reaction to events in the Iran-Iraq War and the Persian Gulf during 1987 focused on three issues: unilateral military initiatives by the United States that might further fuel the conflict; the feasibility and desirability of carrying out a UN-sponsored arms embargo directed at both belligerents; and the problem of Canadian-made arms and components and multiple-use technologies being transferred to the local combatants.

Ottawa expressed concern with respect to U.S. military intervention in the Gulf that the U.S. helicopter gunship attack on the *Ajr* could not be defended under international law. Canada feared that unless Washington clarified its objectives in the Gulf and restrained itself from threatening Iran, its allies would be less inclined to send additional naval support to the Gulf and would not feel obliged to support an arms embargo. Though generally supportive of the U.S. reflagging policy, Ottawa also worried that an extended show of force by Washington could lead to a confrontation with the Soviet Union.

In terms of support for sanctions, Secretary of State for External Affairs Joe Clark argued in a September 22 speech to the UN General Assembly that he fully supported efforts by the UN to use sanctions to help end the Iran-Iraq War. Clark noted that the peace mission of the UN secretary-general "was not as successful as we all had hoped" (*Globe and Mail* 1987a). Under these circumstances, it was reasonable for Canada to support sanctions on arm sales to the belligerents. Ottawa insisted, however, that such sanctions would have to be carried out within the UN framework and with the full support of the Security Council.

The transfer of military-related equipment to Iran and Iraq during 1987 was both a domestic and international problem for Canada. Ottawa released only fragmentary information about its willingness to approve the export of military and military-related equipment to Iran. According to documents obtained by the *Globe and Mail*, twenty-four permits for exports to Iran were issued in 1986 (1987b). Canadian government controls over military-related exports were so weak that Canadian industries at times supplied equipment used by armed forces on both sides of the Iran-Iraq battlefield (*Globe and Mail* 1987c).

Throughout 1987, Canada supported UN efforts to bring about a resolution to this conflict but undertook no direct third-party initiatives with the disputants. Lacking sufficiently strong links to Teheran and Baghdad, Canada was not well positioned to make any credible offer of "good offices" to the parties. The conflict in the Gulf seemed to most Canadian policy makers to fall within the purview of geopolitical competition between the superpowers, thereby suggesting that Canada could do little to affect regional developments in any meaningful way. However, given Iran's geopolitical significance, many Canadians believed that the United States should be encouraged to re-establish a presence in Iran as a necessary precondition for advancing the peace process.

Central America

In contrast to the worsening situation in the Persian Gulf in 1987, developments in Central America pushed local states in the direction of designing and implementing their own regional peace plan. Early in the year it appeared as though all Central American governments were under siege. In El Salvador, discontent with President Duarté's rule became more widespread and militant (*Christian Science Monitor* 1987g). In Guatemala, President Cerezo sought military assistance to cope with leftist insurgent attacks, massive labour unrest and the worst human-rights record in the Western Hemisphere (*Christian Science Monitor* 1987h). In Nicaragua, the Contra rebels began focusing their attacks on rural projects, while in Honduras, the government bought F5 jets from the U.S. to counter Nicaraguan moves to acquire MIG-21s from the Soviets (*Christian Science Monitor* 1987i). Together these developments seemed to promise another year of rising tensions. However, the controversy over Nicaragua and other regional political-military conflicts was suddenly eclipsed by two diplomatic initiatives in early August: on August 5 the United States announced a new American peace plan for the region drawn up by Speaker of the House of Representatives James Wright; two days later the five Central American presidents upstaged the Reagan/Wright plan with a peace plan of their own — a modified version of Costa Rican President Arias's initiative of February 1987.

From Contadora to Guatemala: 1983-87

The Guatemala peace plan of August 7 spearheaded by President Arias (who won the 1987 Nobel Peace Prize for his efforts) represented the culmination of a four-year search by the governments of Central America to find a diplomatic solution to their many overlapping conflicts. During this time, efforts for a negotiated settlement were associated with the Contadora Group, led by Mexico, Colombia, Panama and Venezuela. Concerned with the stalemate over the Contadora process and fearful about the repercussions of the Iran-Contra scandal on U.S. policy in the region, Arias launched his first peace initiative. The key innovation of the Arias plan was its commitment to democratization — freedom of the press, the removal of censorship and the election of a Central American parliament. Mindful of his own country's military vulnerability, President Arias hoped acceptance of his new plan would forestall the Soviet- and Cuban-backed Sandinista regime from threatening neighbouring countries with subversion. Unfortunately, the first Arias proposal suffered from many of the inadequacies found in the Contadora process. The parties were to be subjected to an open-ended negotiation process, inadequate verification provisions and lack of consultation, especially with Mexico, the prime mover behind the Contadora process. Anxious to give the appearance of flexibility, the Nicaraguan government side-stepped outright rejection of the Arias proposal, seeing in it an opportunity to divide U.S. public opinion over aid to the Contras.

The Reagan administration gave a lukewarm response to the first Arias plan. In an effort to reassert the diplomatic initiative, on August 5 President Reagan endorsed the Wright peace proposal. Drawing heavily on the Arias plan, the Reagan/Wright plan called for a negotiated rather than a declared ceasefire, indirect talks with the Contra rebels, the suspension of U.S. military aid and military manoeuvres in Honduras once the ceasefire was negotiated (though humanitarian aid would continue), the termination by the Sandinistas of the emergency law, their restoration of civil rights and their establishing a timetable for new elections. Crucial to the implementation of the U.S. plan was the notion of great power constraint: Washington would only fulfil its part of the bargain if Soviet-bloc military aid to the Sandinistas was terminated simultaneously (Purcell 1987). In putting forward its plan, the administration hoped to ensure the survival of the Contra resistance movement should negotiations break down. At the same time, through this initiative, Washington hoped to rebuild its credibility in the wake of the Iran-Contra Affair. From the vantage point of domestic politics, Nicaraguan rejection of the new U.S. plan would leave Congress little choice but to continue the funding of the Contras. Opponents of Contra aid called the plan a "sham" and its implementation highly unrealistic.

In his response to the Reagan/Wright plan, Nicaraguan President Ortega said he was willing to discuss this proposal along with those of the Contadora Group and President Arias. The Nicaraguan leader also emphasized his refusal to negotiate with the Contra rebels and insisted on direct talks with the United States.

The Guatemala Plan: A Regional Initiative

Whereas the Reagan/Wright plan was aimed largely at ensuring the survival of the Contras, the Guatemalan or Arias plan of August 7, 1987, implicitly rejected all rebel movements and recognized the legitimacy of the Sandinista government.[2] Unfortunately, this plan, like the earlier Arias one, did not provide for penalties in the event of non-compliance. Moreover, the new plan offered no details on the mechanism for concluding a ceasefire. Such ambiguities clearly favoured the Sandinistas over the rebels, since at the beginning of the peace process the rebels would lose all leverage with an immediate ceasefire and the cessation of military aid.

There were four reasons why the Central American countries supported the second Arias plan. First, agreement was perhaps possible in light of diminished U.S. influence in the region in the wake of the Iran-Contra Affair. Second, the Central American leaders were upset with the Reagan administration for not consulting them on the Reagan/Wright plan — a plan they feared the president would be unable to implement because of waning domestic clout. A third factor was the fear in El Salvador and Honduras that Washington would be severely constrained in sustaining its commitment to the Contras. Finally, the Sandinista government in Nicaragua supported the plan because it extended implementation procedures for ninety days; as long as negotiations were in progress, the U.S. Congress would be less inclined to vote additional aid for the Contras.

The November 7, 1987, Deadline: The Problems of Building Momentum

As the November 7 deadline for implementing the Arias plan approached, the Central American countries had taken only some of the steps called for in the peace plan: all had established national reconciliation committees; Guatemala and El Salvador had held talks with guerrillas, while Nicaragua undertook limited press liberalization and announced a unilateral partial ceasefire. The passing of the deadline did little to spur the Sandinista regime towards a more vigorous implementation of the peace plan. Beyond the apparently non-negotiable nature of the Sandinista revolution, the key stumbling block to further progress at the end of 1987 remained the issue of simultaneity: as of November 7, all five Central American presidents were supposed to call on outside powers to stop funding irregular forces in the region. This meant, of course, the cessation of U.S. aid to the Contras. At the same time, the Hondurans warned that if the Sandinistas failed to comply with the peace plan, Honduras would not feel obliged to remove the Contra presence from its territory.

In Guatemala, the peace process bogged down with no progress towards a ceasefire with the local guerrillas. Worse still, given each Central American state's differing perceptions of the regional situation, Guatemalan officials argued that since there was so little fighting in Guatemala, there was no real need for a ceasefire agreement (*Christian Science Monitor* 1987j). By contrast, in El Salvador, President José

Napoléon Duarté decreed a broad amnesty, held preliminary talks with guerrillas and promised to proceed with a unilateral nationwide ceasefire. However, European and Central American diplomats were suspicious of any unilateral Salvadoran initiatives, since the ceasefire was designed to fail while giving Duarté the appearance of compliance (*Christian Science Monitor* 1987k).

Nicaraguan leaders argued that while "aggression" by the United States continued, Managua was not ready to lift its state of emergency or decree an amnesty. President Ortega stressed that any additional steps would only be taken within the framework of simultaneity. Nevertheless, in order to prevent another infusion of aid to the Contras, the Sandinistas dropped their long-standing refusal to open contacts with the rebels and agreed to mediated indirect talks.

President Ortega Goes to Washington

On November 12 President Ortega and the leader of the Contra rebels met separately with American House Speaker Wright. On this occasion Contra leaders argued that while they might agree to the technical terms of a ceasefire agreement, they would not agree to its implementation until the Sandinista government complied with those elements of the Guatemala accord that would allow Contra leaders to return home and participate in local politics (*New York Times* 1987b).

During his four-day trip to Washington, the Nicaraguan president outlined a ceasefire proposal for consideration by Contra leaders. Ortega also agreed to have Miguel Cardinal Obando y Bravo, the Roman Catholic primate of Nicaragua, serve as the intermediary between his government and the Contras. It was agreed that the talks would take place in Santo Domingo, capital of the Dominican Republic (*New York Times* 1987c).

An Uncertain Start for Mediation

On December 1 the Contras announced their own ceasefire plan, rejecting Ortega's proposal. In addition to complying with the terms of the Guatemala plan, the Contras called for hostilities to be ended from December 8, 1987, to January 17, 1988, with simultaneous talks on political issues. The Contras also insisted that rebel troops would remain in control of more than 77,700 square kilometres of Nicaragua and that air, land and sea corridors could be established to supply rebel troops with non-military supplies (*New York Times* 1987d).

For the first time since the Nicaraguan civil conflict began almost six years earlier, Sandinista government officials opened indirect talks with Contra leaders on December 3 under the auspices of Cardinal Obando. It was Obando's task to reconcile the narrowly focused technical ceasefire proposal offered by the Sandinistas (how the Contras would lay down their weapons) with the far broader Contra proposal. The latter stipulated that while a ceasefire is in place, the Sandinistas must make sweeping political changes (*New York Times* 1987e).

The first round of talks between the Sandinistas and the Contras broke down when the Nicaraguan government rejected Obando's proposed truce during which Nicaragua would decree a general amnesty, end press restrictions and lift the state of emergency. The Contras accepted the proposal, but the Sandinistas argued it was incomplete because it did not include an end to all outside support for the Contras. Though the two sides could not agree on a second round of talks, Obando was able to persuade Nicaraguan leaders to accept direct talks between the two factions' technical experts to discuss ways of arranging a Christmas truce (*New York Times* 1987f).

Only three weeks after the talks began, they collapsed on December 22 when the Contras launched a large military operation in the northeastern mining districts of Nicaragua. In conjunction with their attacks, the Contras called off the peace parley in Santo Domingo. Contra leaders refused to meet a U.S. lawyer and a West German politician representing the Sandinistas, insisting instead on face-to-face discussions with at least one Sandinista official. Cardinal Obando acknowledged that the talks had reached an impasse, but he hoped to arrange further talks in 1988. Responding to the rebel attack and the impasse in negotiations, the Nicaraguan government accused the Contras of seeking to influence the debate in the U.S. Congress on the renewal of financial support for the rebels.

Soviet-American Competition and Collaboration in the Region

Beginning in 1985, the Soviet Union shipped helicopter gunships and transport helicopters to the Sandinista government. The helicopters were used to transport troops around the country and to attack the rebels from the air. To offset the technological logistical advantages afforded to the Sandinistas, the Reagan administration supplied the Contras with $100 million, which began to reach the rebels by late 1986. With this money the Contras established an aerial resupply system to sustain themselves in Nicaragua and thereby maintain continuous political and military pressure on the Sandinista regime as well as on the Soviet Union (Purcell 1987). In December 1987 the extent of Soviet involvement in Nicaragua became more ominous when a former senior Nicaraguan Defence Ministry officer, Major Roger Miranda, who defected to the United States, revealed that Moscow was preparing to send large quantities of new weapons to Nicaragua despite provisions of the new regional peace accord. Miranda also suggested Nicaragua was training Salvadorean guerrillas with the knowledge of Cuba and the Soviet Union (*New York Times* 1987g).

In the wake of Miranda's disclosures, Washington chose not to query Moscow about the possibility of basing MIG-21s in Nicaragua. The Reagan administration hoped to use these revelations to ensure continued U.S. funding for the Contras. However, at their December summit in Washington, Mikhail Gorbachev apparently told President Reagan that Moscow would be willing to halt aid to the Sandinistas provided the United States ended aid to the Contras.

In the context of U.S.-Soviet competition in Central America, Washington faced some difficult choices at the end of 1987. However obliquely conveyed, the Soviets appeared to be signalling that they would prefer to avoid paying for a second Cuba if there was a reasonable diplomatic alternative. But as the Nicaraguan defector candidly argued, the Sandinista military's five-year plan showed that if the United States insisted on stepping up military aid to the Contras, the Soviets were prepared to respond in kind (*New York Times* 1987h).

Endgame for U.S. Credibility in Regional Diplomacy: The Release of the Iran-Contra Report

On November 18 the congressional committees on the Iran-Contra Affair released their final report on how $48 million raised from arms sales to Iran had been diverted to the Contras. The committees' investigations revealed "that of the $16.1 million profit from the sale of arms to Iran about $3.8 million went to support the contras" (*New York Times* 1987i). The release of the congressional report undermined U.S. diplomatic credibility in both Central America and the Middle East. With the charge levelled against the Reagan administration that it had willfully circumvented the law in its efforts to fund the Contras, the gulf between the Sandinista government and Washington widened even further. Believing the administration had every intention of continuing its support for the Contras, the Ortega government had little incentive to advance the peace process through direct or indirect talks with the rebels. Ironically, it may be within the context of this U.S.-Nicaraguan deadlock, where each of the disputants fears disengagement from the conflict will result in a loss of face, that a third party like Canada might play a pivotal role.

The Clark Trip to Central America: A New Degree of Assertiveness? [3]

On his November trip to Central America External Affairs Minister Joe Clark suggested that Canadian soldiers could serve as peacekeeping observers in ensuring compliance with the Central American peace plan (*Ottawa Citizen* 1987a). Clark's remarks seemed to point towards a more active third-party role for Canada. Until the minister's trip, the Canadian position had been that expertise and technical advice would be offered to the Central Americans as they devised enforcement mechanisms for their new accord. To lend further support to the peace process, Clark said it may be necessary for Canada to admit Nicaraguan Contra insurgents into Canada as part of a general peace settlement (*Ottawa Citizen* 1987b). External Affairs officials noted, however, that according to current Canadian refugee policy, political refugees accepted into Canada must be non-combatants. Accepting Contra guerrillas would necessitate a change in the rules.

Within the region, Nicaraguan President Ortega reacted favourably to Clark's visit and supported a leading role for Canada in the peace process. Noting that Nicaragua would like to have security zones along its borders with Costa Rica and Honduras, Ortega suggested that Canada could play an observer role in preventing border incursions. However, in addition to supporting the peacekeeping component of the peace process, the Nicaraguan president appealed for more foreign aid. In response to Ortega's call, Clark said Canada could not increase its development assistance substantially but would make any additional commitments contingent upon further progress in implementing the Guatemala plan (*Globe and Mail* 1987d). While the full implications of the Clark visit to Central America remain to be determined, Canadian policy appeared less

timid and more assertive in 1987. More important, at the end of the year
Canada was well positioned to play a facilitative role in advancing the
peace process in Central America.

Southern Africa[4]

The situation in Southern Africa remained fundamentally unchanged in
1987: the conflicts in the region neither escalated significantly nor
moved any closer towards resolution. Despite increased economic
difficulties, South Africa continued its policy of destabilizing its neighbours through its extensive military activities, particularly its support for
the National Union for the Total Independence of Angola (UNITA) and
its military bases in Southern Angola (*South* 1988: 35).

Within South Africa itself, black-on-black violence rose significantly
during the year (*Christian Science Monitor* 1987l). The white regime of
President Botha responded to the growing unrest by adding still tougher
measures to the government's state of emergency policy (*Christian
Science Monitor* 1987m). Bolstered by the May 1987 gains in its
parliamentary majority, the government strengthened its commitment to
stamping out radical black intimidation and made clear it would deal only
with those black leaders willing to engage in power-sharing negotiations.
As the Botha regime moves to shore up its negotiating position, there is
little likelihood that internal oppression will be eased. No doubt the white
regime will aim to establish a parliamentary structure that will ensure
white dominance but offers enough to tempt black leaders to participate.
Whether the two sides can limit their self-destructive behaviour and
strengthen the will to collaborate remains to be seen.

Beyond the immediate borders of South Africa, the Front-Line States
continued to cope with their cruel dilemma. Heavily dependent on South
Africa economically and vulnerable to continuous exploitation by the
Botha regime, the Front-Line States proved unable to disengage themselves from Pretoria — a key precondition for ending apartheid. Worse
still, severe economic difficulties in Mozambique, Angola and Zambia
prevented these states from making credible the threat to impose their
own economic sanctions against South Africa.

Perhaps the most ominous development in the region was the growing
U.S.-Soviet competition in Angola and Zimbabwe. The conflict in
Angola intensified during the year as Washington stepped up military
support for UNITA, the anti-government rebel movement. At the same

time, the Soviets continued to pour heavy equipment into Luanda. Recent efforts by U.S., Angolan and rebel officials to find a solution to this ten-year conflict have succeeded only in highlighting Angola's dependence on Moscow. The Soviets have insisted they will not disengage from Angola so long as the U.S. continues to provide military backing to UNITA. The central challenge confronting Angola's leadership in 1987 was how to negotiate an end to the war with U.S.- and South African-backed insurgents in order to enlist Western aid to resolve the country's deepening economic crisis. In July, Washington argued that if Angola was prepared to link a total Cuban pullout to an end to South Africa's dominance and military presence in Namibia, the door to improved diplomatic relations would be opened (*Christian Science Monitor* 1987n). Unfortunately, Angola remained hopelessly tied to Soviet military support throughout the year.

In Zimbabwe, another of the Front-Line States, the prospects for regional instability increased with Harare's request for a squadron of MIG-29 fighter planes from Moscow. This request probably had its source in Zimbabwe's resentment over the Reagan administration's policy of "constructive engagement," through which Washington appeared to be siding with the white government in South Africa. While Moscow adopted a cautious approach towards the racial conflict in South Africa in 1987 and the associated regional unrest, a major arms sale to Zimbabwe (still under negotiation at year's end) would represent a major departure for Soviet policy in the region. Should Zimbabwe prove capable of countering South Africa's preponderant military power, Moscow could, in one bold stroke, undercut the U.S. position in the region and bolster its own standing in black Africa (*Christian Science Monitor* 1987o).

Ironically, in the complex chess game of superpower competition in the Third World, in 1987 the United States further contributed to the very conditions it hoped to avoid. Rather than forcing the Soviets out of the region, the Reagan administration, through its tacit support of Pretoria's policy of regional destabilization, merely provided Moscow with the opportunity to significantly improve relations with Zimbabwe at the expense of the United States. At the close of 1987, the Reagan doctrine of containing Soviet expansion in the Third World appeared to be without substance.

Commonwealth Heads of Government: The Search for a Multilateral Consensus

The Commonwealth Heads of Government Conference in Vancouver, October 13-17, 1987, focused on the ways in which increased pressure could be brought to bear on the white regime in Pretoria, primarily through intensified economic sanctions. Prime Minister Mulroney, a strong critic of apartheid, led the campaign to strengthen the Commonwealth's sanctions policy and pledged to keep Canada "on the high ground" in the international campaign against South African apartheid by vigorously promoting punitive economic sanctions (*Globe and Mail* 1987e). In opposition, Britain's Margaret Thatcher reiterated her long-standing view that additional sanctions would only hurt black South Africans. Fearful that the sanctions issue would tear the Commonwealth apart, its leaders decided to work around Britain's stubborn stance, calling for broader sanctions and steps to ensure that existing measures would be carried out more effectively. The decision as to what sanctions to apply was left to individual countries.

As part of his strategy to avoid another confrontation over the issue, Mulroney asked the foreign ministers of Australia, Britain, Canada, Guyana, India, Nigeria, Tanzania, Zambia and Zimbabwe to consider how best to proceed. Despite British opposition, the leaders agreed to establish an eight-member group chaired by Canada's Joe Clark (and excluding the British foreign secretary) with a view to providing "high level impetus and guidance" on the Commonwealth's approach to apartheid.[5]

The Vancouver conference also produced agreement on increased aid to the embattled Front-Line States for transportation and communication projects that would reduce their reliance on South Africa. For its part Canada pledged $20 million towards rebuilding the Limpopo railway line connecting Zimbabwe to the port of Maputo in Mozambique. Prime Minister Mulroney stressed, however, that Canada would not provide military aid to the Front-Line States: "We are not going to be offering military aid. We feel that Canada's role is in areas dealing very much with the building and strengthening of those economies [of South Africa's neighbours]" (*Globe and Mail* 1987f). Ottawa did agree to support the other foreign ministers in approving $44 million in aid for South Africa's 25 million blacks (Mackenzie 1987).

Agreement on issues of aid did little to defuse the bitter division between Britain and the rest of the Commonwealth over apartheid. To emphasize how successful sanctions had been, Prime Minister Mulroney insisted that Canadian sanctions had caused a 50 per cent reduction in trade between Canada and South Africa during the first half of 1987. Quick to refute Mulroney's claim, the British, using International Monetary Fund figures, argued that Canadian exports to South Africa had actually increased by 46 per cent between 1985 and 1986 (Mackenzie 1987).

The release of the figures by Britain was clearly intended to embarrass Mulroney and undermine Canada's growing influence in the Commonwealth. After the conference, Zimbabwe's prime minister, Robert Mugabe, suggested that Canada was taking over from Britain as the effective leader of the group. Clearly Prime Minister Mulroney adopted a strong position in Vancouver, at least at the rhetorical level. To some, however, Canadian actions at the conference could merely be construed as another attempt to preserve the unity and values of the Commonwealth rather than a serious change in policy towards South Africa. Perhaps with its newly found leadership role in the Commonwealth, Canada will move beyond the policies of its major allies, Britain and the United States, and adopt a more proactive approach to the numerous conflicts in Southern Africa.

The Limits of Multilateral Conflict-Resolution Efforts

Western policy on Southern Africa lacks coherence. As Roger Martin states:

> The U.S. is simultaneously arming UNITA, claiming a mediating role in Namibia, imposing tough sanctions on South Africa "to end Apartheid," cutting aid to Zimbabwe, and refusing it to Mozambique. Meanwhile, Western Europe aids all the Front Line States, especially Mozambique, and is applying weaker sanctions to South Africa with no clear objective in view, Scandinavia is demanding mandatory sanctions, while Britain's Mrs. Thatcher denounces the very principle of sanctions, is regularly insulted by Mugabe and Kaunda in consequence, yet applies them, and alone trains the Zimbabwean and Mozambican armies to resist South African-inspired pressure. (1987: 401)

The Western approach to Southern Africa must begin with a sense of the real limits of Western influence in the region. At best, the West retains only the threat of sanctions against South Africa and can control to a degree the rate and scope of military and civilian aid for the Front-Line States. Even these instruments are likely to prove insufficient if well-intentioned third parties fail to focus on those steps that will prevent further escalation of the conflict. The immediate goal must not be "ending apartheid" and overthrowing the white government in South Africa but rather protecting the neighbouring Front-Line States from economic and military destabilization. This may mean applying mandatory economic sanctions should South Africa engage in unprovoked economic aggression against its neighbours. At the same time, to deter military aggression, Western states, including Canada, may have to offer greater military assistance to the Front-Line States. In sum, as 1987 came to an end, the harsh reality of South African economic and military power and geographic advantage vis-à-vis its neighbours proved once again to be the most important factor in blocking conflict-resolution efforts.

Conclusion

What conclusions can be drawn about the three major regional conflicts discussed above and did Canada make any significant contribution to their resolution?

In the Persian Gulf, we witnessed a rapid escalation of the conflict along with increased great power and UN intervention. At the end of 1987, neither Iran nor Iraq believed the war required less costly approaches to conflict management. At various moments during the escalation of the Gulf tanker war, opportunities for a breakthrough seemed possible, especially with the September visit by the UN secretary-general to Teheran and Baghdad. Each party required a face-saving solution to relieve its predicament — a perfect opportunity for third-party intervention — yet no outside actor, including the great powers, proved capable of convincing the parties to de-escalate the conflict.

Interestingly, the most dangerous regional conflict in 1987 was the one from which Canadians seemed most removed. While the Canadian government supported UN mediation efforts and made clear its concerns to Washington regarding the dangers of U.S. unilateral military initiatives, Ottawa felt no urgent need to take a more active role in efforts to control the Gulf War. Nor was Canada encouraged by other Western or Middle Eastern powers to become more actively engaged. The Iran-Iraq conflict retained a low priority on the Canadian foreign policy agenda in 1987 and was not an issue that received significant attention by non-governmental organizations.

In contrast, the conflict in Southern Africa remained stable throughout the year. Growing unrest among South African blacks continued, and to the chagrin of many both within and outside the region, the white regime in Pretoria maintained its strategy of regional destabilization while strengthening the state of emergency locally. Under these conditions of neither conflict escalation nor de-escalation, there were no opportunities for a settlement breakthrough.

In terms of the perceived urgent need for third-party intervention, the South African case in 1987 represented a classic example of mismatched intentions. Outside powers, especially the Commonwealth countries, were willing to intervene but one of the key disputants, South Africa, proved resistant to Western urgings. With the conflicts in the region driven largely by the dynamics and spillover effects of internal South African politics, efforts by third parties to redirect and resolve the conflict have been shunned. When one of the principal parties to the conflict retains significant power and resource advantages over the other disputants, receptiveness to third-party efforts designed to undo such advantages will likely be negligible.

While Southern Africa as a region rich in mineral resources has been of long-standing strategic interest to both superpowers, neither the U.S. nor the U.S.S.R. has sought to intervene purposively to de-escalate the conflict, perhaps because neither perceived the other to be taking any provocative steps in 1987 that might undermine existing regional footholds. To the extent that great power geopolitical competition in the region remains stable, the likelihood of, and incentive for, great power mediation is likely to remain low.

While the great powers declined to undertake active conflict-resolution efforts in the region during 1987, Canada did assume a leadership role at the Vancouver Commonwealth conference to urge more punitive sanctions against South Africa. How do we reconcile *low* near-term prospects for conflict settlement with an active interest by Canada in promoting strategies for resolution, including the imposition of sanctions? Canada clearly saw an opportunity to play a leadership role in 1987 in addressing the South African problem through the Commonwealth conference. Encouraged by other Commonwealth members and by various non-governmental constituencies at home, Canada seized the chance to distinguish Canadian policy on South Africa from those of

Britain and the United States. At year's end, however, this heightened profile and new sense of opportunity remained to be converted into the kind of leverage necessary to bring about a significant reduction in the Southern African conflict.

Despite the fact that Central America in 1987 was plagued by armed struggle, human-rights violations and severe economic crisis, the region groped towards implementing a regional peace plan designed to de-escalate local conflict and reduce opportunities for superpower med-dling. By year's end, opportunities for a significant breakthrough seemed reasonably good.

Though outside powers like the U.S. were anxious to impose their own peace formula on the conflict, the Central American states rejected such external overtures, preferring instead to receive outside diplomatic and economic support (as distinct from peace proposals) for a peace accord designed by the protagonists themselves. For the most part, this approach to regional conflict resolution was treated favourably by the international community, though the United States feared it might legitimize the continuation of the Sandinista regime in Nicaragua.

Fearful that it might be excluded from the peace process in Central America, the Reagan administration felt compelled to offer its own peace plan — one that would ensure the survival of the Contra resistance in Nicaragua and more generally safeguard U.S. hegemony in the region. Given that third-party conflict-resolution efforts may be about power politics as much as peacemaking, the incentive for a great power to intervene diplomatically in regional disputes within its sphere of influ-ence is likely to be considerable. During the December Reagan-Gor-bachev summit in Washington, the Soviet Union expressed interest in de-escalating the conflict and supporting the Guatemala accord on a "recip-rocal basis." However, as was the case in the Persian Gulf, the Reagan administration refused to acknowledge a potential Soviet role in the peace process. For many in the U.S. administration in 1987, it was better to live with the conflict in Central America than to pave the way for greater Soviet influence in the region.

In its long-standing support for the Contadora process, Canada has implicitly rejected a third-party role for the great powers in Central America. Suspicious of American motives in the region and fearful of superpower "globalization" of regional conflict, the Canadian govern-ment has tended to strongly support indigenous initiatives like the Guatemala plan. In adopting this approach, Canada has created a unique role for itself in promoting a regional settlement. Because of its commitment to development assistance and international peacekeeping, Canada is seen internationally as a credible and influential actor in Central America. Thus, Canada is well positioned to provide technical and logistical support for ceasefire observation and verification missions. At the same time, through development assistance, Canada maintains close contact with all states in the region and can therefore hold out the possibility of greater assistance to those parties that comply fully with the Guatemala plan. Given that Central America continues to enjoy high salience on the foreign policy and development assistance agendas of the Canadian government and is given strong public articulation by numerous non-governmental organizations, Canada has a unique opportunity in this particular regional conflict to advance the peace process.

4

Call to Arms: Canadian National Security Policy

FEN OSLER HAMPSON

The Conservative government's White Paper on defence dominated the political agenda in Canadian national security policy in 1987. The White Paper charted a dramatic new course for Canadian defence policy, one intended to catapult Canada into the ranks of great maritime powers. Its bold vision of the future struck some observers as almost un-Canadian. But at the year's end, the White Paper's future was still in doubt and its geostrategic assumptions were in danger of being undermined by the growing thaw in East-West relations dramatized at the December Washington summit between U.S. President Ronald Reagan and Soviet General Secretary Mikhail Gorbachev.

Given the Mulroney government's own uncertain political future and its bottom place in the polls, it was far from certain whether Defence Minister Perrin Beatty would be allowed to complete the ambitious course he charted in June with the release of the defence White Paper. There were tough political and bureaucratic battles to be fought against formidable opponents in the Finance Department and Treasury Board intent on trimming government spending and bringing the federal deficit under control. The minister of national defence and his deputies were quickly forced onto the defensive by a bureaucracy and a Canadian public unaccustomed to the Reagan-style "call to arms" and the rhetoric of deterrence that peppered the White Paper. The arguments for a defence build-up, no matter how modest within the East-West balance of power, were threatened by public demands for new social programs, farm subsidies and better day care. The superpower arms control agreement on intermediate-range nuclear forces (INF) coupled with the growing thaw in East-West relations and the euphoria over the Washington summit virtually ensured that the government's attempts to sell a defence build-up to Canadians would be made doubly difficult. What were the key themes of the White Paper? What were the issues in the ensuing debate? That is the subject of this chapter.

The White Paper

Perrin Beatty's White Paper on defence was the first to be issued in sixteen years, the last having been published in August 1971. That earlier White Paper followed a major review of Canadian foreign and defence policy in 1968-69. The 1970s witnessed a substantial attrition in Canadian forces: the Canadian commitment to Europe was cut in half, and the overall size of Canadian forces was reduced by 17,000. There was also a decline in the percentage of the federal budget and of the gross domestic product spent on defence. The portion of the defence budget that went into new equipment also dropped. Capital equipment spending fell from 20 per cent of the federal budget in 1962-63 to 9 per cent in 1972-73. It increased to 20 per cent in 1982-83 (in contrast to a 25 per cent average for the other members of the North Atlantic Treaty Organization [NATO]). These increases reflected acquisitions of the new CF-18 fighter and CP-140 Aurora long-range patrol aircraft, the Canadian Patrol Frigate Program, and modernization and updating of Tribal Class destroyers in June 1985 (Government of Canada 1987a: 1, 43).

The 1987 White Paper pointed a stern finger at the lamentable decline in Canada's ability to meet existing and ongoing defence commitments and to reverse equipment obsolescence and "rust-out." It predicted that "if 'rust-out' were permitted to occur, either by intent or neglect, the loss of equipment in the 1990s would by itself dictate a new, greatly diminished defence role" (Government of Canada 1987a: 46). But the government was not about to let this happen. It would "alter some commitments to bring them more into line with resources, while improving the effectiveness with which remaining commitments are carried out." Defence spending would be kept at a base rate of annual real growth of 2 per cent over the next fifteen years.

The key elements of the procurement program in the new White Paper were as follows:

- purchase of a second batch of six frigates beyond the six currently under construction and selection of a replacement helicopter for the Sea King;
- deployment of fixed sonar systems for the Arctic and greater emphasis on underwater detection;

- phased acquisition of a fleet of ten to twelve nuclear-powered attack submarines to be on station in the northeast Pacific, Canadian Arctic and North Atlantic;
- development of an effective mine-countermeasure activity for clearing Canadian ports and shipping lanes;
- completion and modernization of radar coverage of Canadian coastal airspace and upgrading of existing airfields in the North to function as Forward Operating Locations for CF-18 interceptors and Dispersed Operating Bases or Airborne Warning and Control System (AWACS) aircraft;
- acquisition of six additional long-range patrol aircraft and modernization of the fleet of Tracker aircraft; and
- development of space-based or space-related systems for surveillance, communications, navigation, and search and rescue.

In addition, there are plans to create additional brigades from the reserves and to establish a northern training centre in the 1990s to improve combat readiness of Canadian forces. Canada's current commitments to Europe include one Canadian Mechanized Brigade Group and one Canadian Air Group in Germany. The Canadian Air-Sea Transportable (CAST) Brigade Group and two Rapid Reinforcement Fighter Squadrons that are stationed in Canada are committed to Norway in times of crisis. Canada is also committed to providing a battalion group and a fighter squadron, stationed in Canada, to Northern Europe. However, these commitments will change.

The White Paper outlines government plans to consolidate Canadian forces in Europe because "widespread land and air force commitments...represent a dilution of valuable combat resources, and cannot reasonably be supported or sustained from an ocean away in the event of hostilities." These problems are especially acute in the case of the CAST commitment to Norway. The force would take several weeks to get there, "making timely deployment questionable....Moreover, once deployed, it would be extremely difficult to reinforce and resupply, particularly after the start of hostilities" (Government of Canada 1987a: 61). This was borne out at NATO exercise Brave Lion conducted in 1986. After two years of planning, it still took the military twenty-one days to get to Norway (Centre for Foreign Policy Studies 1987: 7). Henceforth, the CAST force would be committed to Germany to create a division-sized force of two brigades. Two fighter squadrons will also be shifted from Norway to Germany (for a total of five). Canada, however, will maintain its battalion-sized group commitment AMF(L) for service on the northern flank or for deployment in Denmark.

The White Paper also proposed plans to augment Canadian reserves. These forces were cut during the 1960s and 1970s on the grounds of cost and because the Trudeau government felt that they would contribute little to national defence in the event of nuclear war. Reserve strength would be increased to 90,000 personnel. University training programs that existed before the 1970s would be reactivated. The White Paper aims to reduce the distinction between reserves and regulars by integrating the two forces more closely together.

Outer space is another important priority in the White Paper: "Space will increasingly be utilized in support of national defence aims. Canada's priorities for military space activity — surveillance, communications, navigation and search and rescue — flow naturally from our geography." The government's key objectives include the following:

- monitoring research (and possible development) of ballistic missile defence (BMD) and related systems;
- development of space-based surveillance to detect, track, identify and assist in the interception of aircraft and cruise missiles, as an improvement, or as a successor, to existing systems, and to conduct surveillance of Canada's maritime approaches and its remote and Arctic areas;
- development of a satellite communications capability that will provide strategic and tactical secure communications to Canadian sea, land and air forces worldwide and interconnection to allied communications systems; and
- participation and contribution to national and international space programs in navigation and search and rescue in order to enhance Canadian forces and navigational and search and rescue capabilities.

Although the Department of National Defence (DND)

> supports the closest practicable coordination and cooperation between civil and defence space activities [with the Ministry of State for Science and Technology]...considerations of national security and the sensitivities of our allies make it essential that defence space activities and projects be planned, managed and executed under DND control separately from the civil space program. (Government of Canada 1987b: 4)

Process

The key players in the drafting of the White Paper were Defence Minister Perrin Beatty and his assistant deputy minister, Robert Fowler. Their efforts were supported by General Paul Manson, chief of defence staff, and Dr. Kenneth Calder, now director-general of public policy. The exercise began in earnest in January 1987, although much of the groundwork had been laid in the fall of 1986 in the form of preparatory and lead-up studies. There was some consultation with the Department of External Affairs which was invited to comment on various sections and drafts of the White Paper.

Many of the central ideas in the White Paper are not new. This is especially true of its most controversial recommendation concerning the acquisition of nuclear-powered submarines. In the early 1950s when the United States was first getting into the nuclear-powered submarine business, the option was also explored in Canada but was ultimately rejected as too risky and expensive (*Financial Post* 1987: 55). Thoughts of buying exotic technologies continued into the 1960s but had to be put on hold because of budgetary pressures and restraint. Liberal Defence Minister Jean-Jacques Blais was the first to explore the idea in a serious way, but it was the former Conservative defence minister Erik Nielsen who initiated a full-scale, in-depth analysis of the option within the Department of National Defence. A working group was established to study the issue and it had already completed a number of follow-on studies when Perrin Beatty entered the portfolio in June 1986.

These studies had shown that nuclear-powered submarines were relatively superior to high-cost diesel-electric submarines and would meet Canada's three maritime roles: anti-submarine warfare, convoy patrol and surveillance. Furthermore, nuclear-powered submarines would be able to perform these missions in all three oceans, whereas diesel-electric submarines would not be able to operate under the ice because they have to resurface to recharge their batteries. Nuclear-powered submarines are also faster and would be able to cover much larger stretches of the ocean than diesel-electric submarines. Studies also showed that Canada would need ten submarines, at a minimum, in order to have five submarines on continuous patrol. In addition to performing their maritime defence role in Canadian waters, the submarines could also be used during wartime to convoy surface ships along the Atlantic sea lanes and for combat duty along the Greenland/Iceland/U.K. gap.

Thus, much of the important groundwork had already been laid, and the challenge was really to get the minister and the new assistant deputy minister to accept the department's recommendations. They did so eagerly.

Although cabinet accepted "in principle" Perrin Beatty's White Paper on defence so that the report could be tabled in Parliament, it was not without a fight. Secretary of State for External Affairs Joe Clark was reportedly unhappy with the overall thrust of the paper, in particular the recommendation to buy nuclear-powered submarines. Michael Wilson, minister of finance, apparently also had reservations about the cost of the envisaged program. None of these criticisms, however, were strong enough to block cabinet approval.

The strongest criticism of the White Paper, of course, came from the opposition parties and from peace groups when it was finally tabled in the House of Commons. The New Democratic Party (NDP) responded by issuing its own working paper on defence, while the Liberals objected to the overall philosophy and thrust of the White Paper but failed to present a comprehensive alternative of their own.

NDP Response to the White Paper

The NDP's response to the White Paper begins by arguing that the global situation now is "entirely different" from the period following the Second World War when Canadian forces were necessary to help secure the defence of Europe. "Canada's participation in NATO was real and important," says the NDP response; however, the world situation has changed:

> Canada can now make a more effective contribution to peace and security outside of NATO. Western European countries have rebuilt their economies and possess strong defence capabilities. The stationing of one Canadian brigade and some CF-18s in Europe is no longer militarily significant. It is simply expensive symbolism. (Blackburn 1987: 6)

But then the NDP paper changes gears and in language that is strikingly similar in tone and substance to the White Paper itself argues that "Canada is neglecting its primary responsibility, which is protection of our territorial integrity in Atlantic Canada, on the Pacific coast and in the Arctic, which has gained new military and strategic importance" (Blackburn 1987: 6-7).

There is perhaps more emphasis on arms control in the NDP's paper. It suggests that Canada should encourage new agreements to reduce existing nuclear stockpiles, including cruise, short-, medium- and long-range missiles. It also proposes that the government should put an end to cruise-missile testing in Canada and prohibit practice runs by strategic bombers over Canadian territory (p. 9). However, the rest of the NDP's response resonates strongly with the military proposals of the White Paper. It emphasizes the need for surveillance, warning and interception systems to "guarantee that no first-strike across Canadian territory would go undetected." Canada should also purchase a second and perhaps third batch of frigates for maritime control as well as new helicopters to replace the aging Sea King, should install fixed seabed sensors off Canadian waters and at key choke-points in the Arctic, and should buy surface icebreakers. Where the NDP parts company from the Conservatives is in advocating replacement of the North American Aerospace Defence Command (NORAD) with an agreement under which "Canada would assume total responsibility for the conventional defence of its portion of the northern half of North America" (p. 11). Nor should Canada take part in the American Strategic and Air Defence Initiatives. Canada should not buy nuclear-powered submarines, argue the NDP, because the costs are too great and there are risks of environmental accidents. Instead, the NDP would have Canada purchase twelve conventional submarines and new aircraft for northern patrols. In addition, Canada should acquire minesweepers to keep Canadian ports and coastal waters open in the event of war. Troops should be refitted with new equipment and provided with air transport to move on short notice. And the current force should be supported with reserves "trained and prepared to assume vacated domestic positions on short notice" (pp. 18-23).

Although the NDP is on record as favouring Canada's withdrawal from NATO, its response to the White Paper carefully skirts around the issue. And the NDP's promises to buy more equipment are to some extent undermined by its expressed intention to reduce military spending on capital equipment projects by 50 per cent.

Liberal Party Reaction

The Liberal Party's response to the White Paper was led by Douglas Frith, the Liberal's defence critic. On submarines, Frith stated:

I reject the assertion that the only method of addressing the security issue in the Arctic is the acquisition of nuclear powered submarines....The Liberal Party has maintained that the pursuit of national security can only be successful if it is synonymous with the pursuit of international security. It has been a Canadian tradition never to attempt to enhance security through a unilateral, military measure. I view the acquisition of nuclear powered submarines as a unilateral, military approach to a sovereignty and security issue....It is our view that a combination of detection devices with increased air patrols and surface ships, such as the icebreaker and frigates, can provide a visible security presence in Canada's Arctic. I believe that in the long run a combination of conventionally powered submarines, frigates, and air patrols will be a much more cost-effective way of dealing with the security problem which exists in the Arctic than the acquisition of 10 to 12 nuclear submarines. (Government of Canada 1987c: 6780)

On Norway, Frith challenged the withdrawal of the CAST commitment

because all the Nordic countries, including ours, have the same long-term geopolitical concern about the militarization of the Arctic. And because of those Arctic geopolitical interests, I would redeploy the existing forces on the southern flank into the north, being sure to keep our commitment to Norway.

Frith condemned the White Paper's narrow focus on defence:

Defence policy has to be viewed in a wider context of global security, and global security is best achieved by arms control, by peace initiatives. I don't feel that External Affairs was closely consulted on this paper. It seems to me that (a) Joe Clark lost the battle in cabinet on nuclear-powered submarines, and (b) our government's stated position is not to become involved in Star Wars, and yet the...document...clearly leaves the door open....[These] are glaring examples of where External Affairs' views have not been taken into account. (Frith 1987: 24)

Domestic Political Reaction

The peace movement was just as vocal as the parliamentary opposition, with much of its criticism directed at the submarine deployment issue. Some peace activists argued that submarines were a waste of money when budgets for social programs were being cut by the federal government (*Vancouver Sun* 1987). Others viewed the White Paper as "a blatant

imitation of the annual Pentagon publication *Soviet Military Power*,"
which "assumes that Canada's security interests are identical to those of
the United States and other NATO allies" (Johnson 1987).

Ernie Regehr, head of Project Ploughshares, had this to say about the
White Paper:

> Mr. Beatty's White Paper is leading us, perhaps unwittingly, toward direct
> support for star wars and nuclear war-fighting strategies....The call for
> Canadian clarity on deterrence is not a plea for nuclear threat and counter-
> threat as the ultimate basis of security, rather it is caution that an abandon-
> ment of basic deterrence in favor of nuclear war-fighting strategies promises
> even greater insecurity and would make the quest for disarmament a fond
> hope. (Regehr 1987: 1, 3)

Phyllis Creighton, a member of the General Synod of the Anglican
Church of Canada and secretary of the Toronto chapter of Science for
Peace, observed: "It is a disturbing document that fans cold war fears and
hatred, marching to the warmongers' drum with a repeated refrain of 'in
event of war.'"

> [It] identifies the USSR as the "enemy" into the far future in a fashion that
> can no longer be tolerated. From the perspective of the fragile blue ball that
> the astronauts showed us, the one human family of which we are a small part
> must turn away from militarism and point instead toward peacemaking and
> reconciliation. (Creighton 1987: 5, 6)

William Epstein, chairperson of the Canadian Pugwash Group and
senior special fellow at the UN Institute for Training and Research,
believes that the Canadian White Paper proposes "the wrong policy, for
the wrong purpose, at the wrong time." It promotes the arms race and
"does not rule out direct Canadian involvement in the U.S. strategic
defence initiative." Epstein belives that plans to buy nuclear-powered
submarines represent "a stark abandonment of previous Canadian policy
that atomic energy should be used for exclusively peaceful purposes"
going back to the Three Power Declaration of November 1945 in which
Canada committed itself "to prevent the use of atomic energy for
destructive purposes and promote its use for peaceful and humanitarian
ends." According to Epstein, this

will be the first time that any non-nuclear party to the nuclear Non-Proliferation Treaty has decided to use nuclear energy for military purposes. While this may not be contrary to the letter of the Treaty, it is certainly contrary to its spirit....it seems clear that this first-time by Canada of nuclear energy for military purposes will tend to weaken the entire non-proliferation regime. It will create difficult problems for the International Atomic Energy Agency's safeguards system and for Canadian compliance with it. It could encourage other parties to do likewise. (Epstein 1987: 6)

Steve Shalhorn of Greenpeace Canada tackled the argument that submarines would help to assert Canadian sovereignty in the Arctic. According to Shalhorn, Canada's "trouble with the United States is a political, legal problem that's not going to be solved by submarines." The submarines would make

Canada...the sixth country in the world to use technology for military purposes....it violates the NPT [Non-proliferation Treaty] mainly through the fueling arrangements. Submarines use enriched fuel....Currently, a clause in all Canadian uranium export agreements says that uranium cannot be enriched for military purposes. And their practice has been to include the fuel for nuclear-powered submarines in the definition of "military purposes." (Shalhorn 1987: 28)

The Canadian Centre for Arms Control and Disarmament (CCAD), an independent arms control group in Ottawa, also argued that the decision to acquire nuclear-powered submarines would "degrade Canada's effectiveness in nuclear non-proliferation diplomacy, as Canada would have to exempt the high-enriched, weapons-grade uranium fuel for the submarine reactors from international safeguards." Withdrawal of the CAST commitment was criticized "as harmful to Canadian dialogue with Nordic countries on arms control in the Arctic." Planned Canadian participation in the U.S. Air Defence Initiative (ADI) was criticized by CCAD because of "the programme's close links with U.S. Strategic Defense Initiative research on ballistic missile defence" (CCAD 1987: 4).

But not everybody was against the White Paper. The Business Council on National Issues, composed of the chief executives of 150 leading Canadian companies, hailed the White Paper on defence as "a long-overdue, bold and imaginative attempt to give defence policy the priority it deserves." The council endorsed the government's decision to purchase nuclear-powered submarines and to increase the size of reserves, but it questioned "certain gaps and oversights" in the paper. "The critical issue of strategic defense is largely ignored, even though deployment by the United States would have a profound impact on Canadian security and Canada's defence policies and priorities." The council also believed that the government had underestimated the costs of a nuclear submarine program. It expressed some concern that the government had potentially undermined the viability of its new defence policy by unduly exposing the financing of the program

> to the ebb and flow of the political process. A sounder approach would have been to set out a firm commitment to a higher level of real annual growth in defence spending over the proposed 15-year period. This would not only have been more forthright, but would also have lessened to some extent the possibility that the urgently needed measures set out in the White Paper may be jeopardized by domestic political considerations in the future. (*Ottawa Citizen* 1987a; Matas 1987)

Editorial opinion varied. Raymond Giroux of *Le Soleil* argued that "the debate was as much political as it is military," and that

> his promotion of Canadian sovereignty in the face of the growing interdependence of the North American economies will contribute to an essential rebalancing of influences. This is because, despite the affirmations of the White Paper that give priority to security over sovereignty, the militarization of the seas, especially the Arctic Ocean, would serve the country's political independence most of all.

Jean-Claude Leclerc of *Le Devoir* expressed the view that the White Paper is inspired by the desire to express Canadian sovereignty, but "it is also a long avowal of the weakness of the country and its inability to defend its borders. So why keep large forces in Europe when there are not enough in the country itself?" Columnist Richard Gwyn of the *Toronto Star* suggested that instead of arming itself, Canada should work towards an Arctic disarmament conference, a proposal put forward by Ron Purver of the Canadian Institute for International Peace and Security (CIIPS). This would involve convincing "the superpowers to negotiate limits on the kinds of weapons systems they might use in the Arctic...[including] a cutback in the number of attack submarines by both sides...and a ban or deep cuts in sea-launched, cruise missiles" (Gwyn 1987).

Surveys of public opinion painted a confused picture of Canadians' attitudes towards the White Paper and towards the decision to buy nuclear-powered submarines in particular. A March 1987 survey conducted by Decima Research Ltd. for the Department of National Defence asked Canadians the following question:

> If Canada is to build submarines to defend Canadian sovereignty in the Atlantic and the Pacific and particularly the Arctic, most experts feel that these submarines would have to be nuclear-powered — although they would not be armed with nuclear weapons — to do the job effectively. Some people say that if the submarines need to be nuclear-powered in order to do the best job then we should go ahead and build that type of submarine. Others say that we should under no circumstances build submarines which are nuclear-powered. Which one of these two points of view best reflects your own? (CIIPS 1987a: 260-62)

In the survey, 59 per cent of those polled said that Canada should build nuclear-powered submarines, while 40 per cent said it should not. In a related question, 45 per cent of those polled said that "Canada should build its own submarine force to patrol our Arctic waters," while only 12 per cent believed that Canada should rely on the United States to do the job.

A later survey conducted in June by the *Toronto Star* asked a representative sample of Canadians whether "Canada should buy nuclear-powered submarines to defend Canada's claim to the Arctic?" This time only 42 per cent of those polled said yes, while 55 per cent answered no. However, a *Globe and Mail*/ Environics poll conducted between May 25 and June 10 found that 50 per cent of Canadians approved of the government's plan to buy ten nuclear-powered submarines, while only 39 per cent disapproved. The polls were obviously receiving mixed and confusing signals.

In the debate about the White Paper, a number of important issues have been raised concerning the costs of the program, particularly expensive items like submarines, who will build the submarines, whether the technologies and systems will address the perceived threat in the Arctic, and the reaction of Canada's allies and the Soviet Union to the White Paper. We will consider each of these in turn.

Cost

The White Paper is to be financed out of minimum annual budget increases of 2 per cent over the fifteen-year period, with extra funding for big-ticket items on a case-by-case basis. The basic problem is that the re-equipment program, according to Department of National Defence estimates, would require, on average, at least a 5 per cent annual budget increase after inflation. With a current budget of $10.5 billion a year, this would come to more than $500 million each year (*Financial Post* 1987: 45).

The cost issue was explored by the government earlier in 1987 before the White Paper was published. DND devised a series of fifteen-year budget projections for discussion in the cabinet subcommittee on defence. The formula called for average annual increases of between 5 and 5.25 per cent, after inflation. Cabinet rejected the spending proposal as too ambitious. Beatty then responded with a "minimum viable program." This was the department's fall-back position that envisaged a 3 per cent after-inflation budget increase in the first three years and a 4.5 per cent budget increase for the remaining twelve years of the fifteen-year plan. But again this was deemed too expensive, and all Beatty could wrest from cabinet was a commitment to 2 per cent increases with a provision for a case-by-case review of major projects (*Financial Post* 1987: 47).

There is additional danger that Canada is committing itself to hard-ware without worrying sufficiently about logistics, operations and main-tenance, training and modernization, and re-equipment of current forces. For example, the Leopard I tanks that Canada bought in 1976 will need a refit in several years and their 105 mm guns will have to be replaced with a heavier bore in order to meet Soviet advances in range and anti-armour capabilities. Reassigning the CAST brigade to Central Europe means that it will have to be equipped for a heavy-armour role. The brigade currently has no tanks and insufficient armoured personnel carriers. Canada's ground forces in Europe will also require heavy transport trucks, short- and medium-range anti-armour weapons, nuclear and biological warfare decontamination equipment, mechanical digging equipment, artillery-delivered mines, and a host of other equipment for the modern conventional battlefield if they are to remain effective fighting forces.

Costly procurement programs would further erode the support system for Canadian forces, particularly during a period of mounting fiscal austerity. In his 1987 report, Auditor General Kenneth Dye attacked the creaky support system of the Canadian armed services and charged that the Canadian military would not be able to supply its troops in a sustained conflict. The auditor general said that the support system is still based on the thinking of the immediate postwar era — that is, on the assumption that the next war would be brief, global and thermonuclear, with limited participation by troops. After a short period of time, fighting troops would find themselves without adequate ammunition, food, spare parts, evacuation systems for the wounded and the whole range of combat necessities (Macdonald 1987).

According to Charles Doran of the Washington-based School for Advanced International Studies at the Johns Hopkins University,

> If Canada really is going to buy a Class 8 Icebreaker, finance new frigates, update Tribal Class destroyers, provide replacements for lost CF-18s, assume its share of the costs of the North Warning System, properly equip its European forces, increase its reserves to 90,000 men, all on a budgeted two per cent annual increase in defence spending after inflation, magic will have to be performed. In the absence of magic, political leverage to increase budgets must suffice, and that too, in Ottawa as in Washington, is in short supply these days. (Doran 1987: 9)

These expenditures pale in comparison to the costs of the submarine program. Although initial estimates put the cost of the submarine fleet at $5 billion, the Department of National Defence was later forced to revise its estimates upward. Capital costs of ten to twelve submarines were later put at $8 billion to include the costs of training and construction of submarine support facilities. Even this figure has been challenged by a number of analysts. The Canadian Centre for Arms Control and Disarmament argues that DND would have difficulty holding the price down to $8 billion, not only because of construction costs associated with shore and support infrastructure, purchase of nuclear fuel from abroad, and training crews, but also because the hulls of the submarines would have to be upgraded for under-ice operations in the Arctic (Sallot 1987b). The editor of the respected *Jane's Fighting Ships* magazine estimates the total capital cost of the submarine program to be around $11 billion. DND has responded to its critics by arguing that its own estimates take these factors into account.

Who Will Build the Submarines?

Canada is looking to Britain or France to provide the basic submarine design. The two principal contenders are Britain's Vickers Trafalgar class and France's Cherbourg Rubis class. The submarines, however, would be built in Canada by a Canadian contractor. Of the various groups that have entered the prime contractor competition, none has the experience and expertise necessary to build a submarine, let alone a nuclear-powered one. In regular competitions, DND asks for open bids and then spends a year or more analyzing the bids and reducing the competitors to two groups. The project then moves into the "project definition" stage, during which detailed cost estimates are prepared. A contract is then awarded to the best and most cost-effective design. In this case, the government, anxious to speed up the process, has pushed the submarine program into the project definition stage so that it can make a quick decision on whether to buy a French or British submarine. This has created considerable apprehension among potential contractors, who are leery that the project would move ahead only to be cancelled by a Liberal (or NDP) government in two or three years time. This would have disastrous consequences for all future procurement programs in the Department of National Defence and would be especially harmful to the navy. Canada will have to go offshore to buy major weapons systems for the submarines, although the propulsion systems could be built in Canada if Britain or France is willing to transfer advanced nuclear-submarine reactor technology to Canada.

Because of the transfers of technology involved and lack of experience in submarine construction in Canada, there would undoubtedly be slippages in the construction schedules and cost overruns, particularly if the experience Canadian contractors had with the frigate program is any guide. The frigate program was hampered by the inexperience of navy program officials and shipyard executives who were unfamiliar with warship construction and the tremendous changes in technology that had taken place since Canada last built frigates. Shipbuilders and ship designers had special difficulties with modular construction techniques where the challenge is to cram sophisticated electronics and technology into a small vessel. Said one navy official, "In the final analysis, you need people who have done the job before" (*Financial Post* 1987: 51). This problem is likely to be experienced in spades in the case of nuclear-powered submarine construction.

Technology

According to some analysts, there is a real danger that the current technologies for anti-submarine warfare will become obsolescent over the next decade (Stefanick 1987). The Soviets are making rapid advances in quieting their submarines with new propeller technologies obtained from the Japanese and Norwegians. This will cause problems for existing passive sonar detection techniques, while the danger with active sonar detection techniques is that the hunter risks giving its own position away to the enemy. Canada could find itself in an extremely costly and enormously challenging race to develop new technologies for underwater anti-submarine warfare, a race where it does not have the benefit of twenty or more years of experience, as does the United States.

Mission

Soviet submarines have tended to remain in their Arctic bastions near the Kola Peninsula (adjacent to north Norway). It is possible that Soviet hunter-killer attack submarines (SSNs) would be flushed into the Atlantic in the event of a crisis. But would they go through Canadian waters? The Soviets would have to contend with the American submarine threat off North America, and they might not want to meet that challenge. According to David Cox (1986: 23),

> Given the ranges of the most modern Soviet SLBMs, and the relative protection of home waters, the Soviet marginal ice zone, and the deep Polar basin, the strategic reserve function of Soviet ballistic missile-carrying submarines is better served from the Soviet rather than the Canadian side of the Arctic.

However,

> The future use of the Canadian Arctic for deployments of submarines in a precursor or decapitation role cannot be ruled out, but the distances involved suggest that, for most targets, Pacific and Atlantic deployment would be far more advantageous. This, of course, raises the possibility of greater Soviet use of non-Arctic Canadian coastal waters in proximity to U.S. military targets.

The Canadian Arctic might be useful to U.S. submarines trying to enter Soviet sanctuaries in the Norwegian and Greenland seas, since American SSNs have an under-ice capability. The Soviets in response might try to disperse their own submarines out of the Arctic basin into the Atlantic and Pacific. The Soviets might also try to use Canadian Arctic waters to avoid transit through the heavily defended Greenland/Iceland/U.K. gap. But there they would run into problems. The straits are narrow, and transit is risky and dangerous. Some argue that these straits could be defended by means other than submarines, such as mines (Cox 1986). The problem with mines is seeding them in ice-covered waters. It would require a very large number of mines to cover all of the key choke-points and access routes in Canada's Arctic.

Some also argue that using submarines to protect Canadian sovereignty in the Arctic is questionable. They suggest that sovereignty is best asserted through international law, as in the recently concluded agreement between Canada and the United States on Arctic sovereignty. They also question whether Canada would be prepared to use force to deal with intruders in Canadian waters during peacetime.

The Allies

What are the allies' interests in the White Paper? How will they respond? In the case of Canada's European allies, the obvious emphasis on continental defence may be seen as the beginning of North American isolationism (although Canadian government officials have gone to great pains to argue this is not the case). Earlier in the year Norwegian Defence Minister Johan Holst visited Canada to plead against Canada's dropping the CAST commitment. He stated that "it would be very regrettable for Norway's security to lose the possibility of getting reinforcements from Canada" and that if commitments were to start crumbling the result would undermine Article V of the NATO Treaty, which states that an attack against one ally would be considered an attack against all (*Ottawa Citizen* 1987b). Norway is crucial to a successful defence of Western Europe because of the concentration of Soviet forces on the Kola Peninsula and because it flanks the 1,600-kilometre route that Soviet submarines, surface ships and aircraft must pass in order to reach the Atlantic. If the Soviets were to overrun Norway, they would be able to extend their offensive perimeter and have access to the Atlantic. This would substantially weaken NATO's ability to mount an effective resistance against Soviet and Warsaw Pact forces (Gough and Gravelle 1987). But this avoids the issue of whether Canadian forces would be able to reach Norway in time to help with its defence. Aside from the Norwegians, European governments have greeted the White Paper with only mild interest, and in the case of the British and French, their interest stems from the prospect of contracts to sell submarines to Canada.

The U.S. government, however, is disappointed that the Conservatives have failed to fulfil their campaign promise to increase defence spending by 6 per cent. They are also chagrined by the announced deferral of $200 million from the defence budget in 1987, which meant no real growth in the Canadian defence budget at all. The annual growth rate of 2 per cent called for in the White Paper is still below the 3 per cent real growth rate Canada had committed itself to along with other NATO partners at the defence ministers' meeting in April 1987. The Americans feel, quite rightly, that the 2 per cent objective is not enough to meet the expenditures called for in the White Paper. They also think that the submarine program's costs have been underestimated, based on their own experience with submarine construction.

There was no real opposition in the United States to Canada's elimination of the CAST commitment to Norway. Americans welcomed consolidation just so long as it would not mean a reduction in Canadian commitment to the defence of Western Europe. They are somewhat skeptical of the Canadian decision to acquire twelve nuclear-powered submarines. For example, Congressman Charles Bennett, a Florida Democrat who serves as chairperson of the Seapower Subcommittee of the House Armed Services Committee, observed:

> The potential addition of a dozen Canadian nuclear attack submarines to the already outnumbered North American Treaty Organization's submarine fleet would seem a pretty good idea. But would adding anything but the best submarines being built in the West today make much of a difference in combating an ever-improving Soviet submarine force? Canada does not appear ready to spend enough money to buy such a capability. (Bennett 1987)

In the Pentagon, the chief opponent to the submarine program is apparently U.S. Admiral Kinnaird R. McKee, director of the U.S. Naval Nuclear Propulsion Unit (*Financial Post* 1987: 47, 49). However, some of the younger commanders apparently believe that the United States can use all the help it can get to meet the growing threat from the Soviet Union. Some Canadian officials have talked openly about a "NORAD under the sea" that would establish a working relationship between Canadian and U.S. fleets. But the United States is not keen about implementing an integrated command structure governing NORAD relations, and the U.S. Navy has historically been the most independent-minded branch of the armed services. Formal cooperative arrangements also might worry Europeans, concerned about the development of a fortress North America.

Although U.S. official reaction has ranged from opposition to approval, it is generally believed, even by those who support the proposals, that the White Paper's program cannot be funded within the 2 per cent real growth in the defence budget. Americans worry that capital expenditures would eventually force Canada to cut back on its defence efforts elsewhere, including troop commitment in Europe.

> Many Americans therefore do not believe that the Canadian government will follow through on its promise, or hope that it will not. Some are actively searching for ways to persuade Canada to alter its commitment. Many in the United States, as in Canada, see the proposed nuclear-powered submarines as tied up with the question of Arctic sovereignty. This nationalist Canadian concern can appear aimed more at the United States than at the Soviet Union, and can seem to involve ambivalence about defence cooperation with the United States, or even anti-Americanism. (Leyton-Brown 1987: 4)

Writing in the *Armed Forces Journal International*, U.S. defence analysts Steven Canby and Jean Smith (1987: 16) commented: "Still, Canada, a nation of 25 million and among the world's most prosperous, will field an army of but two brigades, a tactical air force of five squadrons, and an air defence force of but three squadrons totalling less than 54 interceptors. Why Canada gets so little bang for the buck (after adequate funding for modernization and sustainment) is the unanswered question of Canadian defence." Canby and Smith complained that the White Paper only increases the Canadian defence budget "marginally and focuses on outputs but does not increase them." But they believe that recognition in the White Paper that Central Europe is the "center of gravity in the balance of power" constitutes a positive development in Canadian defence thinking.

The outstanding questions have to do with the future of defence cooperation with the United States. Would there be a "North American Naval Cooperation Command"? There would obviously have to be some coordination of movements of submarines in coastal and Arctic waters, since these areas are also patrolled by American submarines. U.S. Admiral Carlisle Trost, chief of naval operations, reported to the U.S. Congress in February that American "submarines [were] routinely deployed into Arctic waters [during 1986] where they might be expected to carry out wartime campaigns and battle plans in support of the maritime strategy" (Arkin and Shalhorn 1987). Contingency plans would have to be worked out for crisis situations. There would have to be some agreement on areas patrolled and defended by the two navies. In the words of the U.S. Navy's submarine chief, "Somebody has to make sure that two friendly submarines aren't in the same points of ocean at the same time. We work very closely in command post exercises. We share to a degree what waters we will stay out of during times of war." This might be done within the NATO framework, but a special agreement between Canada and the United States might also be required. Paradoxically, this might result in closer ties with, rather than greater independence from, the United States.

Soviet Reaction

The Soviets have not spoken out publicly against the White Paper, but it is clear from their official statements that they do not like it. The Soviet Union let it be known that it had secretly proposed an Arctic cooperation treaty with Canada in February but had not received a reply. The draft treaty calls for exchanges on environmental protection and Arctic navigation. It would recognize the right of each country to enact laws to control pollution and govern navigation in Arctic waters adjacent to its territory. Although the proposed treaty made no mention of military activity in the Arctic, the announcement came on the heels of a speech given by Soviet General Secretary Mikhail Gorbachev proposing measures to turn the Arctic into a " zone of peace." Gorbachev proposed that the Warsaw Pact and the North Atlantic Treaty Organization should scale down their military, naval and air force activities in the Baltic and Greenland, and in the Norwegian and the North seas. He also suggested that if the political climate were to improve, the Soviet Union would open its northern shipping lanes to foreign vessels (Sallot 1987a). Soviet Embassy officials have suggested that Canada might apply the same logic in reconsidering its proposals to increase military spending in the Canadian Arctic (Hunter 1987).

Continuity and Change

One of the major problems with the White Paper is its lack of congruence with current fiscal realities. It is useful to recall the fate of the defence White Paper presented by Liberal Defence Minister Paul Hellyer in 1964. Hellyer also sought a 2 per cent annual growth in defence expenditure to modernize Canadian forces, of which no less than 25 per cent of the defence budget would go to new equipment, but he underestimated the effects of inflation and the costs of modern weapons systems. The capital portion of the defence budget declined from 19.9 per cent in 1965-66 to 14.2 per cent in 1969-70. This forced manpower reductions from 126,474 in 1962 to 110,000 in 1967 (Kemp 1987: 464-65).

How different is this White Paper from earlier ones in terms of its geostrategic orientation? There is obviously some continuity with previous rhetoric. It is useful to recall the defence priorities of the first Trudeau government, announced on April 3, 1969. These were (1) the surveillance of Canadian territory and coastlines to protect national sovereignty; (2) the defence of North America in cooperation with U.S. forces; (3) the fulfilment of such NATO commitments as may be agreed upon; and (4) the performance of such international peacekeeping roles as Canada may assume (Kemp 1987: 465). These priorities are not very different from those in the new White Paper. However, Trudeau restructured the Canadian commitment to NATO by cutting Canada's European contingent of 10,000 troops in half and leaving just three squadrons of CF-104 Starfighters (something that is not envisaged in the current White Paper). Canada's overall troop personnel was reduced to 83,000 and then to 79,000 in 1974 (a trend the current White Paper seeks to reverse).

Threat Assessment and the Changing Environment of East-West Relations

There is the prospect that the White Paper's geostrategic assessment may become outdated in the changing environment of East-West relations. Comparing the situation to 1971, when the last defence White Paper was issued, the new White Paper argues that the key assumptions in 1971 were overly optimistic.

> Sixteen years later, it is evident that the great hopes of the early 1970s have not been realized. As anticipated, mutual stable deterrence between the superpowers has endured, although at much higher levels of forces....Despite some initial successes, however, arms control has so far proven to be much more difficult to achieve than many had anticipated. (Government of Canada 1987a: 1)

This judgment comes at the time of a major breakthough in U.S.-Soviet relations, with the agreement scrapping intermediate-range nuclear missiles between ranges of 500 and 5,000 kilometres signed by U.S. President Reagan and Soviet leader Gorbachev at the December 7-10 Washington summit. For a while, the summit had seemed in jeopardy when Gorbachev made his attendance conditional on agreed limits to testing of technologies for strategic defence, a demand that was later dropped. As negotiations continued well into the eleventh hour, the key stumbling block was how to deal with verification and compliance provisions of the agreement. The main point of contention concerned the information the Soviets were said to have provided on the number and location of their SS-20 missiles that have not been deployed. Additionally, the United States was anxious to block any Soviet effort to modify the SS-25, a longer-range weapon, for theatre nuclear roles.

Under the treaty, 429 U.S. Pershing II and ground-launched cruise missiles in four NATO countries and 470 Soviet SS-20 and SS-4/5 missiles would be destroyed for a total of 2,611 missiles in all, including short- and medium-range missiles deployed and in storage. The treaty also contains a novel and stringent set of requirements for on-site inspection lasting thirteen years. Each party has the right to conduct inspections at all missile operating bases, missile support facilities and certain missile-production installations by means of continuous monitoring. The treaty also establishes a Special Verification Commission to resolve questions relating to compliance with the treaty (*New York Times* 1987a: A24-25).

There was strong support from the allies for the treaty, but NATO defence ministers also said that NATO should continue to modernize its short-range and battlefield nuclear arsenal in the face of Warsaw Pact conventional and nuclear strength (*Globe and Mail* 1987). Among the options under consideration is the deployment of cruise missiles at sea and on B-52 strategic bombers, which could be flown from the United States or from West European bases for raids into Warsaw Pact territory (Bennett 1987).

The Washington summit failed to see a major breakthrough on strategic weapons and space-based defences. Gorbachev did not give up his opposition to the Strategic Defence Initiative (SDI), nor Reagan his commitment to it. However, the Soviets displayed sensitivity and skill in reaching out to the U.S. audience. They asked for specific limits on the kinds of weapons that could be tested as part of SDI research and for a U.S. commitment to abide by the strict interpretation of the Anti-Ballistic

Missile (ABM) Treaty, which, in the Soviet view, prohibits many forms of SDI testing (Thatcher 1987). At the October 22-23 meeting between U.S. Secretary of State George Shultz and Soviet Foreign Minister Eduard Shevardnadze, and again at the Washington summit, the Soviets stated they were no longer demanding strict limits on all forms of SDI testing. (The Reagan administration claims that the language of the ABM treaty and the negotiating record supports a "broad interpretation" that would permit expanded testing of SDI components.)

At the year's end, it was also apparent that the superpowers had resolved some of their differences on counting rules for offensive weapons. The Soviets reversed their earlier refusal to consider strategic sub-limits under the overall reductions agreed to at the Iceland summit in October 1986. (Those reductions would have brought strategic stocks on both sides down to 6,000 warheads and 1,600 missile and bomber launchers each.) At the Shultz-Shevardnadze meeting in Moscow, the Soviets offered new limits on the numbers of warheads in three categories: 3,000-3,300 on intercontinental ballistic missiles (ICBMs); 1,800-2,000 on sea-launched ballistic missiles (SLBMs); and 800-900 on air-launched cruise missiles. The U.S. proposal included a total ceiling for ballistic missile warheads of 4,800; a maximum of 3,000-3,300 of those could be ICBM warheads, with a maximum of 1,650 allowable on heavy missiles or missiles carrying more than six warheads apiece (the Soviet's SS-18s and mobile SS-24s, and the United States's MX missiles) (Pond 1987). These differences arose from Moscow's dependence on ICBMs, which account for 64 per cent of its strategic inventory, versus Washington's greater reliance on SLBMs (58 per cent) and bombers (22 per cent). However, at the Washington summit, negotiators reached a compromise agreement to limit ballistic missile warheads to 4,900 apiece within the overall limit of 6,000 warheads (*New York Times* 1987b: A22-23). This latter limitation does not cover sea-launched cruise missiles (Soviet Embassy 1987: 5).

Although a superpower arms control agreement on strategic and space weapons still seemed a long way off, the Washington summit marked the beginning of an important thaw in U.S.-Soviet relations. Gone was the rhetoric of the "evil empire" and American unwillingness to do serious business in arms control. In this changing environment, it may be difficult for the Canadian government to persuade Canadians that a defence build-up is necessary to address the Soviet threat, although Canadian attitudes are decidedly ambivalent. In a national poll conducted by the Canadian Institute for International Peace and Security, 71 per cent of those polled said that the West should *not* try to increase its military strength in order to prevent war with the Soviet Union (CIIPS 1987b: 2). However, in the same poll, when it came to Canada's military strength, 63 per cent felt that Canadian defence forces should be larger and 58 per cent agreed with the statement that "the Soviet military threat is constantly growing and represents a real, immediate threat to the West."

At the year's end, the White Paper on defence was eclipsed somewhat by the debate over free trade. The growing preoccupation with the future of the Canadian economy temporarily put defence issues on the back burner as the Mulroney government battled for free trade and its own political future.

PART

III

International Political Economy

5

The World Economy: Consultation Without Performance

JOHN M. CURTIS

After several years of steady, if uneven, growth in many regions of the world, the world economy started showing serious cracks in 1987.

Starting with Brazil's announcement in February that for an indefinite period it would cease to pay interest on the medium- and long-term debt that it owed commercial banks, the debt crisis — never resolved but out of the headlines for several years — intensified. Current account imbalances continued to worsen during the year, with the deficit characterizing the United States' position offset by surpluses in Japan and, increasingly, in the Federal Republic of Germany. Inflation and interest rates, while low compared to their levels of the early 1980s, began rising sharply by mid-year, raising fears and expectations of poorer performance with respect to both indicators. Exchange rates, so carefully crafted by the Group of Seven (G-7) countries as part of the Louvre Accord in February, shifted dramatically during the course of the year, with the U.S. dollar recording postwar lows in terms of both the Japanese yen and the West German mark by year's end. Growth in employment and in gross national product (GNP) more generally showed signs of levelling off and then of slowing as the year progressed, notwithstanding the fact that some countries had been very late in joining the post-1982 recovery while some regions and countries had scarcely participated at all in the recovery.

The most spectacular of all the economic events of 1987 occurred on October 19 when the world's stock markets, a symbol of confidence and a leading indicator of economic activity, interrupted their upward movement that had gone on for up to fifty months with a sudden, dramatic decline of historic proportions. Stability was re-established only by major increases in the world's liquidity, which had the effect of forcing interest rates down and restoring confidence. Within a month, it was clear that the crisis had passed, although billions of dollars of paper wealth had disappeared with unknown consequences for consumer and investment spending throughout the world economy.

This record of unsustainable performance at the international macro-economic level, with its inherent underlying conflict between the market and the national and international policy makers, between the United States on the one hand and Japan and West Germany on the other, and between the creditors of the North and the debtors of the South, was overlaid by an impressive and intensive amount of international economic consultation and coordination over the course of the entire year.[1]

The program of the multilateral trade negotiations (the MTN or the Uruguay Round), for example, was agreed to in late January following intensive negotiations. The U.S.-Japanese "summit" on the dollar/yen exchange rate relationship, also in January, was followed in late February by the Louvre Accord on the stabilization of exchange rates. The International Monetary Fund (IMF) Interim Committee meeting in April had as its major subjects exchange rate and debt issues once again. During May the Organization for Economic Cooperation and Development (OECD) ministers meeting in Paris addressed an array of major international economic policy issues, including trade, debt and structural adjustment. Later that same month, the Cairns Group of agriculture ministers met in Ottawa to give further momentum to the substantive reform of the agricultural trade system. The leaders of the seven largest Western industrialized nations (G-7) met in Venice in June, where again the central agenda items were agricultural trade and exchange rates. Participants in the IMF's annual meeting, held in Washington in September, also discussed exchange rate developments, trade imbalances and debt burdens. It was only fitting that, in a year of frequent and intensive discussions between high-level national actors on global economic policy issues, the G-7 should close the year with a joint communiqué reaffirming the central thrust of the Louvre Accord: "to cooperate closely in monitoring and implementing policies to strengthen underlying economic fundamentals to foster stability of exchange rates" (*Financial Times* 1987).

It is unclear, however, whether these "consultative goods" being supplied by national governments, or by the international economic institutions of which they were members during 1987, met the real demand for effective progress on a range of global economic issues. Indeed, central to any analysis of the world economy in 1987 and of Canada's role within it must be an appreciation of the disturbing trends and underlying conflict surrounding the "economic fundamentals." As described in the following pages, the record of economic performance in 1987 gave rise to some serious questions about the effectiveness of the efforts of the major multilateral and national economic policy institutions and policy makers during the year. Indeed, the distance between economic reality and the capacity to effectively deal with this reality appeared to grow in 1987. In the end, the market, however imperfectly, appeared to have emphatically and spectacularly overruled the policy makers and some of the processes they had set in place in response to the unsustainable economic trends and developments that had emerged worldwide over the past half-decade and more.

The Major Indicators

While the final figures for the year 1987 will not be available for some time, it appears that overall world economic growth remained quite high. For the developed countries as a whole, growth was close to 2.4 per cent over 1986, and for developing countries about 3.3 per cent, reflecting primarily the strong performance of the newly industrialized countries (NICs) in Asia. Within the OECD countries more specifically, gross national product growth is estimated to have remained at about 2.75 per cent, down only slightly from 1986. Thus, as Table 5-1 (page 98) indicates, 1987 represented the fifth year of overall economic expansion.

Employment growth paralleled to some extent the economic growth registered in most of the world's economies. Rates of unemployment reached five-year lows in Canada and the United States in the course of the year, while the historically high rates in Western Europe, which had plagued that region for a decade or more, finally began to show some improvement in at least several countries. See Table 5-2 (page 98).

Interest and inflation rates, while behaving much better than earlier in the decade, stopped falling rapidly in 1987 (see Table 5-3, page 99). In certain countries both indicators began to rise significantly. With respect to interest rates, both short- and long-term rates in the United States and in related international money markets moved up strongly in the second and third quarters of the year and only began to recede when the supply of money was increased following the stock market crash. The impact of increasing interest rates earlier in the year was significant — the bond market, for example, was weak for the balance of the year. In several other important countries, however, the experience was different. Rates in Germany and Japan, for example, influenced partly by the wishes of

Table 5-1
Annual Changes in Real Output, 1982-87 (in percentages)

	1982	1983	1984	1985	1986	1987[a]
World[b]	0.7	2.6	4.5	3.3	3.2	2.8
Industrialized Countries	-0.3	2.7	5.0	3.1	2.7	2.4
Developing Countries	1.6	1.6	4.1	3.3	4.0	3.3
Other Countries	3.7	4.2	3.3	3.6	4.1	3.6
OECD	-0.5	2.7	4.9	3.2	2.8	2.8
United States	-2.5	3.6	6.8	3.0	2.9	2.8
Japan	3.1	3.2	5.1	4.7	2.4	3.5
Germany	-1.0	1.9	3.3	2.0	2.5	1.5
France	2.5	0.7	1.4	1.7	2.0	1.5
United Kingdom	1.5	3.3	2.7	3.6	3.3	3.8
Italy	0.2	0.5	3.5	2.7	2.7	2.8
Canada	-3.2	3.2	6.3	4.3	3.3	3.8
Other OECD	0.8	1.6	3.4	3.3	2.7	2.5

[a] 1987 estimates by the International Monetary Fund for world indicators and the OECD for OECD indicators.
[b] Annual changes in the world output measures annual changes in GDP (or GNP) for industrial and developing countries and real net material product for other countries. Industrial countries include all G-7 countries as well as other major OECD members. Developing countries include all other International Monetary Fund members. Other countries include the U.S.S.R. and other countries that are not members of the Fund.
Sources: *World Economic Outlook, Revised Projections by the Staff of the International Monetary Fund* (Washington, D.C., October 1987); *OECD Economic Outlook* (Paris,

Table 5-2
Unemployment Rates in the OECD Area, 1982-87[a]

	1982	1983	1984	1985	1986	1987[b]
OECD	8.4	8.9	8.5	8.4	8.3	8.00
United States	9.7	9.6	7.5	7.2	7.0	6.25
Japan	2.3	2.6	2.7	2.6	2.8	3.00
Germany	6.7	8.2	8.2	8.3	8.0	8.00
France	8.2	8.4	9.9	10.2	10.5	10.75
United Kingdom	10.4	11.3	11.5	11.6	11.8	10.75
Italy	8.5	9.2	9.3	9.3	10.1	10.75
Canada	11.1	11.9	11.3	10.5	9.6	9.00
Other OECD	10.4	11.7	12.1	12.1	11.7	11.50

[a] Unemployment rates as reported by individual countries. For unemployment rates standardized by OECD to facilitate cross-country comparisons, see *OECD Economic Outlook* (December 1987) Table R17.
[b] OECD projections.
Source: *OECD Economic Outlook* (Paris, December 1987).

Table 5-3
Interest Rate and Consumer Price Index
Movements in 1987

Selected Interest Rates

Wednesday	3-Month Canadian Treasury Bills	Euro-U.S. Dollar Deposits in London 3 Months	U.S. Government 5-Year Bond Yield
January	7.24	6.34	6.63
February	7.78	6.53	6.72
March	6.80	6.59	6.84
April	8.08	7.16	7.93
May	8.19	7.41	8.28
June	8.29	7.29	7.94
July	8.97	7.10	8.16
August	8.99	7.10	8.36
September	9.35	8.43	9.21
October	7.84	7.91	8.43
November	8.31	7.66	8.41
December	8.41	7.53	8.32

Percentage Changes from Previous Period Consumer Prices

	1982	1983	1984	1985	1986	12 Months to Oct.' 87
United States	9.1	3.2	4.3	3.5	2.0	6.1
Japan	2.7	1.9	2.2	2.1	0.4	0.5
Germany	5.3	3.3	2.4	2.2	-0.2	0.9
France	11.8	9.6	7.4	5.8	2.7	3.2
United Kingdom	8.6	4.6	5.0	6.1	3.4	4.5
Italy	16.3	15.0	10.6	8.6	6.1	5.3
Canada	10.8	5.9	4.3	4.0	4.2	4.3

Sources: *Bank of Canada Review*; and *OECD Economic Outlook* (Paris, December 1987).

the domestic authorities in those countries to instil more domestic stimulus into their economies, continued to fall. In other countries there was little movement either way.

More troubling than these interest rate changes were developments concerning prices (see Table 5-3). With respect to almost all key countries for which there are data at present, prices as measured by the consumer price index (CPI) rose substantially during 1987. In the all-important case of the United States, the rate in 1987 was more than double that in 1986, although there appeared to be some deceleration very late in the year. While this increase during 1987 is explicable partly in terms of the rising cost of imports in the United States, it did indicate a turnaround of inflation performance, which in turn affected expectations adversely. Inflation performance elsewhere, while poorer than in the previous one or two years, was not as serious, although policy authorities began to warn of impending damage in the course of the year.[2]

Public sector deficits presented an even more mixed picture. While still severe, the fiscal deficit of the United States showed major improvement in 1987. As a per cent of nominal GNP, the U.S. deficit declined to an estimated 2.4 per cent, the lowest level since the late 1970s. Canadian performance in this regard improved dramatically also, as did that of several other smaller OECD countries. Japanese and German deficits, however, increased, albeit marginally, reflecting the desire of these two countries to provide extra fiscal stimulus to their economies. As with inflation, public sector deficits in 1987 did not present as major a public policy problem to the global economy as they had earlier. But other issues had become relatively more serious.

The Problem Indicators

Current account, exchange rate and external debt developments preoccupied policy makers throughout the year (see Table 5-4 and Figure 5-1, pages 101 and 102). With respect to the international trade situation, the best that might be said was that the current account indicators did not significantly worsen in 1987. Nor did they improve. With respect to the United States, the current account deficit that had become a major problem from 1982 onward continued to deteriorate notwithstanding a dramatically lower exchange rate for the U.S. dollar and sharp improvements in productivity.[3] Each month's release of U.S. trade numbers became major market and media events and led to many legislative proposals in the U.S. Congress to inhibit imports in some way or to more actively expand U.S. competitiveness.[4]

Elsewhere, the surpluses in the two major surplus countries — Japan and West Germany — continued to increase, although at a slower rate than had been the case in 1986 and in earlier years. These continuing surpluses as well as those of certain Asian NICs became the focus of heated attention in the United States in particular, with calls for dramatically increased domestic stimulus in both Japan and Germany, substantial appreciation in the value of the Korean won and the Taiwan and Hong Kong dollars, and accusations of unfair trade practices with respect to virtually all of its trading partners. Other countries' positions varied, with Taiwan in particular recording large surpluses in 1987 while most other countries continued to suffer ever-greater current account deficits. Clearly, fundamental worldwide imbalances were in evidence, as they had been for the past four years, and they were, if anything, getting worse. These imbalances were reflected in many ways. Most importantly, they contributed to the volatility in the international values of various exchange rates.

Exchange rate trends under way since February or March of 1985 continued. The U.S. dollar and its Canadian counterpart were weak from the beginning of the year to the end, with major purchasers of the currencies, especially of the U.S. dollar, increasingly becoming central banks rather than private holders (*Globe and Mail* 1988). The yen and the deutschmark mirrored some of the North American dollars' weakness, the yen rising about 25 per cent against the U.S. dollar in the course of the year and the deutschmark about 15 per cent.

Table 5-4
General Government Financial Balances, Surplus (+) or Deficit (-) as a Percentage of GNP/GDP

	1982	1983	1984	1985	1986	1987[a]
United States	-3.5	-3.8	-2.8	-3.3	-3.5	-2.4
Japan	-3.6	-3.7	-2.1	-0.8	-0.9	-1.2
Germany	-3.3	-2.5	-1.9	-1.1	-1.2	-1.7
France	-2.8	-3.2	-2.7	-2.9	-2.9	-2.8
United Kingdom	-2.3	-3.6	-3.9	-2.9	-2.6	-2.1
Italy	-11.3	-10.7	-11.5	-12.3	-11.2	-10.3
Canada	-5.9	-6.9	-6.6	-7.0	-5.5	-4.4

[a] OECD projection.

Source: *OECD Economic Outlook* (Paris, December 1987).

The rate and the circumstances of the changes among and between these three major currencies had market and other analysts guessing throughout the year. Many questioned the ultimate impact of the various current account imbalances on both domestic and international growth and on prices. Uncertainties prevailed throughout the year, with the situation becoming even more volatile and less certain by the end of the year.

Somewhat more certainty, if not a very tentative optimism, surrounded the debt situation.[5] Total external debt continued to increase, with developing countries owing some $100 billion more at the end of the year than at the beginning. The debt situation varied by country. Some countries, such as South Korea or Taiwan, were seemingly in a better position to manage their debt than Brazil or Mexico, for example. Still, there were several encouraging signs, especially in light of serious problems surrounding Brazil early in the year over both rescheduling of

Figure 5-1
Current Account Balance of OECD Countries as a Percentage of GNP/GDP

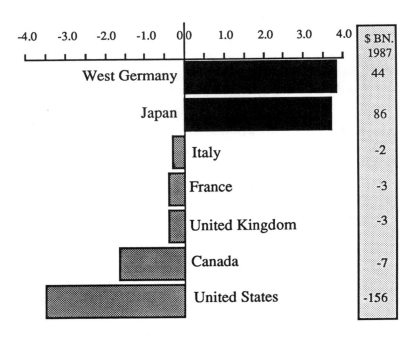

loans and the payment of interest to commercial banks. A new IMF lending facility was finally agreed upon; the World Bank's new focus on structural adjustment lending was re-emphasized by the Bank's new management and by its country stockholders; many Western banks wrote down a large portion of their outstanding less-developed-country (LDC) loans; and towards the end of the year the United States and Mexico had agreed upon a debt-bond swap and underwriting arrangement of possible relevance to other indebted countries. Very serious problems remained, but the will to tackle them on the part of both the debtors and the creditors appeared to be slightly stronger by year's end.

Overwhelming all else in the course of the year was the almost simultaneous crash in stock market values in every corner of the world. Beginning during the second week of October 1987, market jitters climaxed on October 19 (Black Monday) when stock market values fell by the largest one-day amount ever. The causes of the stock market crash were many: over-priced stocks, continually poorer monthly U.S. current account data, rising prices and interest rates, and general uncertainty about national and international economic policies. The timing of the crash, however, remains a mystery. Certainly, instantaneous electronic information and communication systems and the lack of trading margins appear to have aided the process. However, the trigger for the crash itself has yet to be found and agreed upon definitively (*Wall Street Journal* 1987).

The impact of the loss of billions of dollars of paper values as a result of the stock market events in October also remains to be seen. What is clear is that the market in this case, as in the case of exchange rate values, intervened and forced policy makers to act quickly and decisively. The underlying economic situation was not rectified completely, nor was an entire set of new economic policies agreed upon internationally. Nevertheless, monetary policy in several key countries changed abruptly, and confidence quickly returned to the markets. The crisis, by and large, passed by the end of the year; it seemed that 1929 was not to be repeated.

Implications for Consultation and Coordination

With the international consultative process engaged as strongly as ever over the course of 1987 but the accompanying underlying overall economic performance of the world economy less than fully satisfactory, the question arises about improving the effectiveness of such international consultation and coordination or of abandoning such coordination altogether. While an academic view has risen in recent years suggesting that no coordination is better than poor or misdirected coordination (Dornbusch 1987), the reality of the current and prospective political environment is that attempts at such coordination will occur. The task, therefore, is to improve such consultative and coordinating activities by recognizing the economic and political opportunities and constraints of each country and of the international system as a whole and by acting at both an international and national level more quickly and more ambitiously.

In this latter area, serious efforts are being made to strengthen the various international economic institutions and the rules and disciplines that underlie them. As noted above, the World Bank is in the throes of a major restructuring of both its priorities and its personnel to better reflect in particular the structural adjustment requirements of economic development. A new lending facility to assist the developing countries in most serious financial difficulties has been established within the International Monetary Fund, and intensive discussions about expanding the Compensatory Financing Fund (CFF) are under way.

Perhaps the most significant development in 1987, however, was what appeared to be an emerging international consensus that the General Agreement on Tariffs and Trade (GATT) — the underlying institution and set of agreements governing the international trade system — should be strengthened. Proposals to reform the GATT take many forms — many outside the public eye as part of the work of the Negotiating Group on the Functioning of the GATT (FOGS) within the multilateral trade negotiations — but they all appear to revolve around making the GATT a stronger trade policy organization (Camps and Diebold 1983). Parallels with some of the IMF functions have been drawn, including an expanded role for ministers. Improved coordination between the GATT and the international financial institutions has also been called for. Underlying institution-building in this area has been the reality that the international rules and disciplines governing trade need to be strengthened and modernized both in areas that had been negotiated in the previous rounds and in the "new" areas such as services, trade-related intellectual property and trade-related investment measures. The work plan and agenda for achieving these objectives were agreed upon early in the year, as noted earlier, and negotiations carried on in fifteen MTN Negotiating Groups throughout 1987. In the background, protectionist pressures and proposals, and occasionally actions, rebounded across the world economy. But notwithstanding the deteriorating world economic situation, such protectionism appeared on balance to get no worse during the year. Indeed, events such as the initialling of the elements of the Canada-U.S. free trade agreement early in October 1987 and its signing early in 1988 signalled that these forces could and would be resisted.

With respect to the macro-economic side, international coordination in 1987 took a less structured institution-building approach. The questions faced were no less serious than those in the trade field — ranging from the impact of the fall of the U.S. dollar to the role of the now-rapidly depreciating key reserve currency in the financial system, and to the mobilization of international financial institutions and of official bilateral aid to replace commercial bank lending in the debtor nations. Institutions and processes such as the G-7 and the annual summit of the seven leading industrialized countries, as well as the IMF/World Bank and the OECD, continued to address both these and other issues, as did bilateral and smaller group forums.

Much of this activity, however, often appeared to be ad hoc and crisis driven, and the results overall not all that satisfactory, as the earlier sections of this chapter demonstrate. What appeared to be required for the future, given the events of 1987, was even more focus on international institution-building and on leadership, including the capacity for significant and timely policy action. The lessons of 1987 clearly showed that in the absence of well-timed or sufficient action by policy makers, both national and international, the market with all its bluntness would instead do much of the coordinating.

6

Weathering the Storm: North America in the Global Economy

MURRAY G. SMITH

Macro-economic policy as conducted by the major industrial countries during the 1980s created massive imbalances in global trade and payments. These imbalances have placed severe stress on Canada's bilateral economic relations with the United States and threaten serious problems for the multilateral system. As indicated in the preceding chapter, during 1987 these imbalances reached flood tide, creating economic and political crosscurrents in the global economy. Starting with the Plaza Accord in September 1985 and again at the Tokyo summit in 1986, the Louvre meeting in February 1987 and the Venice summit in 1987, the major industrial countries avowed their intentions to coordinate their monetary and fiscal policies with a view to reducing global trade and current account imbalances while maintaining non-inflationary growth. Although the major countries during 1986 had implemented policy moves considered to be in the right direction — the United States had reduced its budget deficit, while Japan and West Germany had moved to cut interest rates — the results can at best be judged as mixed during 1987. The reversal in U.S. fiscal policy after several years of expansionary policy, combined with a shift towards neutral fiscal policies after sustained contraction in Europe and Japan, had produced a dramatic reversal of the appreciation of the U.S. dollar from March 1985 through early 1987, but the U.S. nominal trade deficit actually increased in 1987.

Two years of depreciation of the U.S. dollar failed to reverse the nominal global trade imbalances during 1987 for several reasons. First, the conventional J-curve mechanism predicts that the U.S. nominal trade deficit (and other countries' surpluses) would expand, not contract, after the initial depreciation because U.S. exports are priced in dollars, while imports tend to be priced in other currencies. Second, the J-curve mechanism was exacerbated because world trade had not fully adjusted to the previous appreciation of the U.S. dollar and because creeping protectionism in sectors such as automobiles and steel attenuated the initial response to exchange rate changes. Third, the limited success in achieving coordination of monetary and fiscal policies of the major industrial countries meant that although there was some convergence, economic growth in Japan and West Germany remained weaker than in North America. Thus, all of the burden of adjustment in trade flows fell on exchange rates (Lipsey and Smith 1987). As a result of these factors, global imbalances, particularly the nominal U.S. deficit, continued to deteriorate.

The lack of progress in reversing nominal trade imbalances resulted in the persistence of the political pressures on trade relations that were originally generated by the appreciation of the U.S. dollar. Yet the perceived failure of the depreciation of the U.S. dollar to reverse the trade imbalances seemed to intensify political pressures on bilateral trade relations and the trading system.

Creating the Imbalances

Although they have been operating more or less in tandem, two distinct macro-economic factors can be identified that gave rise to the global current account imbalances of the mid-1980s. The first factor that must be considered is the impact of the shift in monetary policy undertaken by the central banks of the major industrial countries at the beginning of the decade. Virtually in concert, they tightened domestic monetary policy in an effort both to contain and to lower inflation. The result was a dramatic slowdown in world economic activity during 1980-82 and the first declines in the value of world trade since the 1930s. Nominal and real interest rates reached historic peaks for most countries during this period. The results were sharp decreases in investment activity, a contraction in household spending on consumer durables, and weak markets for resource commodities.

Over the first half of the decade, this austere and concerted monetary program was successful in arresting and lowering inflation in the industrial countries. Indeed, the decline in the rates of inflation in the Canadian economy, and also in the U.S. economy, in the 1980s — about ten percentage points — is comparable to the price deflation experienced in the 1930s. The transition to a low inflation environment was particularly painful for Canada both because of Canada's dependence upon resource commodities, which experienced real price declines, and because domestic inflation in Canada proved to be more tenacious than in other economies, notably that of the United States.

The transition to a low inflation environment would have been painful for industrial and resource sectors in North America even without any other complicating factors. Particularly for the Canadian and U.S. resource sectors, the trend towards lower real commodity prices, which has been associated with the disinflation process, would have caused considerable difficulty. The resource sectors of the United States and Canada experienced an especially joyless recovery, however, because of a second macro-economic factor — divergencies between the fiscal policy of North America on the one hand and of Europe and Japan on the other. Starting in 1982, the United States, and also Canada, embarked on a policy of fiscal expansion through rising full-employment budget deficits. At the same time, the European and Japanese economies were pursuing restrictive fiscal policies by moving towards a surplus on their full-employment budgets. Furthermore, significant disparities in the rates of economic growth were associated with this divergence in fiscal policies. The result was a sharp deterioration of the external balance positions of North America and a corresponding shift to surplus by most other major industrial countries.

These two macro-economic policy divergencies affected economic activity in the summit countries through several channels. One channel was the exchange rate. Efforts to finance the U.S. and Canadian budget deficits put upward pressure on interest rates in their capital markets and thus increased capital inflows, which in turn appreciated the U.S. dollar against all major currencies from 1980 to 1985. The Canadian dollar declined against the U.S. dollar during this period but appreciated against other major currencies. When adjusted for the higher rate of domestic inflation in Canada, the increase in Canada's effective real exchange rate was significant, although less dramatic than that experienced by the United States.

In addition to the exchange rate effect, the transmission of high real interest rates through global financial markets also contributed to divergencies in economic growth and trade performance. The European and Japanese economies were experiencing contractionary effects on domestic demand from the move towards budget surplus, but they did not enjoy the declines in real interest rates that might have been associated with these changes in their domestic fiscal policies. Instead, high real interest rates emanating from North America acted both to slow the pace of recovery in their economies and to curtail the increase in private sector capital spending that ordinarily would have been associated with their own fiscal policy measures. Japan and Europe, like Canada, expanded their exports of products such as automobiles to take advantage of the consumer-led recovery in the U.S. economy.

During the early to mid-1980s, the global trend to disinflation, combined with the strong U.S. — and to a lesser extent Canadian — dollar and the divergence in economic growth performance, placed severe stress on those parts of the North American economy that were producing primary resource commodities. Canada found itself in a position not unlike that of other highly indebted resource-producing nations in the Western Hemisphere; it had to sustain large trade surpluses, despite the deterioration of its export prices, in order to service its foreign liabilities. The problems of the debtor countries only served to deepen the crisis in the North American resource sector.

Disparities in the macro-economic policies of the major industrial countries predictably produced a substantial divergence in external current account positions. Japan and Western Europe moved towards larger and larger trade and current account surpluses, while the United States, and also Canada with a lag, moved towards large current account deficits. In the case of the United States, these macro-economic stresses fanned protectionist fires, particularly in the resource sectors. There was greater pressure for the application of U.S. fair trade laws, as well as increasing resort to escape-clause actions and voluntary export restraints, which were used to institute managed-trade regimes in major industrial sectors. At the same time, the United States resorted to export subsidies in agriculture, ostensibly to combat European and Japanese agricultural policies, but Canadian agriculture was caught in the crossfire in the ensuing subsidy war.

The delayed response of the U.S. trade deficit to the declines in the U.S. dollar against the currencies of some of the major industrial countries since March 1985 heightened protectionist pressures during 1987. Yet this delayed response was entirely predictable for several reasons. First, the pattern of relatively weak economic growth in Europe and Japan had persisted, in part because of the cautious monetary and fiscal policies of those countries. Second, the adverse effects of the appreciation of the U.S. dollar through the first half of the decade was not fully reflected in the U.S. trade position. Therefore, the traditional J-curve effect, which leads to a short-term deterioration of the trade balance in response to a depreciation in the currency, was exacerbated by the lag in the response to the previous appreciation. Third, the U.S. dollar declined dramatically relative to the currencies of Japan and Germany, but the movement was much less dramatic against other currencies. A broad-based measurement of effective exchange rates suggests that the devaluation of the U.S. dollar was about 20 per cent from March 1985 to March 1987.

Trade policy factors also influenced the response of the U.S. trade account to the depreciation of the U.S. dollar. The voluntary export restraint arrangements in key industrial sectors reduced the impact of exchange rate movements on trade volumes in the short term. Under the export restraints, foreign producers limited their export volumes and took higher profit margins from their sales in the United States. As their costs rise because of appreciation of their domestic currencies, foreign producers tend initially to absorb the impact by lowering their profit margins. It is only when the exchange rate has moved a sufficient amount — to a level where their domestic costs necessitate a price increase in the U.S. market up to a level that makes the export restraint arrangements no longer binding — that the exchange rate movement begins to have a significant effect on trade volumes.

Finally, the prolonged period of dollar overvaluation distorted investment decisions. It appeared more attractive to invest offshore instead of investing within the United States. It will take years of new investment to catch up, but the slow response of the U.S. trade balance to exchange rate movements does not provide a basis for pessimism about the long-term competitiveness of the U.S. economy. Many believe that the movement in the exchange rate will not restore external balance in the U.S. economy. Views were similar during the 1970s when there were those who thought that energy prices would rise exponentially and that demand and supply would not respond to those price increases.

Americans can learn from an examination of the Canadian economy. During the 1970s, Canada ran a large current account deficit relative to the size of its gross national product (GNP) and increased its net foreign indebtedness considerably. Today Canada's foreign debt amounts to about 30 per cent of GNP. At present, Canada is simultaneously running a substantial surplus in merchandise trade along with the large deficit in its current account. In future the United States will be obliged to service its mounting foreign liabilities, thus necessitating a trade surplus.

As a debtor nation, Canada continued to run a trade surplus of about 2 per cent of GNP in 1987, despite the substantial current account deficit of about 2 per cent of GNP. All of Canada's trade surplus came from its trade with the United States, as Canada ran a trade deficit with the rest of the world. This heavy dependence upon trade with the United States makes Canada vulnerable to U.S. protectionism as well as to the possibility of a sharp recession in the U.S. economy, which seemed to be heralded by the stock market crash in October 1987.

Trade Policy Pressures

During the 1980s, and particularly for much of 1987, unilateral measures under the U.S. trade laws have been judged by U.S. private interests and by Congress to be the most effective vehicle for resolving trade disputes and the best means to discipline the unfair practices of trading partners. The global imbalances of the 1980s, and the associated rise in U.S. protectionism, have created severe stresses in bilateral economic relations between the United States and its major trading partners, including Canada, and stretched the fabric of the world trading system. Since U.S. protectionism has been channelled into complaints about unfair foreign practices, the threat to impose penalty duties affects adversely the investment climate in Canada and unleashes pressures on Canadian governments. Thus, the rules and procedures governing the bilateral application of import relief laws were central Canadian concerns in the Canada-U.S. trade negotiations.

The pressures of U.S. protectionism have manifested themselves in a variety of ways. There has been a spate of actions filed under the existing U.S. trade laws, as well as political pressures to alter U.S. trade legislation and administrative practice to make it easier for domestic petitioners to obtain relief from import competition.

Countervailing Duties

The use of subsidies and the procedures governing the application of countervailing duties were key issues in the Tokyo Round. The United States sought to discipline the use of subsidies by other countries, while other countries sought to limit the application of U.S. countervailing duties. The European Community was unwilling to negotiate any rules that could limit subsidies under either the Common Agricultural Program or the industrial policies of member states. For its part, the United States was unwilling to implement the injury test in the application of its countervailing-duty law. Under the compromise achieved in the Tokyo Round, the United States introduced the injury test for countries signing the General Agreement on Tariffs and Trade (GATT) subsidies code, while the definition of countervailable subsidies was broadened. Under present U.S. practice, countervailing duties can be imposed on any domestic subsidies that are not widely available, although recent decisions by the U.S. Court of International Trade cast some doubt on even this latter qualification. The trend towards a broadening of the U.S. definition of a countervailable subsidy operates as an increasing constraint on the domestic policies of governments in Canada.

The two bills introduced into the Ninety-ninth Congress in the United States represented a continuation of the trend towards redefining unfair trade. Both bills were intended to overturn the U.S. International Trade Administration's *Softwood Lumber* decision of 1983, which found Canadian stumpage policies not to be countervailable subsidies under U.S. law. In addition, a new type of "resource-pricing subsidy" was proposed in the omnibus trade bill — H.R. 4800, legislation that was passed by the House of Representatives but was not taken up by the Senate. Nevertheless, the result desired by some U.S. lumber interests was achieved in October 1986 when the International Trade Administration of the Department of Commerce reversed its previous ruling and, in a preliminary determination, found that the stumpage practices of provincial governments were countervailable subsidies. Fearing that appealing this decision would be risky and subject to delay, the Canadian government chose to negotiate an out-of-court settlement on December 30, 1986, rather than pay hundreds of millions of dollars in duties to the U.S. Treasury.[1] Although the Commerce Department rationalized its reversal of the 1983 decision on the basis the *Cabot Corp.* decision by the Court of International Trade, this unilateral redefinition of subsidy serves to underline the ambiguity of the statutory criteria for imposing countervailing duties.

The Omnibus Trade Bill

The opening of the 100th Congress in January 1987 was marked by avowals by the Democratic leadership that an omnibus trade bill would be passed in 1987. After the Democrats gained control of the Senate in the mid-term elections, the new majority leader, Senator Byrd, pledged that the Senate would promptly take up the trade bill — H.R. 3 — which was one of the first bills introduced into the House of Representatives. The initial version of H.R. 3 closely resembled the previous omnibus trade bill, H.R. 4800, and, in particular, it contained a resource-pricing-subsidy amendment to the countervailing—duty law. Many amendments were made to the legislation, most of which were intended to make it easier for U.S. claimants to obtain relief from import competition. The House of Representatives passed its version of the legislation — amounting to 958 pages — by April. The House bill was taken up quickly by the Senate Finance Committee, then the Senate version — 1,053 pages — was hammered out in lengthy debate on the Senate floor. By the time Congress rose for the summer recess, the Senate had passed its version of H.R. 3. Both the House and the Senate bills were highly protectionist, but not in the same ways (IRPP 1987).

Instead of attacking resource subsidies directly, the final versions of the House and Senate bills propose a more generic approach. Both the House and Senate versions of the trade bill, which were passed in the summer of 1987, include the following special rule to guide the interpretation of U.S. countervailing-duty law: "(B)...the administering authority...shall determine whether the bounty, grant, or subsidy in law or in fact is provided to a specific enterprise or industry, or group of enterprises or industries."[2] This general statutory language is intended to guide the interpretation of the concept of specificity in U.S. countervailing-duty law. The report of the House Ways and Means Committee offered the following explanation for this new special rule:

With regard to the so-called specificity test, subparagraph (B) would require the administering authority to determine whether benefits *actually conferred* accrued to a specific enterprise or a group of enterprises or industries rather than merely examining the legal nature of the subsidy program and the "nominal" availability of such benefits. This, in effect, codifies the finding of the Court of International Trade decided in *Cabot Corp.* v. *United States*, that the Commerce Department had been interpreting the concept of "specificity" and "general availability" in an unduly narrow manner....The Court in *Cabot* provided a sound interpretive rule to be applied in those cases where broadly available benefits are at issue. The test for such programs is whether there is a sufficient degree of competitive advantage in international commerce being bestowed upon a discrete class of beneficiaries that would not exist but for government action. This necessarily involves subjective, case-by-case decisions to determine whether there is such a discrete class of beneficiaries. (U.S. Congress 1987: 123-24)

The Ways and Means Committee offered the following reason for the new statutory provision on specificity:

> The Committee is encouraged by the Commerce Department's recent preliminary affirmative determination in *Certain Softwood Lumber Products from Canada* as a reflection that the Department is beginning to take a broader perspective on its interpretation of the specificity test in dealing with resource-type products in light of the court's holding in *Cabot*. It now appears that a special provision dealing with resource input products is not necessary for such an input product to be countervailable if the Department properly applies the specificity test. (p. 126)

The House version of the bill goes further than the Senate version by including a set of rules to guide the calculation of "preferentiality" and by codifying the Commerce Department methodology for calculating subsidies that was used in the *Softwood Lumber* case.

The proposed standard for countervailing duties in the omnibus trade bill is directed at a variety of government policies, not just alleged resource subsidies. In the committee's own words, a "subjective case by case examination" of any "competitive advantage that would not exist but for government action" is a broad and ambiguous standard to apply to a mixed economy in the late twentieth century.

When Congress returned from the summer recess, a conference committee was organized involving over 200 members to negotiate the joint version of the legislation. Not only was the conference exceptionally large, the trade bill involved more than twenty committees in both chambers, creating complicated jurisdictional wrangles. Fortunately from the point of view of Canada and other countries, the conference committee quickly bogged down in the complex task of reconciling the two bills and negotiating the required political compromises.

Beyond the technical complexity of reconciling the two versions of the trade bill, economic developments reduced the political pressure to produce a trade bill. The most dramatic development was the crash in the stock market in October, a crash that evoked the folk memory of the Smoot-Hawley tariff that followed on the heels of the stock market crash of October 1929. Not only was the Smoot-Hawley tariff recognized as a factor contributing to the Great Depression, but neither Smoot nor Hawley was re-elected. A more subtle development was the decline in the U.S. dollar, which improved the competitiveness of U.S. producers and stimulated growth in U.S. exports. In real volume terms, the United

States experienced export-led growth in 1987 in an economy close to full employment, despite the fact that the nominal trade balance deteriorated.

The recent turmoil in financial markets appears to have cooled the ardour of Congress for tough new trade legislation. More importantly, the turbulence in financial markets has provoked a temporary flash of sanity in Congress: the recognition that the real source of the U.S. trade problems is the U.S. budget deficit. Yet even if this new-found perspicacity of Congress is sustained, the unwinding of global economic imbalances could have disruptive consequences for Canada and produce new strains on its global economic relations.

Unwinding the Imbalances

At the close of 1987 the global trade and payments imbalances appeared to have stabilized, with indications that they are likely to contract in 1988. The reversal of the tide of trade flows and the pattern of exchange rates and interest rates associated with that reversal have important implications for Canada's economic relations.

The growth trend in production and trade required in the United States and Canada is clear. Over the next few years, aggregate consumption in the United States needs to grow about 1 per cent slower than aggregate production — with the reverse true for Europe and Japan — generating a shift towards external balance. Canada, for its part, must expand offshore exports, exploiting the lower value of the Canadian dollar against the currencies of other major industrial countries in order to move towards surplus in overseas trade. If the U.S. economy slips into a prolonged recession, for example, the adjustment process could be painful for Canada.

Even if the pace of adjustment is difficult to gauge, the sectoral pattern of trade shifts can be anticipated with some certainty. The resource sectors, having endured seven lean years, could prosper under any scenario, except a deep global recession, because the decline in U.S. and Canadian dollars has improved commodity prices in dollar terms. At the same time, the slowdown in consumer spending will reduce demand for automobiles just when additional capacity for North American assembly is coming on stream. Thus, the locus of U.S. protectionism could shift into the automotive sector. As Paul Wonnacott (1987) has argued, the Canadian automotive industry could be the major beneficiary of the Canada-U.S. free trade agreement because the agreement will prevent catastrophic outcomes such as countervailing-duty cases against Canadian-based automotive exports.

For the moment, it appears that the political momentum behind the U.S. trade bill has waned. The glowing embers of U.S. protectionism could be reignited, however, if the nominal U.S. trade deficit fails to enter into a sustained decline in 1988. Furthermore, consideration by Congress of the proposed Canada-U.S. free trade agreement could become entangled in manoeuvring between Congress and a lame duck president over the trade bill.

Although the decline in the U.S. and Canadian dollars could ease recent stresses in bilateral resource trade, the appreciation of the Japanese and European currencies is likely to make Japan and Europe less inclined to consider trade liberalization, particularly for their highly protected agricultural producers. Access to offshore markets will become of greater importance to Canada, even if the free trade agreement goes ahead as planned, because of the realignment in exchange rates. But chances for an "early harvest" on agricultural trade at the GATT ministerial meeting in late 1988 appear increasingly fleeting.

Although buffeted by heavy weather in 1987, the Canadian economy was able to slip through the shoals of U.S. protectionism relatively unscathed. New perils await in 1988, but if the monthly U.S. trade deficit begins to decline, overall trade relations between Canada and the United States could improve in the year ahead. The realignment of exchange rates and the reversing tide of global trade flows, however, could create new stresses within the automotive sector in North America and between North America and the other major industrial countries over world agricultural trade.

PART

IV

International Development

7 | The Environment and North-South Conflict

JOHN T. O'MANIQUE

In 1987 the population of our planet exceeded five billion. It had doubled since 1950. Also in 1987, the long-standing debate of global proportions on the impact that further development would have on the planet's ecosystem was renewed in a fresh and focused way. The central issue is whether present development strategies are in conflict with the environment. If such a conflict exists and is not resolved, then the possibility of further conflict among nations along a North-South axis, brought about by the stresses created by negative developmental impacts on the ecosystem, arises.

The question of conflict between development and environment, although very complex, is basically empirical and can be analyzed in a disinterested way. In contrast, the question of possible international conflict over the negative environmental effects of development is not only a complex empirical issue but one that also has a normative dimension, which makes objective analysis and assessment very difficult. This chapter will, nevertheless, explore the 1987 revival of the development/environment issue and attempt some analysis of the conflicts that could arise from it.

The Development/Environment Conflict

Early in 1987 the World Commission on Environment and Development (WCED), a distinguished international panel of scientists, government officials, and development and environmental experts chaired by Gro Harlem Brundtland, prime minister of Norway, submitted its report, *Our Common Future*, to the United Nations. The message of the WCED is that economic growth is needed for development, but growth, in its present forms, puts tremendous strains on the environment. The challenge is to provide the material bases for development without destroying the ecosystem, the source of that material base — in other words, to provide sustainable development. The commission argues that a united, cooperative effort will be required of the nations of the world to meet this challenge.

The debate that had emerged from the earlier warnings of limits to growth, almost twenty years ago, was emotionally charged. Many from the South interpreted the ecologists' messages as a threat to their development—"Now that we have reached high levels of affluence," the North seemed to be saying, "material growth can cease and we can enjoy our wealth in a clean environment." With good reason, those who needed more growth and those who supported them objected to this message. With the renewal of ecological concern and explicit discussion of the development/environment problem, the debate will again be intense. It will be difficult to analyze and assess the problem and discuss solutions in a disinterested way, and some might avoid the issue altogether.

The first studies of limits to growth focused on the ecological problem alone. Development was included only as a component of projections such as the following: "If trend x continues into the future, then the consequence will be y." This was not a prediction. No one was saying that x would continue or y would occur. Nor was this a normative proposition. The projection was silent on the value of x and y; it did not say what either x or y ought to be. The overall conclusion was obvious: "In a finite world, material growth will eventually reach a limit, and if the growth is exponential, it will reach its limit faster." But there were no predictions as to when various limits would be reached. Yet these essentially empirical, non-normative analyses — leading to projections, not predictions — were interpreted widely as forecasts with ethical and often anti-developmental ramifications.

The Brundtland Commission report explicitly confronts both the ecosystem and development impacts and does so empirically and normatively. The empirical projection is that if present development trends continue, serious environmental damage will result. The commission's normative position is also very clear: development for all people in the world is good and hence ought to occur. The WCED calls, therefore, for a revival of economic growth, especially in the South. The dilemma is this: development requires a healthy environment, but growth can damage the environment — hence, the need for a new kind of growth.

The conflict between development and environment arises from the accelerating increase in population and from the fact that, through development, more of people's material needs or wants are being satisfied. Since 1950, the world's population has doubled, but mineral production has grown threefold and manufacturing sevenfold (WCED 1987: 206). This dramatic increase in industrialization, so far concentrated in the countries of the North but also growing in the South, places a great strain on the capacity of our planet to provide resources and to absorb waste, and in some instances has done damage to its life support system. We are familiar with global effects such as the possibility of adverse climatic changes arising from the huge amounts of carbon dioxide released into the atmosphere by the burning of fossil fuels and from the depletion of the ozone shield by other industrial gases, which could increase the incidence of cancer and adversely affect the oceans' food chain. We know, moreover, of the high rate of destruction and marginalization of agricultural land and of deforestation throughout the world.

We also hear regularly about more local effects, such as the Three Mile Island and Chernobyl nuclear reactor accidents, the Bhopal pesticide factory leak, the chemical discharge into the Rhine River and the Mexico City gas tank explosion. Closer to home we are concerned about acid precipitation, toxic materials in the Great Lakes and a range of pollutants in our water, air and food chain (see chapter 10). Some of these problems are due, in part, to natural causes, but we also must attribute them to the development practices of our own species. Even much of desertification can be explained in terms of a range of inappropriate human activities that compete and collaborate with climate in destruction. There is clearly a conflict between us and our planet — between development and environment.

Measuring the Development/Environment Conflict

How concerned should we be about the possible negative impact of development on our environment — about potential conflict between economic and ecological objectives? Should we, like the Brundtland Commission, be so concerned that we would argue for major changes in development strategies involving significant new forms of international cooperation, or can we continue to concern ourselves only with the economic dimension of development and hope that present approaches will see us through? The empirical question is: can our ecosystem provide the resources for, and absorb the residues from, whatever processes are required to effect an acceptable level of development for our species and sustain that level of development?

This is a huge and complex question with so many variables that a clear and simple answer is impossible. We do know, however, that development involves industrialization, which uses energy, and that energy consumption is central to the ecological problem. To approximate an answer to this question, this chapter offers an analysis of the relationship between development and environment, using energy consumption[1] as the common variable between economic development and environmental impact. The results of the analysis will not only help to confirm that there is a problem worthy of concern but will also shed light on the nature and magnitude of that problem and on how it affects, and is affected by, different levels of development, thereby illuminating the subsequent discussion of related North-South conflict. The assumptions underlying the analysis are that economic growth, measured by gross domestic product (GDP), is related to increased energy consumption and that increased energy consumption is related to some of the most serious ecological problems. The relationship between economic growth and energy consumption is twofold. First, it is assumed that growth is associated with industrialization, which is fuelled by energy. (Industrialization includes manufacturing, mining, construction, and the production/supply of electricity, water and gas.) Second, increasing wealth is associated with rising energy consumption not directly related to the production process. This non-productive energy would include fuel for private transportation, electricity for domestic lighting, and the like.

The relationship between energy consumption and ecological problems is also twofold. First, the quantities of certain important types of energy that our planet can supply, fossil fuels in particular, are limited. Non-renewable energy stocks will eventually be depleted, and accelerated use will hasten the depletion date. As stocks dwindle, costs rise, causing possible economic crises perhaps long before the last drops are used. Second, and probably more important, many of the negative impacts on our environment, some of which were discussed above (global heating, acidification, ozone destruction, various air, land and water pollutants), are directly or indirectly related to energy consumption. Energy consumption is only a surrogate variable for the complex set of ecological problems, but it could be indicative of their general magnitude.

Trends and Relationships

Let us first assess the recent trends in and relationships between growth and energy consumption and then make some projections of these two variables into the future. An analysis of sixty-four developing countries and sixteen developed market economies for which there are relevant data confirms the role of industrialization in development. It indicates that the correlation between growth in GDP and growth in industrialization between 1965 and 1980, for all categories of countries, is very high. There would appear to be little doubt that economic growth and industrialization go hand in hand. The relationship between industrialization and increases in commercial energy consumption is more complex. The earlier stages of industrialization are less tied to increases in energy consumption than are later stages. In developing countries, during relatively high-growth periods, at all income levels, growth in energy consumption is greater than industrial growth, which in turn is greater than growth in GDP. In the developed market economies, growth rates of GDP and industrialization are about equal, and increases in energy consumption somewhat lower.

During the period of recession from 1980 to 1985, the rate of energy consumption decreased in virtually all countries. In the poorest countries this decrease was closely associated with a slowdown in industrialization, while in wealthier countries and especially in the developed market economies, growth rates in industrialization and in GDP were much higher than those of energy consumption, owing perhaps to their higher levels of efficiency and reductions in non-productive consumption on account of cost.

Economic development in the poorest countries (where gross national product [GNP] per capita is less than $400 [U.S.]) is already heavily dependent on industrialization, even though these countries are at a pre-industrial stage with emphasis on agriculture and infrastructure. There is, however, not yet a strong connection between economic growth and increases in commercial energy consumption. (We should note once again, however, the major role played by non-commercial energy in these countries.) Industrialization becomes a more dominant factor in the economic development of middle-income countries and becomes more closely related to energy consumption.

This analysis gives rise to some interesting and relevant hypotheses. First, energy efficiency (defined simply as GDP growth/energy growth) increases as GDP rises. The poorest countries are an exception to this. There, the early stages of economic development seem to involve relatively low energy consumption. Possible explanations for this include these countries' continuing reliance on non-commercial energy; the concentration of development in agriculture and infrastructure, which may be less energy intensive; and the relatively low levels of non-productive energy consumption.

Second, among developing countries, energy efficiency falls during slow-growth (recession) periods. In the developed market economies, decreases in energy consumption were much greater than was the drop in economic growth during the 1980-85 period. In the developing countries, however, growth rates of GDP fell more rapidly than those of energy use. China, whose energy efficiency improved remarkably during the recession, is not really an exception, since it is relatively isolated from the global economy.

With the links between economic development and energy consumption confirmed and some of their characteristics noted, we will now project these variables into the future to shed light on the development/environment dilemma.

Projections

The question to be considered now is, how much energy would be consumed by a world in which a "good" level of economic development had been obtained throughout? We obviously cannot predict what that consumption would be, but we can project actual trends to gain some insight into what it might be if recent conditions persist into the future. We will choose a GDP of $4,000 (U.S.) per capita as the level of "good" economic development. This is approximately the present position of Spain and could, with proper distribution, provide a good life for all. We will use the same aggregations as above and assume a GDP per capita growth rate of 5 per cent per annum for all developing countries throughout the period. Given the projections for population growth in the developing countries over the next fifteen years, this could require GDP growth of around 7 per cent and hence may not be possible initially; but as steady states in population (net reproduction rate of one) are anticipated to be reached by these countries between the years 2000 and 2040, an average rate of per capita growth of 5 per cent, if somewhat optimistic, could be possible over the long period in question.

At this rate, the low-income countries (considering them as a unit) would achieve a GDP per capita of $4,000 (U.S.) in 57 years (57 years from the base year, 1985; that is, the year 2042), the lower-middle-income group in 34.5 years, and the upper-middle in 18.5 years. The assumptions upon which the related energy consumption projections are made are based on an analysis of the actual consumption rates from 1965 to 1985 and include adjustments for the variations in energy efficiency. They are also adjusted for population, using United Nations' population projections. As countries reach the $4,000 plateau, all growth rates go to zero; the projection tells us only what energy is required to get to this level of economic development. Given these assumptions, in the year 2042 our projected "developed" South is consuming almost twelve times its present amount. If the North were to increase consumption by only 1 per cent per year during this period, the global consumption in 2042 would be more than four times the present. If there were no growth in energy consumption in the North, the global increase would be just less than fourfold.

Assessing the Projections

These projections support the hypothesis of a development/environment conflict. Given the degree of damage to our planet's ecosystem brought about by present levels of energy consumption, the consequences of a fourfold increase in that same pattern of consumption could be seen as disastrous. The pattern of consumption — that is, the relative amounts of the various energies used — is an essential factor in determining environmental impact.

The pattern during the 1980s is as follows: oil, 41 per cent; coal, 23 per cent; natural gas, 17 per cent; renewable energy, 17 per cent; and nuclear, 2 per cent. Estimates of the capacity of our planet to supply fossil fuels suggest that this pattern cannot be maintained. Oil is in shortest supply, followed by gas and then coal. A calculation based on data from sources used by the Brundtland Commission (WCED 1987: 171) indicates that, considering supply, the following would be reasonable increments to achieve the fourfold increase of our projection: oil, 1.9-fold; gas, 4.1-fold; coal, 6-fold; nuclear, 36-fold; and renewable, 4.6-fold. These increases in fossil fuel use, and especially in the use of coal, by far the "dirtiest" of the three, would cause severe environmental problems, the most noteworthy being global warming, acidification of the environment and industrial pollution, concentrated in urban areas. One study referred to in the WCED report (p. 172) expressed concern over the risks of global heating at half the energy consumption levels of our projection.

In 1986 there were 366 working nuclear reactors in the world; a 36-fold increase would bring that number to over 13,000. U.S. Nuclear Regulatory Commission estimates of the risk of serious radioactive release resulting from component failure for light-water reactors, if applicable to all 13,000, would put the probability of such an accident at one in seventy-six years. The Three Mile Island and Chernobyl accidents, however, were caused by human failure, which cannot be predicted a priori. They did occur after 2,000 and 4,000 reactor-years respectively; at that rate, there would be 6.6 accidents per year among the 13,000. Along with the growing risk of accident, nuclear energy presents risks associated with nuclear waste disposal; increases of the magnitude projected above could push this risk to very high levels. Finally, the most unpredictable and most dangerous risk associated with nuclear energy lies in the use that terrorists could make of nuclear plants, fuels or residues. A small quantity of plutonium in the hands of any terrorist could produce disastrous consequences. As availability increases, so do the odds of nuclear blackmail.

While accurate predictions are still not possible, it seems most likely that the cumulative impact of the projected energy use would be harmful to our environment in at least some of the ways noted in this paper, if not in others, including some not yet conceived of. Many of these negative effects would have no regard for national boundaries and many would endanger the capacity of our planet to sustain life or would directly threaten health or life. How, then, can this conflict between development and the environment be resolved?

Conflict Resolution

The challenge is to resolve the conflict in favour of both good human development and a healthy environment. The Brundtland Commission calls for a revival of economic growth, especially in the South, and then proposes a number of measures that it believes will be required if our planet is to cope with this growth. These include a change in the quality of growth to a new kind that will be sustainable; conservation and enhancement of environmental resources; sustainable population levels; orientation of technology to environmental factors; integration of ecology and economics in decision making; reformation of international economic relations; and greater international cooperation (WCED 1987: p. 363ff.).

The solutions put forward by the commission are very general in nature. In the light of the above analysis, we will look at some more specific possibilities for sustainable growth through changes in energy consumption and the prospects for their success. The reduction of energy consumption through greater efficiency is one obvious solution. The above projection, however, already takes present variations in efficiency into account and, if anything, inflates the capacity of developing countries to become more efficient. The greatest growth is in the South, where at present there is the least efficient use of energy and the least pollution control. These characteristics are, in fact, officially reinforced within the development process. Equipment and procedures, obsolete because of their inefficiency in the North, are provided to and used by the South. Pollution control is considered to be a luxury that the South cannot yet afford. As part of a solution, the North would have to subsidize the extra costs to the South of higher efficiency and better pollution control.

A second approach to resolving the conflict would be to alter the pattern of energy consumption — to use higher proportions of energies that are less harmful to the environment. As stated above, however, availability of energy at acceptable cost is a major factor in determining the mix and proportions of the kinds of energy used at any time; the present trend is towards increasing use of more ecologically harmful coal and risky nuclear energy. This second approach, then, would actually be a trend reversal that would at first increase energy costs and eventually deplete oil and then natural gas, simply delaying the basic problem. Nevertheless, because delays provide time for other solutions to emerge, the North should give the South financial and technological support in shifting to relatively cleaner energies.

In the long run, the only ecologically acceptable shift in the energy-use mix is towards a greater proportion of renewable energy. Solar, biomass, wind, water, geothermal — these sources are not only renewable but also, with some exceptions, environmentally safe. In the projection above, renewable energy moves from 17 per cent of the total to only 20 per cent. To hold the increases in coal consumption to 100 per cent and nuclear to 300 per cent, use of renewable energy would have to rise twelvefold during the projection period, to 50 per cent of total consumption. The North should support research and development in this area for North and South.

A third solution would simply be a reduction of energy use with no increase in efficiency, that is, an actual reduction in production and in non-productive consumption. The question here is, what effect would this have on development?

The projection was based on actual trends relating energy consumption to economic growth and took into account to some extent the variations in these relationships. Do these variations include the possibility of much higher GDP growth to energy consumption ratios? We must recall that economic growth is related to energy use through both production processes and non-productive consumption. The latter is more a consequence of GDP than a cause, and thus reductions in this area (for example, in transportation) could be effected without negative impacts on economic development and probably with positive impacts on development itself. In many instances, reductions in the non-productive consumption of energy would involve changes in objectives and lifestyles. The South is, to a very great extent, following the high personal consumption pattern of the North. The use of private cars rather than public transport is perhaps the most obvious case of an energy-consuming/environment-polluting trend exported from North to South. The world's largest city, Mexico City, is now choking on its own exhaust. In these areas, the North could assist through support for research, appropriate technology transfer and development, and also good example.

Good development could also be based on less energy-intensive production, but this would also require changes in present development objectives and in lifestyles. There are indigenous and ecologically sound development models now being applied on a small scale in some developing countries. Examples of the Gandhian approach to rural development can be found in India and of the Buddhist way in Sri Lanka — both having high development to economic growth ratios. Similar approaches have existed and flourished in the North as well, the Mennonite communities of southern Ontario being one example. These kinds of development are ideal solutions to the problem but are not seriously considered by most development planners and policy makers, North or South.

The ultimate resolution to the conflict would perhaps come from a complex set of approaches and adjustments, including those just reviewed. This is not now being done and probably will be done only incrementally in response to actual crises. In the words of the Brundtland Commission:

The period ahead must be regarded as transitional from an era in which energy has been used in an unsustainable manner. A generally acceptable pathway to a safe and sustainable energy future has not yet been found. We do not believe that these dilemmas have yet been addressed by the international community with a sufficient sense of urgency and in a global perspective. (WCED 1987: 169)

Given the assumption that the present path leads to serious environmental problems in the long term, what might arise in the shorter term if we do not cooperatively address this dilemma? Again, prediction is not possible, but the prospect of North-South conflict arising out of the development/environment conflict does emerge. Extending our projection to encompass this potential conflict is not pleasant but is perhaps necessary if we are to have a complete picture of possible consequences of present development trends.

North-South Conflict

In our projection, most of the increase in energy consumption is in the South. In 2042 the South would use three-quarters of the world's energy, an almost exact reversal of the present proportions. The South itself would be using about two and a half times the current world total, suggesting that energy use for developing countries alone could cause environmental problems regardless of the extent of ecologically motivated adjustments in the North. The solutions, as discussed above, would require expensive and unpopular combinations of controls, efficiencies, altered and reduced objectives, and changed lifestyles that, without the kinds of support from the North proposed above, might not be adopted. The resulting serious environmental threats would be global, but they could be seen by the North as originating in the South and might thus cause conflict along North-South lines.

What would be the consequences of future environmental threats that could be attributed to growth in the South? The North will not likely tolerate damage to its own well-being. The South, for its part, will not easily forgo development opportunities that the North has already had in abundance. In a worst-case scenario, is it possible that to protect Northern vital interests — whether of the West, the East, the superpowers themselves, individually or collectively — military action could be taken? This is done at present by the superpowers to protect their economic and related ideological interests; a new dimension of ecological threats could easily increase international tensions and shift them more to the North-South axis.

Less-extreme responses could include economic and legal action to impede or adjust growth in the South. The North could reduce or control the flow of investment to the South so as to retard certain environmentally damaging lines of development. It could achieve similar objectives by reducing or controlling the export to the South of industrial inputs — capital equipment, technology, spare parts, raw materials, energy — through pricing, the imposition of export duties or simply embargoes. And it could very easily confine official development assistance to ecologically sound targets.

Retardation of those production processes of the South that damage the environment could also be achieved by a reduction of their imports to the North. This would perhaps be tied to greater tendencies towards Northern self-sufficiency and isolation.

At present, some local environmental problems in the North are solved by exporting them to the South, where pollution controls are weaker and health standards lower. As the people of the North demand greater environmental protection, many ecologically harmful industries, rather than pay the costs of high environmental standards, may move from North to South, carrying the harmful processes with them — and, perhaps, do this in the name of development.

Any of these measures would be seen by the South as unfriendly at best and by some as attacks on their sovereignty, easily leading to further deterioration of relations and increased tensions. Conflict related to increased nuclear energy use in the South could be especially acute. Threats of nuclear accident, of waste disposal problems and especially of terrorist use of nuclear energy would be of great concern to the North, particularly in times of international tension or heightened terrorist activity. A range of responses from economic to military could be envisaged.

It is obvious that these Northern responses to environmental threats are all in opposition to the current dominant free market approach to development. They could, therefore, create serious conflict within the North itself, depending on how divergent were the perceptions of the problem and the agreements on the solution. Massive interference in the market and rejection of the law of relative comparative advantage would cause deep ideological conflict in the power centres of the North.

Attempts by governments to control large transnational corporations would themselves be major conflicts.

The above discussion has focused on conflicts related to environmental degradation. The depletion of energy supplies, especially if allowed to happen without cooperative plans for adjustment and alternatives, could lead to conflict over the remaining scarce resources. Energy now is seen by world powers as a vital interest that should be protected by military force if necessary. The threat of such military force would increase as energy supplies decrease. This could increase tensions anywhere in the world, but given the shift in energy use from North to South, it would be especially intense along the North-South axis. Our economic and ecological projections were extended to the political arena to give us some idea of what might happen if there is no resolution to the development/environment conflict; in the conclusion of this chapter, we will look for solutions in actual development approaches.

Current Approaches

The market economies of the North, and in particular the United States, are encouraging the South to follow a market-controlled industrial growth path which, in itself, would have little or no concern for the ecosystem. The World Bank, a dominant force in development and now virtually controlled by the United States, is promoting this development philosophy — essentially the philosophy of the Reagan administration.

The 1987 issue of the Bank's annual *World Development Report* had as its central theme industrialization and foreign trade, which, it argued, are together the key to economic growth and development; ecological issues are ignored. The problems identified are economic obstacles to growth, in particular, trade barriers and undue government intervention in the marketplace. The solutions are free trade and free markets. Economic efficiency is promoted; ecological efficiency is not mentioned.

Can open and free markets (if such could exist) provide us with environmental protection? It is difficult to see how a pure free market development strategy such as that advocated in the *World Development Report* (1987) would not lead towards a worst-case future. Economic growth through industrialization, directed by market forces — by short-term profit and instant gratification — has to date increased the ecological threat while resisting the required controls. This narrow economic and laissez-faire approach, which promotes bilateralism, competition and minimum state intervention, is in direct conflict with the Brundtland Commission's call for a multilateral cooperative strategy that would require state involvement and intervention. It is, nevertheless, a very popular and powerful position in much of the North and South.

The pure free enterprise approach, however, is now being touched, and perhaps modified, by environmental issues. Within the World Bank itself there is evidence of environmental concern that is not reflected in its own report discussed above. Some two years ago a reorganization of the Bank was initiated that has led to about 500 layoffs, many of these being economists. It has also resulted in the creation of forty new positions in seven new divisions devoted to environmental matters. Ecological concern was not absent previously — ecological assessments have been a part of World Bank projects for some time — but it is clearly receiving more emphasis now. It would appear that this increased interest in the environmental dimension of development arose from an awareness within the Bank that since it is the poorest who suffer most from environmental problems, the Bank must concern itself with these problems if it is to do its job. At the same time there was pressure from outside — from developing countries, from the "like-minded" countries of the North and from the environmental lobby of the United States, transmitted to the Bank through Congress and the U.S. administration.

How is one to interpret this intrusion of ecological concerns into economic issues and predict its results? There would appear to be a real commitment to the ecological dimension within the Bank, shared and promoted by its president, but the *World Development Report* might still reflect mainstream Bank thinking. Whether the basic approach to development will shift will largely depend on the effectiveness of the newly hired environmentalists.

However, even if the World Bank's philosophy does change, there is no guarantee of a positive ecological effect on development. The World Bank is perhaps the single most influential body in the area of economic development, but even its role is just a small part of the whole. Its example might augment its influence, but one must assume that development paths will be determined primarily by nation-states. Taking the most cynical perspective, one could see these legitimate environmental concerns being used for their own economic purposes by those who control the Bank. We know that, at present, the United States opposes, with considerable success, support to development projects that might result in competition with U.S. industry; it could, alone or in concert with other powerful members from the North, use environmental standards to further such control. If this were the case, it would be a clear instance of North-South conflict arising from double economic and ecological standards, which could be applied well beyond the context of the Bank.

The double economic standard of the North, and especially of the United States, already exists. Freedom in trade, in investment and in factor transfers are advocated as general principles of the competitive, free market approach, but, in practice, controls on trade, financial transfers and immigration reduce the freedom of the system and maintain the competitive domination of the North. The principles are applied most often when it is to the advantage of the North, less frequently when they would help the South. A similar and related double ecological standard could be emerging. The United States in particular and other countries of the North to a lesser extent resist solving their ecological problems, including transboundary ones, on short-term economic grounds. But will the North be as tolerant of transboundary ecological problems in the South once they are perceived by the North as threats to itself? A most cynical scenario would have the North applying very strict ecological standards to the South in order to control both pollution and competition for its own ecological and economic advantage.

Concluding Thoughts

At the end of a year that has seen the beginning of a reduction in East-West tensions, it is disturbing to contemplate the possibility of a whole new dimension of conflict. But the possibility is very real. There can be no doubt about the ecological threat itself; it exists and can be measured today. The only question is how much more serious will it become in the future? What is much more difficult to deal with is the question of how peoples and nation-states will respond to the threat.

The development/environment debate is not between growth and no growth, but between environmentally sound, sustainable growth and ecologically destructive, unsustainable growth. This chapter has argued that the attempt to achieve the required levels of economic development by present development strategies would have severe ecological consequences and would be, thereby, not only unsuccessful but also destructive. In assessing possibilities of success or failure, we must avoid doomsday scenarios; we cannot predict the date that the world will end because there will not be a simple, single end. We are dealing with interrelated processes, not independent events. A continuation of the process of unsustainable development would cause ecological problems and consequent international conflict that would themselves retard the process, but not necessarily resolve the conflict. Within unsustainable development, success creates failure in an iterative and incremental way. The question is, how far will we go — how much failure will we accept and how much damage will we do — before we move to a sustainable development path? And might it not then be too late?

Our analysis has shown that sustainable growth is not easily charted, let alone a voyage on which our species will readily embark. The Brundtland Commission's map is very general, but, with difficulty, the appropriate detail could be added. It is most unlikely, however, at this time or in the near future that it would be followed. The response from the powerful market economies of the North to the call for a New International Economic Order demonstrates that there is little hope for the international cooperation, development of international institutions, multilateralism and intervention into economic processes that would be required. The "magic of the market" will provide the solutions.

This sets the stage for an ideological debate between free enterprise and interventionism. Neither side, however, has a convincing position. Excessive individual liberty, especially when motivated only by profit, produces economic growth but does not protect the environment or support sound development. Excessive state control has stifled economic growth while failing to protect the environment. That ideal level of government planning and intervention that would protect the present and guarantee a future for all citizens without destroying individual initiative and freedom has eluded most societies.

But even this freedom-versus-order issue is not the root of the problem. How should we expect world powers to act? Will they behave simply in accordance with their ideological principles? Was the Soviet Union thinking of the values of true socialism when it invaded Afghanistan? Does the United States have any concern about the freedom of Nicaragua while it systematically destroys that country? The effective motive, spread evenly around the globe, is self-interest, but the outcomes depend on power, concentrated in states and large corporations but super-concentrated within the superpowers.

Such a Hobbesian view dashes the apparent optimism of the Brundtland Commission (WCED 1987: 41), at least in the short term. It may well be that as concern for the environment emerges, such concern will be used, as suggested above, to the advantage of the powers of the North — and in particular of the North-West. The competitive mode will

continue, with stuttering development, ecological degradation and resulting conflict. At some point, however, our species, being rational, will
respond in its own self-interest to the increasing frequency and severity
of ecological disasters and development failures and will evolve the
cooperative approach to sustainable growth. The Brundtland Commission captures the essence of the present situation in one little sentence:
"The Earth is one but the world is not" (WCED 1987: 27). We might add:
The Earth will make the world either one or none. Our planet might force
us to abandon all that divides us and isolates us and could destroy us. To
survive we must transcend ideology, chauvinism and imperialism and
become a community. This will happen too late for many, but not,
perhaps, too late for our species.

8 Canada and North-South Conflict

DAVID R. MORRISON

Conflict between the North and the South has not been as visibly intense in the 1980s as it was in the 1970s. In the previous decade, the countries of the South were able to work out a common agenda for international structural change despite their growing economic differentiation and ideological and regional conflicts. The self-confidence that culminated in the demand for a more equitable New International Economic Order (NIEO) reflected an overestimate by the South of its bargaining strength, as the rather indifferent response of the industrialized countries to the "North-South dialogue" indicated. However, any hope for an NIEO evaporated in the early 1980s in the wake of the worst global recession in fifty years, the collapse of oil and other commodity prices, an enormous debt overhang in Africa and Latin America, growing trade protectionism among governments in the North, and, within many of the latter, a neo-conservatism interested in international development only if state interventionism yields to the "magic of the marketplace."

Many of the impressive economic gains of the earlier period have been lost, living standards among the relatively privileged in many countries have declined, the magnitude of rural and urban poverty, already growing, has intensified, and efforts to achieve enhanced democratization and human rights are endangered. Meanwhile, as noted in chapter 7, the destruction of the human habitat in both North and South continues apace, often in ways that make it appear as though developmental and environmental goals are antithetical to one another. The challenge of finding viable pathways to sustainable development with dignity and justice is greater than ever.

Canada's modest role in confronting that challenge changed very little in 1987. However, it was a year for significant fresh thinking about policies and priorities. Parliamentarians rather than bureaucrats played the leading role in this process. The House of Commons Standing

Committee on External Affairs and International Trade (SCEAIT) completed a far-reaching assessment of Canadian policies and programs in the sphere of official development assistance (ODA); its recommendations and the government's response to them will be examined here in some detail. The chapter will then turn to a discussion of evolving Canadian positions on the international debt problem (the subject of yet another parliamentary study undertaken by SCEAIT's Senate counterpart), trade with the Third World, refugees, and the report of the World Commission on Environment and Development (WCED). The chapter concludes with an assessment of the Mulroney government's record in the sphere of North-South relations.

New Directions in Official Development Assistance?

ODA is but one vehicle for financing international development. In fact, it will never be more than a marginal supplier of the external capital needed; trade, direct investment, and commercial loans will remain much more important in aggregate terms. Canadian ODA, currently running at $2.7 billion (Cdn.), makes Canada the fifth-largest donor among the industrial country members of the Organization for Economic Cooperation and Development (OECD), but that sum represents only about 6 per cent of OECD aid, which in turn accounts for only a fraction of North-South capital flows. However, development assistance does create opportunities for particular sorts of capital and human-resource transfers that many developing countries, especially the poorest, are not able to obtain through other means. In addition, ODA has now assumed a special saliency in the context of the international debt crisis as one means of offsetting the dramatic reversal of resource flows between North and South. Thus, the issue of aid effectiveness is a critical one.

Aid effectiveness is the principal concern of *For Whose Benefit?*, issued by the House of Commons Standing Committee on External Affairs and International Trade in May 1987. Chaired by William Winegard, a former university president elected as a Conservative member of Parliament in 1984, the committee embarked upon the study in the wake of the African famine and the questions that it raised about the efficacy of Canadian aid efforts. Various parliamentary committees and subcommittees had examined aid issues on a piecemeal basis over the years. The most recent was a special House-Senate committee, which reported a year earlier; though concerned with all aspects of Canada's external relations, it was inundated with submissions on North-South issues (Special Joint Committee of the Senate and the House of Commons on Canada's International Relations 1986). However, more than a decade had elapsed since the last comprehensive public review of the ODA program.

Some of the earlier parliamentary studies (notably one in 1981 on Canada's relations with Latin America and the Caribbean) had failed to achieve agreement between parliamentarians from all three major parties who espouse an internationalist perspective and those who hold a more confrontational, Reaganite vision of the world. This time some of the latter were so heavily involved in projects such as restoring the death penalty that they left SCEAIT in the hands of the former. What emerged was a rather remarkable non-partisan consensus that was closely attuned to the concerns of the many non-governmental organizations (NGOs), community and church groups, and educational and other institutions that testified.

The report suggested that "the aid program needs a fresh jolt of political energy." Noting several positive aspects in Canada's performance, it nonetheless concluded that "the aid program continues to betray an ambivalence of purpose and design" (SCEAIT 1987: 3). The mandate of ODA is quite simple:

> to help the poorest people and countries in the world to help themselves. Only by discharging that mandate does assistance serve Canada's long-term national interests, be they defined in humanitarian, political or commercial terms. At the same time, there are many pressures on the aid program to serve other short-term interests, not all of which are consistent with the central purpose of Canada's official development assistance. (p. 12)

This is a refreshing approach in that it rejects the glib assumption often enunciated by governments that there is a necessary complementarity of interest in ODA between developmental and other concerns such as the support of Canadian industries and exports. As far as the committee was concerned, this is an empirical question that must be answered on a case-by-case basis, with basic developmental objectives taking precedence in the event of a conflict. The report recommended that Parliament adopt a legislative mandate for development assistance, in the form of a parliamentary charter, and made proposals for changing priorities, linking aid to human-rights performance, untying more ODA, improving aid organization and strengthening evaluation.

New and Clearer Priorities

A Development Assistance Charter. The Winegard Committee suggested the following as the text for a parliamentary charter:

- The primary purpose of Canadian official development assistance is to help the poorest countries and people of the world.
- Canadian development assistance should work always to strengthen the human and institutional capacity of developing countries to solve their own problems in harmony with the natural environment.
- Development priorities should always prevail in setting objectives for the ODA program. Where development objectives would not be compromised, complementarity should be sought between the objectives of the aid program and other important foreign policy objectives. (SCEAIT 1987: 12)

The government response accepted these three principles and added a fourth:

- Development assistance should strengthen the links between Canadian citizens and institutions and those in the Third World. The Government will therefore endeavor to foster a partnership between the people of Canada and the people of the Third World. (Government of Canada 1987: 41)

While rejecting legislative enactment, the government did promise to "enshrine" the charter in a public statement of policy. At this stage, one can only speculate about the likely impact. However, the fourth principle, laudable at one level and perhaps seemingly innocuous, may be used to justify the primacy of Canadian goods and services, perhaps in certain cases offsetting the intended steering effect of the other principles.

A Greater Emphasis on Human-Resource Development. Historically, Canada's bilateral aid program has been skewed heavily towards the provision of food aid and major capital projects, particularly in the spheres of energy, transportation, and agricultural equipment. With the emphasis in the mid-1970s of the World Bank and other international development agencies upon meeting basic needs, the Canadian International Development Agency (CIDA) began to move more into rural development, health, education and housing. In 1980 CIDA adopted human-resource development as one of three sectoral priorities alongside energy and agriculture. However, bureaucratic inertia and a program tied heavily to Canadian procurement had precluded any dramatic movement in this direction five years later.

In advocating a much greater emphasis upon human-resource development, the Winegard Committee criticized what it saw as "a strong tendency to treat expenditures on capital equipment and infrastructure as productive investments, while expenditures on people, especially the poorest people, are regarded as unproductive social costs" (SCEAIT 1987: 9). The report identified needs for expanded efforts in strengthening the role of women in development (already a strong CIDA priority), improving primary health-care delivery systems and supporting educational development, especially at the primary and post-secondary levels (pp. 24-30).

The government again accepted these recommendations, although the text of the response suggests that the reorientation of practice will not be as substantial as the committee advocated. It also expressed some hesitancy about becoming heavily involved in primary health care, literacy and primary school education (Government of Canada 1987: 43-45). More enthusiasm was expressed for expanded occupational, university and in-house business educational and training programs — all areas where Canadian expertise can be readily called upon and the tying of aid more easily accommodated.

Food Aid and Agriculture. Ever since the Ethiopian famine of 1984-85, the Canadian government has formally acknowledged what critics had been saying for some time: that "food aid *can* be incorporated in a rational development plan, which, by means of judicious technical and structural changes in the agrarian sector, has among its objectives the eventual elimination of the need for such aid" (Morrison 1985: 7). However, the Winegard Committee found Canadian performance still wanting. For the most part, the report noted, food aid is used as a "quick disbursing program transfer that also satisfies high Canadian tying requirements." It went on to recommend that non-emergency food aid not exceed 10 per cent of the ODA budget, and that more resources be devoted to agricultural development (SCEAIT 1987: 57-58).

In response, the government indicated that it intended to continue increasing the food aid budget by 5 per cent a year. Clearly, this use of Canadian surpluses (largely of wheat) is deemed to be too important to domestic interests to consider jeopardizing it. However, the response temporized slightly by agreeing that "food aid is not always the best form of development assistance" and promising to announce shortly "a new food aid policy framework" (Government of Canada 1987: 70).

Reorientation of Country Focus. The Winegard Committee also tackled the question of how to select the countries that would be the primary focus of the Canadian aid program. The existing three-tier system, established in the early 1980s, was subjected to harsh criticism. Ostensibly designed as an attempt to achieve greater concentration of impact and greater coherence of effort in some countries, "the country classification system as now constituted is over-extended." The committee called for the abolition of the existing system and the designation of no more than thirty core program countries on the basis of developmental criteria (SCEAIT 1987: 65-67). The government accepted the recommendation (Government of Canada 1987: 75). It will be fascinating to see whether reinventing the wheel will change its spokes, and how existing core countries will respond if any are dropped.

Human Rights. The other major recommendation for a shift in priorities reinforced the earlier call by the Special Joint Committee for a more explicit link between aid and the human-rights performance of recipients. While mindful of the political and ideological controversy embedded in debates about human-rights violations, SCEAIT came down in support of a set of guiding principles for informing ODA policies (SCEAIT 1987: 26-27). The government expressed skepticism about the possibility of establishing operationally effective criteria, both because international standards are so general and because of "the diversity of legal systems, social values and traditional structures in the countries in which CIDA functions." For similar reasons, and because judgments would be "too subjective," the government rejected a recommendation to establish a public human-rights country classification grid in favour of using diplomatic channels and less formal means of responding to concern about violations (Government of Canada 1987: 50, 52). However, a commitment was given to make respect for human rights a "top priority" in ODA policy and to place more emphasis on human-rights performance in deciding whether or not to proceed with development programs. The government also accepted recommendations to establish a human-rights unit within CIDA and to give CIDA personnel training on human-rights issues (Government of Canada 1987: 50-56; CIDA 1987: 2).

In response to the Special Joint Committee, the government had earlier agreed to set up an International Institute of Human Rights and Democratic Development and had commissioned a special study by two academics (see Côté-Harper and Courtney 1987). The Winegard Committee asked for assurance that the institute would be an independent body like the International Development Research Centre, and not a mere substitute for a comprehensive human-rights policy (SCEAIT 1987: 30). This recommendation was accepted. Subsequently, the special study was published and officials from External Affairs and CIDA began drafting legislation (News Release, Government of Canada, November 13, 1987).

While the committee's recommendations for establishing clear standards for judging human-rights performance and a public classification system were perhaps based on naive assumptions, one can respect its desire to develop a way of making human-rights conditionality meaningful. However, even though the significance of the new policy remains to be judged, it will meet opposition from elements in the business community worried about a potential loss of Canadian export markets (*Financial Post* 1987).

Tied Aid

Another form of conditionality has a long history. The debate between proponents and opponents of "tied aid" has been going on for over twenty years. Critics of the requirements tying Canadian bilateral ODA to the purchase of at least 80 per cent of required goods and services from Canadian sources (with at least two-thirds Canadian content) claim that the resulting technological bias, real costs and lost opportunity costs weaken the value of aid. The North-South Institute (1985: 8) commented in a recent publication: "The bald fact is that the poorest countries and people and the projects that benefit them are rarely the most attractive markets for most Canadian industries, universities and other institutions."

In addition, cogent arguments and research (including some internal government studies) have been advanced to show that much greater untying could be achieved without a resulting detrimental impact upon the Canadian economy. However, policy makers have not been convinced and claim that tying aid does serve the mutual interests of donor and recipient. In any case, so many domestic interests have become dependent upon the ODA program that it is difficult to foresee any dramatic change.

However, while careful to maintain a balance among competing claims, the Winegard report took quite a radical stand in relation to existing government policy. Tied aid should act "as an incentive, not an alternative, to achieving the goal of Canadian international competitiveness....From a development point of view, even more crucial than competitiveness is appropriateness" (SCEAIT 1987: 37). The committee proposed that the 80 per cent rule be relaxed to increase flexibility for developing-country procurement, with the untied author-ity being gradually raised to 50 per cent of the bilateral budget; that tying requirements be waived for some of the least developed countries in sub-Saharan Africa; and that greater untying of food aid be permitted when a neighbouring country has exportable food surpluses (p. 39).

Not surprisingly, the government had trouble with these recommen-dations, but it did give a little ground. The proposal on food aid was essentially rejected, but the government agreed to adapt the policy on tying "while ensuring that the Canadian private sector continues to be involved in development co-operation through the provision of goods and services." Accordingly, the response accepted moving to a level of 50 per cent untying in sub-Saharan countries and some other least developed countries, and to 33 1/3 per cent elsewhere (Government of Canada 1987: 57-58).

Improving Aid Organization and Delivery

Decentralizing CIDA. The Winegard Committee made several recommendations for improving the organization and delivery of Cana-dian ODA. Potentially the most significant one advocated decentraliza-tion to the field. Critics had long been saying that CIDA was far too Ottawa-centred in terms of both decision making and personnel, a theme that ran through much of the testimony to the committee. Noting that CIDA itself had been actively studying and debating the issue for some time, the committee urged movement from discussion to action, arguing that decentralization would do much to streamline a cumbersome, rigid and delay-prone organization that requires a loop through headquarters for almost every decision. A more field-based operation would also permit greater flexibility and responsiveness to local conditions, involve recipients in all stages of the process, foster a greater orientation towards human-resource development and secure more effective coordination of aid efforts with Canadian NGOs and institutions and other donor countries (SCEAIT 1987: 82-84).

In pressing for decentralization, the committee recognized that CIDA's personnel resources are limited and that the exercise has to be undertaken in a cost-effective manner. It suggested creating five or six regional offices in Africa, Asia and the Americas, each headed by a senior official who would have considerable project-approval authority (pp. 86-90). The government accepted the recommendation "in principle" (Government of Canada 1987: 82-84), and has given every indication of "biting the bullet." In the short run, decentralization will be energy-absorbing and could well lead to decreased effectiveness and lessened attention to the other reforms emerging from the review. However, the potential gains are well worth the risk, provided that regional offices and employees are not so lavishly endowed as to force a cutback in real aid.

There is another aspect of decentralization that is not discussed by SCEAIT, but that continues to be a source of concern for those who want to strengthen Canada's ODA effectiveness. More and more of the delivery of the Canadian bilateral aid program has been contracted out to private consultants and firms. While undoubted benefits flow from tapping energies outside public agencies for many types of projects, privatization in certain instances can add an additional layer of red tape to an operation and runs the risk of excessive fragmentation of effort. There has not been a careful analysis assessing the true comparative costs and benefits of employing public servants or private consultants in any given situation.

Other ODA Channels. SCEAIT endorsed Canada's long-standing commitment to the international financial institutions and other international agencies, recommending that about one-third of the ODA budget continue to be allocated to multilateral programs (SCEAIT 1987: 58-60). The report was also enthusiastic about the work of NGOs and other non-profit private institutions, and proposed a substantial increase in funding for them (pp. 91-99, 104). The government responded positively (Government of Canada 1987: 85-89, 91-92).

SCEAIT consistently asserted that the primary thrust of ODA ought to be towards Third World development, and only secondarily towards Canadian commercial and other objectives if these do not conflict with the primary thrust. However, it did suggest that the business community is the most underutilized resource in Canadian official development assistance....The Committee...would especially like to encourage initiatives that involve a more lasting business commitment to developing countries. The Committee is deeply troubled by the apparent tendency on the part of some businesses to look upon CIDA as a convenient source of tied aid contracts where the partnership ends as soon as the money runs out. This is not good enough. (SCEAIT 1987: 99-101)

Long-term commitments were needed through a continuing Canadian commercial presence in some countries. The committee urged greater use of the programs offered by CIDA's Industrial Co-operation Division (INC) that support private sector initiatives aimed at establishing joint ventures or other forms of collaboration leading to investment flows and technology transfer. The government accepted a series of recommendations calling for increased funding for a stronger and more flexible CIDA-INC that would "not sacrifice developmental criteria in the bargain" (p. 103; Government of Canada 1987: 90-91). With a few exceptions, Canadian businesses have seldom set their longer-term horizons beyond Canada and the United States. The policy review and a study by the Conference Board of Canada (*Montreal Gazette* 1987) have thrown out a challenge that may not be met.

Improving Evaluation. Another potentially significant section of the report focused on improving the evaluation of aid effectiveness by better and more-targeted long-term planning, a more open and self-critical policy-making process and a greater use of arm's-length evaluations (SCEAIT 1987: 115-19). The government's reply was generally positive (Government of Canada 1987: 97-101), but it remains to be seen whether the protectiveness and defensiveness that have characterized CIDA in the past will change. There has been an understandable nervousness about the prospect of embarrassing findings reaching the media or the parliamentary opposition. However, for the most part, reservations have been more a reflection of the characteristic caution of the Canadian public service. This trait has an understandable place in many government activities, but it is certainly inappropriate if evaluation is to become a tool for improving ODA performance and for creating more public confidence in that performance. The embarrassing reports already have a way of emerging, but better planning and evaluation could help to ensure that the incidents leading to them would occur less often.

The Debt Crisis

The Third World debt crisis has now been with us for half a decade. Soon after the Mexican bubble burst in 1982, country after country announced that it could not pay its foreign debts on schedule. After initial fears of a global financial panic were assuaged, governments in the dominant countries of the North, led by the United States, took the position that each situation would be best handled on a case-by-case basis, with the principal remedy being the conventional program of adjustment through austerity under the guidance and leadership of the International Monetary Fund (IMF). There was no shortage of suggestions for more-integrated multilateral approaches, but these were generally rejected as unworkable or too costly.

Meanwhile, drastic import strangulation and disastrous drops in living standards occurred within both "epicentres" of the crisis: some seventeen middle-income countries, principally in Latin America, that together owe upwards of $400 billion, mostly to commercial banks; and three dozen low-income countries, mostly in Africa, that owe only about one-tenth of that amount, largely in concessional loans from multilateral agencies and donor countries (Culpeper 1987: 3, 6). The worst crisis is "that of the disadvantaged — the people who have lost jobs, seen their limited purchasing power decline, experienced a deterioration in their already inadequate access to health care and unpolluted water, and so on" (Morrison 1985: 10).

By 1985, it was clear that conventional adjustment strategies were not leading to recovery. The so-called Baker initiative, named for James Baker, the U.S. secretary of the treasury, represented an important breakthrough in American thinking about the debt crisis. While still emphasizing a case-by-case approach, Baker prescribed policies for middle-income debtors that would achieve some growth along with balance of payments adjustment and control of inflation; an ongoing key role for the IMF, but with enhanced involvement in structural adjustment lending by the World Bank and regional development banks; and increased lending by the World Bank — however, the emphasis for the World Bank was even more on adjustment and less on growth (Culpeper 1987: 11-13). Not surprisingly, there was also a strongly Reaganite edge to Baker's call for more reliance on the private sector, supply-side market reform and increased foreign private investment.

Canada's policy on the debt crisis has mirrored that of the United States since the election of the Mulroney government, with perhaps three notable exceptions. First, Canada has been more prepared to carry its proportionate share of funding increases for the IMF and the World Bank; second, a number of measures have been taken to lessen the burden of official debt to Canada of several African countries and a few others as well; and third, Canadian banks have been forced to set aside greater provisioning to cover their portfolios in countries with serious debt problems. In 1987 the Standing Senate Committee on Foreign Affairs (SSCFA) suggested that Canada's stake has several dimensions: lessening the strains on domestic banks (with their $27-billion exposure to problem debtors in Latin America and the Caribbean); strengthening financial institutions and markets around the world; enhancing trade (the value of Canadian exports to the Third World fell from 12.1 per cent of total exports in 1982 to 8.1 per cent in 1985); reducing the risk that processes of democratization in debtor countries will be reversed; and improving Canada's capacity to promote international development (SSCFA 1987: 1, 37, 45-48).

The Senate committee's general recommendations included a call for a more integrated international strategy for handling the debt problem that would guide the case-by-case approach, much more direct involvement by creditor-country governments, including Canada, increased flows of funds from creditor countries and the international financial institutions, consequent higher funding levels for the debt-related programs of the IMF and the World Bank, more effective coordination of Fund and Bank policies, and improved market access to Canada and other OECD countries for the exports of indebted developing countries (SSCFA 1987: 69, 92, 94, 108, 110, 111). While generally supportive of Fund and Bank initiatives, the Senate committee offered a cautionary note on the American-induced ideological bias of conditionality: "It will be important...to temper the conditions that are pressed on debtor countries to adopt economic policies favouring a market economy with an understanding of the differing traditional values and systems of some developing countries" (p. 67).

Addressing the problem of middle-income debtors, the Senate report supported the broad outlines of IMF and World Bank adjustment programs (p. 14). At the Canadian end, it recommended building up the provisioning of domestic banks beyond the level of 10 to 15 per cent of exposure to high-risk debt ordered by the inspector general of banks in 1984. It was noted that some European banks had set aside reserves of about 50 per cent, while the Japanese figure was around 20 per cent; only the American level was lower than the Canadian (principally because American banks are not allowed to write off any provisions as a business expense, compared to about one-fifth in Canada and high levels elsewhere). The committee suggested that Canadian provisioning be increased to 18 to 20 per cent by 1989 and that this be facilitated by enabling the banks to write off a greater proportion as taxable expenses (SSCFA 1987: 39-40, 84-86). "The banks must carry an appropriate share of the cost of handling the bank debt problem, but maintaining the health of the domestic and international economies justifies governments in relieving them of some of that burden" (p. 85). Ultimately, it is likely that much more of the commercial debt will be dealt with in this way by governments.

Turning to the African and other least developed countries, the Senate committee applauded steps that successive Canadian governments had taken to lighten the debt burden of several low-income debtors: the decisions in 1977 to forgive the ODA debt of the least developed countries and from that date to put all CIDA projects in these countries on a straight grant basis; the offer in 1986 of a fifteen-year moratorium on payments of principal and interest of the ODA debt of other African countries where Canada had continued to make concessional loans rather than grants; and the decisions of Canada and some other donor countries, also in 1986, to provide all future aid in the form of grants and to convert to grants the non-utilized parts of development assistance loans. The committee recommended further debt-relief measures, including outright forgiveness in the case of some least developed countries and the extension of support to some non-African countries (SSCFA 1987: 41, 97-98). The government did subsequently forgive the debt of several African countries, announcing these decisions at the Heads of Government Conferences of la francophonie in Quebec and the Commonwealth in Vancouver (*Globe and Mail* 1987b; *Toronto Star* 1987c). (These steps elicited generally favourable responses in the press, except for a questioning of the human-rights record of some of the beneficiaries, such as Zaire.) Also, consistent with its earlier efforts to strengthen the capacity of the IMF and the World Bank to assist low-income debtors, Canada was one of the first Western countries to pledge a full share to the IMF Structural Adjustment Facility (*Toronto Star* 1987b).

North-South Trade

While there have been several positive aspects of Canada's performance on the debt question, at least as it relates to the least developed countries, there has been little movement on trade. The latter is an issue at the forefront of the South's demand for an NIEO in the mid-1970s and remains a matter of intense conflict even though much of the unity and optimism within the Third World has been dissipated by events in the 1980s. What happens in the sphere of world trade is crucial for the recovery of the major debtors and for development more generally. As the Winegard report noted critically, "we still hear far more about how aid can support our exports than about how trade with us can support their development" (SCEAIT 1987: 43).

Canada imports less from developing countries as a proportion of total imports than any other industrial country, and our national policy has been among the most protectionist. One standard explanation for these facts is that the external trade profile of the Canadian economy is closer to that of many Third World countries than to the industrial country norm; Canada wants less of what the developing world has to offer, and has not had much success in capturing markets in the South for what Canada has to offer. Also, domestic political forces continue to ensure that many more resources are devoted to protecting labour-intensive industries such as clothing and footwear than to the retraining and adjustment policies that would be needed in the wake of trade liberalization in these sectors. Canada was again a prime mover behind the renegotiation in 1986 of the Multi-Fibre Agreement (MFA), "the GATT-endorsed system of restraints that discriminates against Third World textile and garment exports to industrialized countries" (North-South Institute 1987: 10).

Although the Winegard Committee recognized the constraints upon any significant change in Canadian performance in the near future, it urged making import promotion a declared objective of ODA policy, particularly in core countries. It also recommended a reduction in protectionist barriers (SCEAIT 1987: 44). The government "accepted" these recommendations, but, as in the reply to the Special Joint Committee a year earlier, the official rhetoric was more positive than what the government can actually be expected to deliver (Government of Canada 1986: 65; 1987: 61-62). However, perhaps judgment should be deferred until we are further into the current Uruguay Round of trade liberalization talks within the General Agreement on Tariffs and Trade (GATT). Heading into these, Canada did help to achieve a modest success that could well redound to the interest of many agricultural exporters in both the North and South: the so-called Cairns Group of fourteen countries managed to persuade the European Community to include agriculture on the agenda, provided that it is not given undue priority (North-South Institute 1987: 10-11).

The emphasis of the Winegard Committee on import promotion was part of a concern to put both sides of the trade ledger into a longer-term perspective, to see trade as a means of promoting development for the poor majorities in the poorest countries with the expectation nonetheless "that a strategic increase in aid and trade involvement in some countries can and should repay long-term dividends to Canada" (SCEAIT 1987: 35). The report was critical of the emphasis in Canadian policy upon immediate returns for domestic interests. It also stressed the danger that a narrow focus upon using ODA for trade promotion may downplay or ignore human-rights considerations. Without these broader concerns, an aid/trade policy "can risk becoming subsidy for mainly commercial transactions that really ought to pay for themselves" (p. 35).

This position reflected an interesting convergence within the committee of "small c" conservative opposition to public subsidies for business and the left-liberal/social democratic critique of how ODA is distorted when it is used as a vehicle for immediate commercial gain. We have already seen how this convergence informed the proposals for greater untying of aid and a longer-term commitment by business to Third World ventures. Other recommendations called for stronger Canadian action within the OECD to discourage mixed credits (a mix of subsidized concessional and commercial terms) for Third World export promotion and for a commitment not to count as ODA any concessional export-financing package unless it meets the criteria of the proposed development assistance charter (p. 42).

Again the government "accepted" the recommendations, but once more the cutting edge of the committee's recommendations was blunted by a response making it clear that practice would not change appreciably (Government of Canada 1987: 59-60). While it is true that Canadian participation in concessional trade financing has been a reluctant response to the aggressive use of this practice by others, notably France and Japan, the general use of aid for trade promotion is simply too strongly entrenched in a web of vested interests to expect otherwise. The government's decision in 1986 to defer action on a proposed aid/ trade fund (inherited from the previous Liberal administration) was a reflection more of deficit cutting and backtracking on aid targets than of any change in policy (Gillies 1987).

The Plight of Refugees

The recent Canadian record on refugees is also a mixed one. There are now over ten million refugees worldwide; most of them are from countries of the South and many of these have fled from civil wars, other manifestations of intense regional, ethnic and religious conflict, and abuses of human rights. Although Canada's contribution to easing the problem has been modest in terms both of admitting refugees to Canada and of relief work abroad, the performance was deemed sufficiently praiseworthy that the country was awarded the international Nansen Medal in 1986 in recognition of national efforts to help refugees. Clearly, this award reflected much good work and human caring, but its announcement came at a time when there were almost daily reports of muddled policies and procedures, of bureaucratic delays in processing refugee claims and of other instances of official insensitivity.

Then in 1987, just when the government strengthened its pledge to make international development policies more attuned to human rights, it also introduced legislation aimed at curbing bogus refugee claims through means that have been criticized as conflicting with the Geneva Convention on Refugees, other international covenants and our own Charter of Rights and Freedoms (Angus and Hathaway 1987). The catalyst of course was the arrival in Nova Scotia in July of a boatload of 174 Sikhs from India claiming refugee status; a year earlier 155 Tamils from Sri Lanka had waded ashore to Newfoundland in similar circumstances. Both events generated popular outrage against those who arranged the transport and organized the trips, giving the government an opportunity to demonstrate leadership by clamping down on human trafficking for profit. However, the cabinet also capitalized on the popular perception that these people were illegal immigrants trying to jump the queue rather than people with genuine claims for sanctuary.

Parliament was recalled in mid-August, five weeks early, and was asked to give speedy approval to the Deterrents and Detention Bill (C-84). Its passage was seen as a higher priority than approval for Bill C-55 (introduced earlier in the year), which was designed primarily to simplify and speed up the refugee determination process, a generally agreeable objective, but which had been criticized sharply for proposing to give to Canadian officials the right to turn back refugee claimants at the border and to deport them to "safe third countries" (Schelew 1987). Bill C-84 met with general support from the opposition and the media for its intent to impose heavy penalties upon illegal commercial smugglers such as those who organized the boat trips for the Tamils and Sikhs, but was denounced for applying these penalties equally to church and other humanitarian groups that have been active in assisting potential refugees to come to Canada. It was attacked as well for provisions that would enable authorities to board and turn back suspicious ships without a hearing, to detain for lengthy periods and without a hearing people who arrived without proper identification and documentation, to deport, again without a hearing, claimants who were deemed to be security risks, and to exercise sweeping search and seizure powers.

The chorus of protests extended to the United Nations high commissioner for refugees, the Tory MP chairing the Standing Committee on Immigration (who was subsequently removed), and several individuals and groups who have said they will proceed with legal challenges under the Charter of Rights (*Globe and Mail* 1987a; *Toronto Star* 1987a). However, the government refused to back down on any of these measures and after some months secured passage of the bill in the House of Commons. At year's end, the bill was still facing a serious challenge from the Liberal majority in the Senate, with little prospect that the minister of immigration would back down in order to end the stalemate (*Toronto Star* 1987d; *Globe and Mail* 1987f).

Environment and Development:
A Preliminary Response to Brundtland

Of all of the challenges that arise in the domain of North-South conflict, none is as important for the future of humankind as developing a more active and better-balanced global strategy for achieving sustainable economic development that respects the limits of nature. *Our Common Future*, the 1987 report of the World Commission on Environment and Development, was discussed in chapter 7. The report says little that is new for students of environment and development. Rather, its importance lies in the fact that it speaks on behalf of an eminent group of people from North and South who served on the commission, chaired by Gro Brundtland, the prime minister of Norway.

In 1972, when the first United Nations Conference on the Environment was held in Stockholm, concern for the environment was viewed by many Third World leaders as a luxury they could ill afford until their countries were much further along the path to industrial development; some complained, not without cause, that the logic of environmentalism in the North appeared to condemn the South to the continuing poverty associated with being "hewers of wood and drawers of water." The Brundtland report reflected considerable political and educational work since then to forge a consensus that the preservation of the environment and the development of the Third World, far from being contradictory, are inextricably linked. This change of consciousness has also obviously been facilitated not only by industrial disasters such as Bhopal and Chernobyl, but also by growing knowledge about the human impact on rural environments that has intensified desertification and deforestation.

It is too soon to predict whether the Brundtland report will go the way of the earlier Pearson and Brandt reports on international development, both of which generated considerable discussion but little action as they moved into the archives of history. Stephen Lewis, Canada's ambassador to the United Nations, stressing the urgency of seizing the moment, regretted that some Third World governments were afraid that the report would be used as a club to keep them from the fruits of industrial development, while some Western governments opposed what they saw as recommendations for meddling with free enterprise (*Globe and Mail* 1987c). Environment Minister Tom McMillan was one of the first national spokespersons to participate in the United Nations' debate on the report in October 1987. He avoided taking positions on many of Brundtland's specific recommendations, but his speech reflected a strong rhetorical commitment to its fundamental premises:

> Surely, the policies of the industrialized world are fundamentally flawed when the interest payments of many Third World countries are larger than the amounts they receive from us in aid. We may not ourselves strip their rain forests of virgin timber. But we certainly bear some responsibility for the conditions that compel those who do. (Environment Canada 1987: 4)

McMillan outlined existing Canadian policies and initiatives, but the only new announcement was an offer to hold an International Conference on Environment and Sustainable Development in Canada in 1992, the twentieth anniversary of the Stockholm Conference (p. 13).

Within the sphere of Canadian ODA, this sort of rhetoric is now informing policy at a general level. While CIDA lagged behind many other major OECD donor agencies (including the American) in establishing procedures for environmental monitoring and assessment (Runnalls 1986), the government did announce in July 1986 the introduction of what was billed as a comprehensive environment and development strategy for CIDA (Ferretti 1987a: 13). A further commitment to put a central priority upon ecological concerns was made in June 1987 (*Ottawa Citizen* 1987a), and details were spelled out in the government's response to the Winegard report (Government of Canada 1987: 74-75), although Schrecker (1987: 34) and Ferretti (1987b) criticized the report itself for a failure to highlight environmental issues. It is too soon to determine what impact the new policy will have upon practice, other than adding a new layer of bureaucratization. However, it may help to reinforce a movement away from large capital projects towards the greater emphasis on human-resource development advocated by SCEAIT.

Beyond the specific question of how to ensure that Canadian aid is geared to sustainable development is the broader one raised by Ted Schrecker (1987: 4): "If relatively rich Canada cannot get its internal act together, our pronouncements on environmental questions will neither have nor deserve much credibility with poor countries which face far harsher tradeoffs between short-term economic policy and resource management objectives." Obviously, the record to date in forest, soils and fisheries management leaves much to be desired, as does the performance in respect to non-renewable resources and energy. Schrecker is pessimistic about the future, in large measure because of the resource dependence of most of the country's regional economies.

> The result is to hasten ecological degradation and inappropriate resource uses: both individual resource users and governments which depend on resource-related revenues for continued solvency, and the superficial health of resource-based economic activities for continued electoral success, neglect long-term conservation measures which are associated with significant short-term (economic or political) costs. (Schrecker 1987: 8)

There is another dimension to the issue of whether Canada will or can give leadership on environment and development. The Brundtland Commission stated: "Among the dangers facing the environment, the possibility of nuclear war, or military conflict on a lesser scale involving weapons of mass destruction, is undoubtedly the greatest" (WCED 1987: 290). It also claims that "four of the most urgent global environmental requirements — relating to tropical forests, water, desertification, and population — could be funded with the equivalent of less than one month's global military spending" (p. 303). This question of budgetary trade-offs was discussed in the special United Nations Conference on Disarmament and Development in August. Secretary of State for External Affairs Joe Clark endorsed the goals of arms reduction and increased ODA, but rejected as simplistic a proposal for a new international agency that would channel military savings into extra development assistance. He noted that while Canada's military spending is four times greater than aid expenditures, twenty-five times more is spent worldwide on arms than on development: "If the rest of the world were operating under the same rules that Canada is operating under, we'd have significantly fewer problems" (*Ottawa Citizen* 1987b). Canada, though hardly "clean," is a relatively minor player in international arms trafficking (Regehr and Epps 1987). However, the Mulroney government is committed to increasing domestic military expenditures more rapidly than ODA, and official regulations governing Canadian participation in the arms trade, such as they are, have become more lax (Schrecker 1987; Gordon 1986).

Conclusion: An Assessment of the Mulroney Government and North-South Conflict

Although there remains a considerable agenda for reform in Canadian North-South policy, the Mulroney government has taken a more consistent interest in this domain than its Liberal predecessor. Pierre Trudeau tended to blow hot and cold on Third World issues, often leaving a series of undistinguished secretaries of state for external affairs to muddle through when his attention was focused elsewhere. Some of the credit for the change must go to Joe Clark, whose steady hand at the helm has been in marked contrast to that of many of his ministerial colleagues; remarkably, he also retreats to the background on occasions when Mulroney wants to appear on the global stage. Moreover, despite the government's preoccupation with the trade negotiations with the United States (or perhaps because the prime minister has pre-empted this issue for himself), Canada's current foreign posture under Clark has a strong multilateral orientation, in which Canada's leadership in North-South matters is a key component.

It was not clear that this would be the case in 1985 when in its Green Paper, *Competitiveness and Security*, the new government "tended to interpret Canada's economic and security interests...in a predominately bilateral, North American framework" (North-South Institute 1987: 1). However, a year later the official response to the Special Joint Committee supported the strong multilateralist position of the committee (Government of Canada 1986: 5). In the meantime, the appointment of Stephen Lewis as Canada's ambassador to the United Nations had given the country a strong and principled voice there, and someone who would go on to play a key role in international initiatives to deal with the human and ecological disasters of sub-Saharan Africa. Although the response to the Ethiopian famine in 1984 was, as elsewhere, "too little, too late," the government eventually responded creatively both by matching private generosity with government funds and by mounting a large-scale relief operation coordinated by David MacDonald. MacDonald, subsequently appointed ambassador to Ethiopia, has helped to keep the continuing African crisis in the consciousness of the public, and CIDA has devoted considerable energy to Africa 2000, a program aimed at improving long-term developmental prospects on the continent.

While Canada has long been a key actor within the Commonwealth and has become the largest donor to Commonwealth technical assistance programs, the strong stand that Clark and Mulroney have taken on South Africa, especially in the context of British Prime Minister Thatcher's firm opposition to further economic sanctions, has enhanced Canada's stature among Third World members. Canadian policy still falls short of the complete sanctions and the break in diplomatic relations sought by the anti-apartheid movement, but it is no longer correct to characterize it by the epithet "commerce over conscience" that Redekop (1985) used to describe the record of the Trudeau era. It is of course easier for a Canadian government to take a stronger stance now than it was a few years ago. The domestic resistance within South Africa is much stronger, solidarity movements in Europe and North America have continued to grow, and campaigns for corporate disinvestment have met with considerable success. However, the government's position is remarkably hard-edged considering the strength of opposition to it among some Tory backbenchers.

The current government's efforts have been instrumental in creating a stronger institutional basis for la francophonie, the organization of

French-speaking countries that may become, like the Commonwealth, an important organization for bridging interests and mediating conflicts between North and South. Canadian credibility in Third World eyes was further strengthened during the summit of la francophonie in Quebec City in September, just as it was when the Commonwealth Heads of Government meeting was hosted in Vancouver in October. The government's stance on South Africa was significant in both cases, as were the debt forgiveness measures and new promises for cooperation in distance education and other spheres.

The policy on Central America has been cautious and ambivalent in contrast with that on South Africa and the associated commitment to increasing support for the Front-Line States.[1] To some extent the Canadian position reflects a polarization within public opinion that is as sharply divided as it is on Southern Africa, but that has many more shades of viewpoint between pro-Nicaragua and pro-U.S. (administration) positions. What has emerged has been fairly soft-spoken support for various efforts to facilitate a peace process (albeit with a more vigorous enunciation late in the year on behalf of the Arias peace plan). In this respect, the government has consistently but rather quietly opposed all foreign military intervention in the region, whether it be American, Cuban or Soviet, and has signalled its "neutrality" by sponsoring modest aid programs in Guatemala, Honduras, El Salvador and Nicaragua. None of this has been very adventurous when set alongside the political and developmental challenges within Central America, and Joe Clark's hand was less steady than usual when he visited the region in late November (*Sunday Star* 1987; *Globe and Mail* 1987d). Nevertheless, in terms of political realities, the policy has been at odds with President Reagan's pet project at precisely the time when the major external agenda for the Canadian government has been the achievement of a free trade agreement with the United States.

In sum, the Mulroney government's record on North-South matters has been mixed. During the past three and one-half years, Canada has projected a forceful presence in the United Nations, while in the Commonwealth and la francophonie it has focused upon developmental priorities, human rights and creative conflict resolution. Policies on the debt crisis of the least developed countries and on the survival needs of sub-Saharan Africa have been creditable. However, the response to other aspects of the debt problem has been inadequate. If the renewed efforts of the major Latin American debtors to develop a common strategy in the wake of the November 1987 Acapulco Commitment are successful

(*Globe and Mail* 1987e), Canada and other OECD countries may soon regret not having taken a more comprehensive course of action. Also, as has been argued above, Canadian policies on trade and refugees leave much to be desired. There is considerable potential for playing a high-profile role in the Central American peace process, but its realization will likely depend as much upon domestic American politics as upon events within the region itself. Whether the rhetoric on the environment will have much significance in practice remains to be seen.

As far as the Winegard proposals for reform are concerned, the initial government response suggested that muddled objectives will continue to characterize the aid program. In trying to cater to all interests, the response blurred the sharp focus of the SCEAIT report, which judged all activities first and foremost by developmental criteria. However, some key elements of the report have become a new orthodoxy — the emphasis on human-resource development and human rights, the desirability for CIDA to decentralize, and the need for more-coherent planning and evaluation of ODA programs. We will see a lot of activity within CIDA in the months ahead, but a big question must be whether the cabinet has the interest and the will to encourage the bureaucrats to push forward. As 1987 drew to a close, the Mulroney government was standing only a little above its low ebb in the opinion polls and was beset by a host of political problems with less than two years before the next federal election. The constituency concerned with international development is vocal and articulate, but it is small. Thus, action on some of the recommendations may be delayed unless Joe Clark sees them as important for the legacy of his stewardship.

PART
V

Canada-U.S. Relations

9 | Canada-U.S. Trade Disputes and the Free Trade Deal

DAVID LEYTON-BROWN

Tensions between Canada and the United States are inevitable and recurrent because of the proximity, asymmetry and interdependence that characterizes their relationship. Among that variety of tensions, trade disputes have been particularly prominent. The free trade negotiations offered an opportunity not only to seek the economic benefits of enhanced market access, but also to manage that form of conflict. Canada did not achieve all that it wanted in that connection from the free trade agreement, but it did obtain a set of dispute avoidance and settlement mechanisms that go substantially beyond the status quo. This chapter will assess the way in which the free trade negotiations between Canada and the United States did and did not contribute to the management of conflict in the trade area.

The importance to Canada of its trade relationship with the United States is well known. The two countries are partners in the largest bilateral trading relationship in the world, and each is the other's largest supplier and customer. In 1986, of the total merchandise trade of $172 billion, Canada exported $94 billion worth of goods to the United States and imported $77 billion worth from that country. In that year, 78 per cent of Canada's total exports went to the United States and 70 per cent of Canada's imports came from the United States, while Canada accounted for 20 per cent of all U.S. exports and 18 per cent of total U.S. imports (Government of Canada 1987b). These figures demonstrate the importance of bilateral trade to both countries and the disproportionate reliance of the Canadian economy on its trade with the United States. The importance for Canada of maintaining or indeed enhancing its access to the U.S. market, and of preserving an atmosphere of stability and predictability in the trading relationship with the United States, is evident.

During this decade, threats to that access, stability and predictability appeared to be on the increase. A growing number of trade irritants hampered Canadian exports, and Canadian business leaders became more concerned about the possible loss of market access that could result from threatened unilateral changes in U.S. trade laws (Leyton-Brown 1987). After much deliberation by governmental and non-governmental bodies, the Canadian government on September 26, 1985, formally requested that the United States and Canada explore the potential for negotiating a comprehensive free trade agreement. These free trade negotiations, which began in May 1986, were not intended or expected to settle the specific trade problems that were immediately before the two governments. Rather, they were a device to establish commitments and mechanisms to avoid or resolve future disputes.

The basis of a free trade agreement was concluded on October 3, 1987 (Government of Canada 1987c), just hours before the expiration of the negotiating authority of the U.S. administration under existing trade law. It dealt with many issues other than the avoidance and settlement of trade disputes, including increased market access through tariff elimination and freer government procurement; special arrangements in specific sensitive sectors such as automobiles, financial services, alcoholic beverages, agriculture, energy and cultural industries; and path-breaking measures regarding services and investment. After more lengthy and difficult deliberations than expected, a final legal text was released on December 11. If approved by the legislatures of both countries,[1] the agreement will come into force on January 1, 1989.

It remains to be seen how certain provisions, such as those with respect to the avoidance and settlement of disputes, will work in practice. It also remains to be seen whether some of those provisions will be altered, or at least reinterpreted, in the process of translating the final text into implementing legislation.

The purpose of this chapter is threefold. First, recent and potential trade disputes between Canada and the United States will be identified. Second, Canadian objectives in entering the free trade negotiations will be clarified so that the results may be compared against them. Third, a preliminary assessment will be offered of those contents of the free trade agreement that bear on the management of trade disputes; this will include consideration of what was achieved, and what was not, with regard to the types of problems that prompted the negotiations.

Types of Trade Disputes

The trade disputes of direct relevance to the free trade agreement have all concerned the security of Canadian access to the U.S. market. There have, of course, been other sorts of disputes (for example, concerning Canadian trade remedies and non-tariff barriers to U.S. imports, or Canada-U.S. competition for export markets, such as those involving agricultural subsidies), and aspects of the agreement bear on these issues. Nevertheless, the predominant concern for Canada was the detrimental impact on investment and employment in Canada of the apparent rise of protectionist pressures in the United States. These include the application of U.S. trade remedies directed specifically against imports from Canada, the application of U.S. trade remedies directed primarily against imports from other countries but which nonetheless affect or "sideswipe" Canada, and the threat or passage of U.S. legislation with protectionist effect that changes the rules by which trade remedies are assessed, or imposes direct restrictions on imports from Canada alone or in combination with other countries.

Trade Remedies Directed at Imports from Canada

Trade remedies, or contingent protection provisions, are established under the U.S. Trade Act in keeping with agreements of the General Agreement on Tariffs and Trade (GATT) to allow for the imposition of countervailing duties, anti-dumping duties, and safeguard quotas or duties and other measures in appropriate circumstances upon petition by private parties through a quasi-judicial process. All of these measures are intended to restore a "level playing field" in the face of unfair or damaging trade practices by other countries.

Countervailing Duties. Countervailing duties may be imposed upon foreign imports found to have materially injured U.S. producers and to be subsidized within the terms of U.S. law. The injury test is internationally accepted, though nationally applied, but the U.S. government has taken it upon itself to define and redefine what constitutes a subsidy. The U.S. system is designed to be accessible to the private interests affected, and the countervailing-duty process may be activated by the petition of any private individual or association.

Once a petition has been filed, two parallel investigations are conducted according to a strict timetable: the International Trade Commission (ITC) makes preliminary and later final determination of the existence of material injury, and the International Trade Administration (ITA) of the Department of Commerce makes preliminary and later final determination of whether the imports benefit from a subsidy above a negligible level. The process is terminated if the preliminary or final determination of injury by the ITC is negative or if the final determination of the existence of subsidies by the ITA is negative. Nevertheless, even if a Canadian company successfully avoids the imposition of countervailing duties, the costs in time and money of fighting the case can be seriously disruptive. Though Canada's success in withstanding countervailing duties has been relatively good, the number of such cases has been increasing, and Canadian businesspeople see the process as a form of harassment by their competitors in the United States.

The most prominent and controversial countervailing-duty case occurred in 1986 concerning imports of softwood lumber from Canada worth almost $4 billion a year (Leyton-Brown 1987: 158-61). Despite the fact that a previous countervailing-duty case had resulted in a negative finding on subsidies by the ITA in 1983, a second countervailing-duty petition enjoyed better success, which many in Canada attributed to politicization of the process. After a positive preliminary finding of the existence of subsidies, which reversed the earlier decision, although neither the facts nor the law had changed, Canada negotiated for the imposition of a 15 per cent export tax instead of the proposed countervailing duty. This case stood as an example of the dangers to Canadian exporters of the U.S. countervailing-duty process.

Anti-dumping Duties. Anti-dumping duties may be imposed upon foreign imports found to have materially injured U.S. producers and to have been sold at prices less than the "normal" foreign market value. According to U.S. anti-dumping law, that normal foreign market value can be established by the selling price of the product in the exporter's domestic market, by the selling price in a single third-country market that meets certain criteria, or by a constructed-cost estimate of the producer's costs plus a minimum of 10 per cent for general expenses and 8 per cent for profit. Like the revised definitions of subsidies under countervailing-duty law, the constructed-cost provision of anti-dumping law was the product of unilateral legislation in the U.S. Congress.

Canadian exporters have been concerned that U.S. anti-dumping actions can prevent them from responding to changing supply and demand conditions in the world market by lowering prices when demand is weak. This certainly has been the implication in the most striking recent anti-dumping case concerning the export of over $400 million a year of potash from Canada (Wilkinson 1987). Following a preliminary determination of material injury by the ITC on March 23, 1987, the ITA announced a preliminary determination on August 21, 1987, which found that Canadian potash was being dumped in the United States and which imposed preliminary duties ranging from 9.14 to 85.2 per cent on different exporting companies. Although the duties against potash have been suspended as a result of an agreement signed by the producing companies and the Department of Commerce in January 1988, the dispute prompted the Saskatchewan government to pass legislation allowing it to restrict production so as to force prices up. This case again typifies the Canadian disquiet with U.S. trade law and with the process by which it is implemented.

Safeguards. Safeguard actions authorized under section 201 of the U.S. Trade Act allow for the temporary imposition of quotas or duties if a disruptive increase in imports is proven to have caused injury to U.S. producers, whether the imports are fairly or unfairly traded. Safeguards are sometimes referred to as escape-clause actions because they allow the United States (or any other country taking such action) to escape from its GATT obligations on a temporary emergency basis. The fact that safeguards can be applied against imports that are not subsidized or otherwise unfairly traded raises concerns about predictability and fairness. The outstanding recent example of a safeguard action directed against imports from Canada was the May 22, 1986, imposition of a five-year tariff on imports of red cedar shakes and shingles from Canada (Leyton-Brown 1987: 161-62). This caused heightened tension and led to Canadian retaliation.

Other Trade Remedies. While countervailing duties, anti-dumping duties and safeguards are the most common U.S. trade remedies that have contributed to disputes between Canada and the United States, there are also some other features of U.S. trade law that could do the same. Section 301 of the U.S. Trade Act authorizes the president to take all appropriate and feasible steps to enforce U.S. rights under any trade agreement, or to counter foreign trade practices that are unjustifiable or unreasonable and that burden or restrict U.S. commerce. In 1987, instead of simply responding to complaints, President Reagan was led by the U.S. deficit to initiate section 301 investigations. Section 337 of the Trade Act provides for remedies against imports tainted with infringement of intellectual property or antitrust laws.

Sideswipe Effects

Canada stands to suffer economically whenever quotas or higher tariffs are imposed by the United States, even if the measures are primarily aimed at reducing imports from other countries. This inadvertent impact on Canada is referred to as "sideswiping." These cases usually arise in the context of safeguard actions, where the surge of imports damaging U.S. producers may be coming from third countries but the safeguard measures restrict Canadian access as well. The outstanding recent example concerned the imposition of restrictions on imports of specialty steel in 1983. Although Canadian exports of specialty steel were neither subsidized nor increasing, Canada still suffered the negative impact of this imposition.

Protectionist Legislation

Two sorts of concerns are raised by U.S. legislative activity. The first involves specific measures to restrict imports or to affect general trade patterns. Again, the possibility of sideswiping exists if legislation intended to affect trade with Japan or the European Community nevertheless has an impact on Canada. Of course, some of that legislation is aimed directly at limiting imports from Canada, such as the series of proposed lumber bills throughout the 1980s. The second involves unilateral congressional action to change trade rules and especially to alter the criteria and processes of the trade remedies mentioned above. The omnibus trade bill now before Congress would do exactly that. It poses an ominous protectionist threat to Canada and other trade partners of the United States if it should be passed into law (see chapter 6 for a discussion of the provisions and prospects of the omnibus trade bill).

Canadian Objectives in the Free Trade Negotiations

Canada's fundamental objective in the free trade negotiations was secure and enhanced access to the U.S. market. Subsidiary objectives ranged from job creation to the protection of Canadian culture and social programs. In the context of this chapter, only the objective of secure access to the U.S. market will be examined fully.

A study prepared in the Trade Negotiations Office at the outset of negotiations, and released by the Department of External Affairs (DEA), focused on the existing and threatened protectionist barriers in the United States.

> Canada requires an agreement that exempts our exports from U.S. protectionist measures aimed at reducing the imports of other countries. Such an agreement should also reduce the severity and duration of any measures aimed specifically at Canada and should limit the ability of the United States unilaterally to determine the terms of cross-border trade. (Government of Canada 1986: 1)

That document went on to specify certain Canadian negotiating objectives (Government of Canada 1986: 3-4):

To secure our market access through:
• new rules and procedures limiting the protectionist effect of trade remedy laws, i.e., exemption from measures aimed at others and a rigorous limitation on the degree and duration of measures which affect Canada; and
• clearer definition of countervailable financial assistance programs (i.e., subsidies) to industry, agriculture, and fisheries so as to reduce the threat of countervailing duties.

To enshrine our market access through:
• a strong dispute settlement mechanism to reduce the disparities in size and power and to provide fair, expeditious and conclusive solutions to differences of view and practice.

It is important to note that the language was carefully chosen to specify that despite public expectations to the contrary, the objectives were limitation on, not exemption from, U.S. trade remedies (apart from safeguard measures aimed at others) and a strong (though not explicitly binding) dispute settlement mechanism.

The importance of this theme of secure access was underscored in the special debate in the House of Commons on March 16, 1987. Prime Minister Mulroney stated: "Our highest priority is to have an agreement that ends the threat to Canadian industry from U.S. protectionists who harass and restrict our exports through the misuse of trade remedy laws. Let me leave no doubt that first, a new regime on trade remedy laws must be part of the agreement" (Government of Canada 1987a: 4146). This was reinforced by Minister for International Trade Pat Carney: "Of the most important things on our agenda for negotiation are dispute settlement mechanisms. We want to replace the existing ones....For example, if the U.S. alleges that our stumpage programs are subsidies, we want an impartial, binational tribunal to deal with the issue, not the U.S. Department of Commerce" (Government of Canada 1987a: 4179). Clearly, the Canadian objectives with regard to secure market access included a binational dispute settlement mechanism, a new set of trade rules jointly derived, and limitation of U.S. trade remedies affecting Canada.

Dispute Settlement in the Free Trade Agreement

The free trade agreement yielded a complex and interconnected set of mechanisms and procedures intended to prevent trade disputes and to resolve those that cannot be avoided. These include general dispute settlement provisions and two special procedures for anti-dumping and countervailing-duty cases and for safeguards cases. Four different types of dispute settlement mechanisms were created: a high-level political body to oversee the implementation of the agreement; binding settlement for anti-dumping and countervailing-duty cases; binding arbitration (either compulsory or mutually agreed upon in different circumstances); and expert panels to make recommendations. In some important ways these mechanisms fall short of what was sought, and indeed of what is objectively desirable, but in the aggregate, they are an improvement over the current situation.

Anti-dumping and Countervailing-Duty Disputes

Because of the political sensitivities attached to the softwood lumber case and the concern about U.S. redefinition of the rules, this issue attracted more attention than the other dispute settlement provisions in the agreement. Unquestionably, Canada achieved less than had been hoped for in this area, but the results are at least potentially better than what existed previously. Three different aspects will be considered here: the binding binational appeal panel, the negotiation of new trade rules, and the constraint upon subsequent legislation.

Binding Binational Appeal Panel. The objective of the agreement is to ensure the impartial application of respective national laws. Producers in each country retain the right to launch complaints under national trade laws against injurious unfair trade practices of dumping and subsidization. After a final determination by the national tribunal, either party has the right to appeal to a binational panel, which will replace the possibility of judicial review (though bias or flagrant misbehaviour of one or more of the panelists may in turn be protested to a newly created binational board of retired judges). The panel, composed of two members appointed by each party from a roster of panelists, together with a fifth member acceptable to both parties (or otherwise selected according to the agreement), will proceed according to a specified timetable to issue a binding decision within 300 to 315 days. The panel may not conduct new hearings on the facts of the case, but it will determine whether the national tribunal's decision was in keeping with that nation's domestic law on the basis of the factual record before it. In its binding decision the panel will either uphold the determination of the national tribunal or remand the case back to the tribunal with appropriate instructions for action "not inconsistent with" the decision.

This part of the agreement is an improvement over the current situation. The final appeal is now to a body that is binational rather than national in composition. The speed with which the binational panel will complete its work will be far preferable to the two to four years that the process of judicial review currently takes in the United States. Furthermore, the knowledge that politically influenced anti-dumping and countervailing-duty cases can or will be overturned by an unbiased binational appeal panel may well serve to deter such cases from being initiated, or such political pressures from being applied. In other words, the mere existence of the binational panel could lessen the likelihood of future cases.

Nevertheless, the agreement failed to achieve many important things. It did not provide for an exemption for Canada from U.S. trade remedy law (this was not the Canadian objective). It did not establish a new binational body to adjudicate disputes and enforce decisions, or even, as some suggested during the negotiations, to make an initial determination before national bodies proceeded with their investigations. Nor did it create a new trade law regime replacing existing national laws with new jointly determined rules (such as the definition of permissible and impermissible subsidies or a mechanism to measure the extent of subsidization, or the replacement of anti-dumping laws with domestic competition and predatory pricing laws). It did not allow the binational panel to challenge the findings of fact or to challenge the national laws on the basis of which the determination was made in terms of their compliance with GATT obligations. Furthermore, it did not include binding determination of cases involving other trade remedy disputes, such as those stemming from sections 301 and 337 of the U.S. Trade Act. Finally, it did not guarantee that Canadian firms would no longer be harassed by the filing of anti-dumping and countervailing-duty complaints, and thus did not absolutely guarantee secure access.

The binational appeal panel is doubly interesting for what it is not. It falls short of the decision-making tribunal that some, like Carney, called for. It is also considerably more than an advisory body that can make recommendations only on those cases both governments agreed to refer to it. An assessment of the worth of this dispute settlement mechanism rests on an assessment of the fundamental nature of the problem to which it responds. On that question there is a profound difference of opinion as to whether the issue is U.S. trade laws or the way they are applied. Some argue that "the problem does not lie in the lack of objectivity in the application of these laws by American courts. The problem lies in the laws themselves" (Rotstein 1987). Others contend that "the source of Canada's recent trade woes has not been unfair American rules but the unfair application of those rules" (Goar 1987). Carol Goar went on to argue that the U.S. regulatory process has fallen prey to political pressure and business influences and that there is no hope of changing the U.S. method of handling trade disputes, which the Congress considers sacrosanct: "So Canada decided to bargain for the next best thing: a chance to overrule these biased judgments."

Negotiation of New Trade Laws. The important objective of a new, jointly determined set of trade rules was not achieved. However, the two governments have realized that this part of their task is unfinished. The agreement provides for a five-year period, possibly extended for an additional two years, for the development of a substitute system of laws in both countries for anti-dumping and countervailing duties. Failure to agree to implement a new regime at the end of the seven years would allow either party to terminate the agreement on six months notice.

Some observers are worried that Canada's bargaining advantages will be greatly reduced once the agreement is in effect and that the negotiation of new trade rules might simply become the ratification of U.S. trade rules. As James Laxer (1987) put it,

> Once the Canadian economy is even more integrated with that of the United States in several years, there will be no turning back. To imagine that Canada will have any clout at that point to extract a favorable set of rules from the United States to replace American and Canadian trade law is to dream in technicolour.

Subsequent National Legislation. Both Canada and the United States retain the right to change their domestic anti-dumping and countervailing-duty laws after the agreement comes into force, but such changes will apply to the other country only if it is specified in the legislation, if the other country was notified of the proposed changes and had the opportunity for prior consultations, and if the changes are consistent with GATT codes on anti-dumping and subsidies and with the object and purpose of the agreement. A binational panel can scrutinize proposed changes and express opinions about their consistency with the GATT codes and with the object and purposes of the agreement, and about whether they would have the effect of overturning a prior decision of a binational dispute settlement panel. If a panel recommends modifications of proposed changes to anti-dumping or countervailing-duty legislation, that will trigger compulsory consultation about a mutually agreeable solution. If no agreement is reached, the offended party may take comparable legislative or executive action, or terminate the agreement on sixty days notice.

Despite the attempts to build in requirements for specification, notification, consultation and retaliatory action up to and including termination of the agreement, it remains possible for the United States to change its anti-dumping and countervailing-duty rules unilaterally. The economic asymmetry may make comparable Canadian action elusive, and termination of the agreement may be even more costly than the effects of the changes to U.S. laws. Only time will tell how much the United States will be constrained from unilateral action.

Safeguards

The agreement recognized the need for emergency measures to remedy serious injury to domestic industry caused by a sudden surge in imports. It established a two-track system for safeguard actions. Both tracks require prior notification of and consultation with the other party, and mutually agreed compensation or measures of equivalent economic effect.

The Bilateral Track. During the transitional phase of the agreement, when injury might result only from the reduction or elimination of duties, the importing country may suspend the reduction of duties and restore the lower of the current most-favoured-nation rate or pre-agreement rate. This may be done only once for each product and for a maximum of three years, which may not extend beyond the transitional period except by mutual consent.

The Global Track.   This provision is designed to minimize the sideswipe effect. Canada and the United States will exclude each other from safeguard actions unless imports from the other country are substantial (that is, greater than 5-10 per cent) and contribute substantially to serious injury or threat of injury. If the other country is excluded from the safeguards, it may be included if a surge of imports from it undermines the effectiveness of the safeguard action. If the other country is included, its imports may not be restricted below the trend of imports over a reasonable recent base period with an allowance for growth. This provision does meet the objective of exempting Canada from U.S. measures aimed at others, unless Canada is part of the problem. Even if that is the case, there is a limit on the extent of action that may be taken.

In the event of a dispute over safeguards (such as whether safeguards were properly imposed, or over the adequacy of compensation), the matter must be referred to binding arbitration. In the event of non-compliance, the other party will have the right to suspend the application of equivalent benefits.

New Legislation

One of Canada's concerns has been the tendency of the U.S. Congress to legislate trade restrictions and to revise trade rules. Provisions of the agreement concerning proposed changes to anti-dumping and counter-vailing-duty laws have been discussed above. More broadly, a set of notification and consultation provisions apply to any legislative or other measures affecting the operation of the agreement. Each government is required to provide written notice to the other party as soon as possible of any proposed or actual legislation, regulation or governmental proce-dure or practice that it considers might materially affect the operation of the agreement. It must also respond to any question, whether or not notification has previously been given.

Either party may request consultations on any matter it considers affects the operation of the agreement, whether or not notification has been given. Both parties have committed themselves to seek a mutually satisfactory resolution through consultations, thus avoiding the need to resort to the dispute settlement mechanisms. If a dispute cannot be resolved through consultations within thirty days of a request for consul-tations, then either party may resort to the general dispute settlement provisions and request a meeting of the Trade Commission (discussed below). These provisions do not prevent the U.S. Congress from initiat-ing legislation that affects Canada, but they do provide a process for avoidance of disputes, and criteria for the resolution of disputes if they do occur.

In the interim, before the agreement comes into force on January 1, 1989, a standstill provision is designed to prevent actions that would make the agreement less likely to be approved. The October 3 agreement reads, "Both Parties understand the need to exercise their discretion in the period prior to entry into force so as not to jeopardize the approval process or undermine the spirit and mutual benefits of the Free Trade Agreement" (Government of Canada 1987c: 32). Letters to this effect were exchanged when the final text was released. The obvious question is what effect this provision will have on the U.S. omnibus trade bill (see chapter 6). The House of Commons Standing Committee on External Affairs and International Trade recommended unanimously on Decem-ber 15 that if the omnibus trade bill is passed without exempting Canada from its protectionist provisions, Canada should withdraw its consent for the agreement.

General Dispute Settlement Provisions

The agreement establishes a set of institutions and procedures for the avoidance or settlement of all disputes respecting any aspect of the interpretation or application of the agreement, except for the special provisions regarding anti-dumping and countervailing duties and safeguards discussed above. The central body is the Canada-United States Trade Commission. This is a political rather than judicial body, with at least one cabinet-level representative from each government. It has the responsibility to supervise the proper implementation of the agreement and resolve disputes that may arise over its interpretation and application. It will operate by consensus and according to a strict timetable.

The Trade Commission will meet at the request of either party. If the commission is unable to resolve a dispute within thirty days, it will refer the matter to binding arbitration if all of its members agree, or either party may request that the matter be referred for examination by a panel of experts. If binding arbitration is agreed to but one party fails to implement the findings of the arbitration panel and no appropriate compensation is agreed to by the parties, the other party will have the right to suspend the application of equivalent benefits.

If the dispute is referred to a panel of experts, a strict timetable will be followed. The panel will be composed, like the binding binational appeal panel, of two members chosen by each government and a fifth agreed to by the commission, the other panelists or by lot. The panel will conduct hearings, make findings of fact, determine the consistency of the disputed measure with the obligations of the agreement, and issue an initial report with recommendations to the parties for a settlement. Within thirty days but after an opportunity for responses from the parties, the panel will issue its final report. The commission will then agree on a resolution of the dispute, which will normally conform to the findings of the panel. Where possible there will be non-implementation or removal of a measure not conforming with the agreement. If the commission is not able to reach consensus agreement on a mutually satisfactory resolution within one month of the panel's final report, the complainant has the right to suspend benefits of equivalent economic effect until the dispute is resolved.

At various points in these dispute settlement provisions, it has been established that in the event of non-compliance or unreconciled disagreement, the other party may suspend benefits of equivalent economic effect. Some dismiss this as without consequence, because of the economic asymmetries between Canada and the United States. Nevertheless, these measures all represent a sincere attempt to create recourse to some meaningful sanction, short of termination of the agreement, to prevent frustration of the principles of the agreement through inactivity.

Conflict Management or Conflict Creation?

It has been argued here that the free trade negotiations were an occasion for the management of trade conflict. The negotiations aimed at producing an agreement that would contain provisions for the avoidance and resolution of the types of trade disputes that have bedeviled the Canada-U.S. relationship in the past.

Paradoxically, but not surprisingly, the free trade negotiations have given rise to new tensions, especially within Canadian domestic politics. The free trade negotiations, and the agreement they produced, have created new issues for federal-provincial and interprovincial conflict. These differences have less to do with the dispute settlement provisions discussed in this chapter than with other elements in the agreement, but they threaten to dominate, and perhaps to worsen, the relationships among the various Canadian governments.

Three provincial governments (Ontario, Manitoba and Prince Edward Island), from three different regions of the country, have clearly expressed opposition to the agreement. Their opposition, like that in the public debate, is based variously on the arguments that the deal is a bad one, giving up too much for too little, that the deal will erode the constitutional powers of the provinces and indeed the sovereignty of Canada itself, and that the U.S. timetable requiring that the agreement be signed on January 2, 1988, does not give Canadians enough time to consider the deal on its merits. During the Ontario provincial election during the summer, Premier David Peterson campaigned on the promise that he would not accept any free trade agreement that did not meet six conditions (Harrington 1987). He promised that Ontario would oppose any agreement that guts the auto pact, reduces Canada's ability to promote and preserve Canada's cultural identity, restricts Canada's right to support industrial development and reduce regional disparities, excludes safeguards for Canada's agricultural industry and the viability of the family farm, prohibits the continued screening of foreign investment to ensure that it is in the interest of Canadians, and lacks a binding independent mechanism to settle disputes.

Opposition to the agreement has come on all of these issues, while its supporters have argued for the economic and political benefits expected to ensue. Premiers Grant Devine of Saskatchewan, Don Getty of Alberta and Robert Bourassa of Quebec have been the most vocal provincial advocates of the deal, but the debate has spread to all sectors of Canadian politics and society. While both opposition parties and many other critics argued that an election, or at least a referendum, should be held on the issue before Canada becomes committed to it, the Mulroney government announced its determination to conclude the agreement in 1988.

The most important conflict, however, is between opposing views of the nature and future of Canada. The domestic debate on the free trade agreement does not fundamentally address questions of the reduction of trade barriers, or even the broad questions of enhanced and secure access to the U.S. market. Rather it centres on the question of the relationship between government intervention and the market and the kind of country Canadians want for the future. The free trade agreement itself raises, but does not settle, this fundamental trade dispute.

Conflicts have also arisen within the United States. Some private interests opposed to the agreement were placated or won over by changes agreed to in the process of translating the initial agreement into the final legal text. Opposition from the maritime shipping industry, one of the most powerful lobbies in Washington, was negated when the provision for future national treatment of shipping was deleted from the final agreement, leaving their national monopoly intact. The U.S. telecommunications industry was brought on board by accelerating the rate of reduction of Canadian tariffs. Nevertheless, several identifiable interests in the United States remain opposed. These are most notably automobile parts manufacturers and certain resource industries, like small oil and gas firms, uranium producers, and copper, lead and zinc mines. There is also some opposition from western agricultural interests (for example, hogs) and the steel and textile industries. All of these interests are sure to lobby Congress to oppose the agreement. Despite these lobbying pressures, congressional opposition to the agreement is more likely to arise from the wider competition between the administration and the Congress over trade policy generally. The Canada-U.S. free trade agreement could be held hostage as a bargaining chip in the struggle between Congress and the president over the omnibus trade bill.

The deep divisions in Canada, and the possibility of congressional opposition in the United States, raise the prospect that the agreement might not receive final approval in one or the other country. If that should occur, Canada-U.S. conflict (not to mention intra-Canadian conflict) would be sure to increase. Not only would the trade disputes the agreement sought to avoid or manage continue (or even increase with growing protectionism in the United States), but recriminations could worsen the atmosphere in which the overall relationship is managed. We could not return to the time before the free trade negotiations began as if they had never happened.

The free trade agreement is a partial success with regard to its objective of secure access, since it provides at least more secure access for Canada to the U.S. market. But the success of the agreement as an exercise in conflict management rests not only on the dispute settlement provisions of the agreement and how they are implemented in practice, but on the domestic and bilateral political developments of the coming year. This story is still unfolding.

10 | Conflict over Common Property: Canada-U.S. Environmental Issues

DON MUNTON

In contrast to a pattern of extraordinary events in trade, finance and arms control, 1987 was a year of non-events in Canada-U.S. environmental relations. The problems remained apparent — acid rain, toxic chemicals, the accumulating wastes of our industrial society. The solutions remained elusive.

A bilateral acid rain accord, once again, did not emerge. Some amendments to the bilateral agreement on Great Lakes water quality were made, but these involved changes more of process than substance to the existing accord. Moreover, the revised agreement was signed with such little fanfare — and in Toledo, Ohio — that the occasion failed to disrupt the year's pattern of *immobilisme* significantly. Indeed, the year was such that its major accomplishment may well have been a bilateral agreement, not on protecting the breeding grounds of the Porcupine Caribou herd per se, but on consulting about protecting it.[1]

It was, nevertheless, a most revealing set of non-events. The past year exposed more completely than could any public breakdown in negotiations the basically conflictual nature of bilateral environmental diplomacy. It revealed more starkly than any opposition questioning the limited range of options open to the present, or to any, government in Ottawa. And it showed more clearly than a gaggle of summits the essentially dependent nature of Canada's relationship in matters environmental with its larger and, apparently unrepentantly polluting, neighbour to the south.

None of this would seem to square well with conventional analyses of Canada-U.S. relations, a set of perspectives holding that these relations are characterized predominantly, indeed fundamentally, by a cooperative spirit, a problem-solving approach and an interdependence of impacts and interests. This conventional view, though indeed open to question, at least casts into perspective the lack of significant advances, let alone achievements, in environmental issues during recent months. As well, this dominant view provides a useful contrast to the trench warfare that stalled any advances on environmental questions.

Canadian-American Relations: Conventional Views

Relations between Canada and the United States would not seem to offer much in the way of insights on international conflict. The two countries' bilateral relationship is usually pictured as a model of cooperation. Their objectives, it is said, are rarely different, let alone contrary. The official rhetoric is seldom harsh, let alone angry. Their negotiations are characterized by a mutual search for compromise rather than by confrontation. In comparison with the relationships prevailing between many countries, that between Canada and the United States seems almost bereft of "conflict" worthy of the term.

A cluster of related propositions about Canadian-American relations emphasizes this "partnership-cooperation" perspective. One set of arguments explains the extent of cooperation between these close allies as the natural result of similar interests, and the irritants that do arise as the result of misunderstandings, of posturing that is not normally taken seriously, or of a few particularly sensitive and emotive questions (Holsti 1971). A related proposition is that conflict management is promoted by a comparatively relaxed, easy-going consultative process and by a unique "diplomatic culture," comprising, among other factors, a common, pragmatic problem-solving approach, a pervasive professional diplomatic ethic, a common language for technical issues, and a set of unofficial understandings and implicit rules for the conduct of relations.

Another, complementary, perspective on Canadian-American bilateral politics emphasizes the highly interdependent nature of the relationship (Keohane and Nye 1977). It holds that the absence of military threats, the lack of issue linkage, and, especially, pervasive transnational ties give rise to processes of accommodation that mute conflicts and facilitate compromises. These processes are marked by a lack of overall issue dominance by the stronger partner, by the pursuit of a variety of state goals across issues but without linkage between goals on different questions, by the increased importance of agenda-setting, by greater influence on the part of transnational actors, and by a changing role for international organizations. One consequence, Keohane and Nye have said, is that in highly interdependent relationships, the smaller power will "win" more often than when less interdependence exists. Analyses of historical cases in Canadian-American relations have tended to support this proposition (Nye 1976; Keohane and Nye 1977, chap. 7).

Common property issues such as found in the environmental area[2] would seem ideal candidates for this partnership-cooperation model. They involve use of shared or common resources — the air, boundary waters and so on — and they reflect high levels of interdependence. They also involve interests that are at least in one sense mutual — preventing the destruction of the resources themselves. When the partnership-cooperation model is applied to Canada-U.S. bilateral environmental issues such as acid rain and the Great Lakes, one would expect that few conflicts would arise, that the two countries would have difficulty settling whatever differences do arise, and that Canada ought to win as often as not. Recent experience with these two major environmental issues suggests a rather different pattern; this chapter will examine these cases and explain why. In the process, it will explore the arguments favouring a distinctly different perspective on Canadian-American relations, one that would seem appropriate not only for these issues but for others as well — such as free trade and defence.

Acid Rain as an Issue

The problem of acid rain is only as new as the industrial age. Although it was discovered — and the term coined — in the 1880s, the phenomenon remained outside the realm of international politics until the 1970s. The term "acid rain" has come to stand for a complex set of physical and chemical phenomena by which gases, especially sulphur and nitrogen oxides, are emitted as a result of combustion and other processes, transformed into acidic compounds while being transported through the atmosphere, and then deposited on land and water surfaces. Acidity is conventionally measured on the pH scale, with low values being highly acidic. Given that rain, snow and dry particles can all deposit these acidic compounds, the term "acidic deposition" is more descriptive and accurate. Given that other substances, particularly toxic chemicals, can also be transported long distances through the atmosphere and pose significant environmental hazards, the phrase "long-range transport of air pollution" will also be used here.

Acid rain was first brought publicly to the agenda of Canadian-American relations in 1977 by then federal environment minister Romeo

LeBlanc. It was, he said, "an environmental time bomb" and "the worst environmental problem [Canada has] ever had to face." His successor, John Roberts, pointing to the fact that about half of the acidic deposition in Canada originates with sources in the United States, noted that others, though not he, were beginning to use the term "environmental aggression" (Munton 1980, 1980-81). If some of the more recent scientific evidence has suggested that this rhetoric may have been a little overblown, that the death toll of lakes, fish, trees and *homo sapiens* is not mounting as quickly as once suspected, then it is also the case that little of the evidence has suggested a problem does not exist.

In the late 1970s Canadian and American government scientists, working as the Bilateral Research Consultation Group (BRCG), produced a survey of the existing scientific knowledge and underscored the extent and seriousness of the problem of acidic deposition. The solution they pointed to was substantial reductions in the emissions that cause acidic deposition. The Canadian government soon set as its objective achieving reductions of 50 per cent in U.S. and Canadian emissions over the coming decade.

After some informal talks, the Trudeau government and the Carter administration signed a joint "memorandum of intent" (MOI) in August 1980 committing themselves to the negotiation of an agreement and the establishment of bilateral working groups and a coordinating committee. Then the 1980 presidential election intervened and the cast of characters changed.

A few negotiation sessions were subsequently held, but there was no progress. The new Reagan administration, espousing an anti-regulatory philosophy, showed little interest in pursuing the goal of the MOI and even less in considering new pollution controls. Indeed, its appointees at the Environmental Protection Agency (EPA) set about turning back the environmental policy clock. The refrain on acid rain became "more research has to be done." And in case that research looked a mite too definitive, senior Reagan political appointees began to rewrite the scientists' conclusions in the final BRCG report (Yanarella and Ihara 1985: 40).

Good science was clearly not enough. Canada's political tactics had already begun to change somewhat, and the process was accelerated by the stalemate in the diplomatic negotiations. Officials in Ottawa and at the Canadian Embassy in Washington began to carry their arguments more often and more directly to the U.S. Congress and to the American public. The style was a distinct contrast to the old sacred cow of Canadian "quiet diplomacy." The new "public diplomacy" was not well received by all who observed these tactics. It was resented most by those against whom it was employed effectively.

Ottawa also pursued two other strategies, one domestic, the other international. Domestically, federal environment officials slowly began patching together an agreement with the seven eastern provinces to reduce Canadian emissions by half. The last provincial government to sign on — coal-producing and coal-burning Nova Scotia — finally did so in late 1987. Internationally, at a major meeting in Ottawa in early 1984, the "feds" were instrumental in founding what became known as the "30 per cent club" — a group of developed states committed to reducing sulphur dioxide emissions within their own territories by at least 30 per cent. The club, needless to say, did not include the United States, although the embarrassed Americans insisted they be invited to the meeting as observers.

The tougher-minded public diplomacy approach vis-à-vis the United States became a casualty of the federal election of September 1984. Along with the Foreign Investment Review Agency and the National Energy Policy, it did not survive the advent of a new friendly style and the declaration of a new cooperative era in Canadian-American relations. It remained to be seen whether American policies — and the all-important bilateral win-loss column — would change as well. Could a victory on acid rain elude the nice guys as surely as it had eluded their pushy predecessors?

Prior to the Shamrock Summit of 1985, Prime Minister Brian Mul-roney identified acid rain as a top Canadian concern. It was not considered one for the United States, and certainly not a concern at all for the Reagan administration. Destined to make no breakthroughs on the issue of acid rain, the leaders' salvage teams came up with what appeared to many observers as a mere face-saving action — the appointment of two "special envoys" to investigate the problem for a year. Acid rain action went on hold, a captive of the summitry schedule.

The envoys, Bill Davis, former premier of Ontario, and Drew Lewis, former transportation secretary in Ronald Reagan's cabinet, reported back as bidden to the following year's summit in Washington. They concluded that acid rain was, indeed, a problem, not a myth, but did not recommend immediate emission reductions. Instead they proposed a major and long-term $5-billion investment by industry and government into research, development and demonstration of so-called clean coal technologies. Both the president and prime minister accepted the report.

Canadian enthusiasm for this seeming initiative, never abundant, quickly disappeared. The relevant U.S. federal funding contained in the 1987 budget turned out to be more "old" money than new and destined largely to developing aspects of coal-burning technology rather than to reducing emissions of sulphur and nitrogen oxides. "Our initial reading of these figures is negative. They didn't give us cause for rejoicing," said Environment Minister Thomas McMillan. "There is, though, a lot of interpretation to be done. The figures don't speak for themselves" (McIntosh 1987). The interpretation did not take long.

Within a few weeks a senior official in McMillan's department had looked closely at the Reagan administration's proposals and found them wanting. He declared that on transboundary pollution flows into Canada, "the sum total of spending will have no effect at all....They have failed to meet their commitment" (Keating 1987). After forceful representations by Mulroney during Vice-President George Bush's visit to Ottawa in February 1987, Ronald Reagan announced in March that he would be seeking full funding for the clean coal technology demonstration program recommended by the envoys.

Despite this more positive note, the third annual Reagan-Mulroney summit of April 1987, to paraphrase McMillan, gave little more cause for rejoicing. Again back in potentially rough Canadian political waters, the president may have felt politically obliged to offer something. Whatever the reason, and after what was apparently a last-minute debate among his advisors, Reagan added to the script of his speech to the Canadian Parliament the meaningless pledge that he "*agreed to consider* the Prime Minister's proposal for a bilateral accord on acid rain" (italics added).

It was not much, certainly not a Reagan-Gorbachev summit-style breakthrough. But for both sides, apparently, it was enough to get the formal talks going again. The next month a team of Canadian officials arrived in Washington for a one-day meeting with their American counterparts — the first such formal meeting during the tenure of the Mulroney government. The Canadians reiterated their proposal for 50 per cent reductions on both sides from 1980 levels. The American side made clear that the president was still "considering" the proposal.

The fundamental opposition of the U.S. administration to any sort of new legislated emission reductions was clearly unshaken. It had been abundantly evident in the early Reagan years under his first administrator of the Environmental Protection Agency, Anne Gorsuch. The opposition remained clear when Gorsuch's replacement, former Nixon EPA administrator William Ruckelshaus, was shot down in his 1984 attempt to bring in a modest package of acid rain controls. And the resistance emerged again within days of Reagan's Ottawa statement.

On April 22, EPA administrator Lee Thomas told a U.S. Senate environment committee hearing that there was no demonstrated need to reduce sulphur dioxide emissions. There was not, in his mind, sufficient scientific evidence to support an acidic deposition control program. "The issue," he said (in none too articulate a fashion), "is one that today I don't have to say I've got to do this today with the scientific information that I've got today" (O'Neill 1987). Two more years of research were needed before any decision was made about emission controls, he added.

Thus articulated by the U.S. official whose role should make him the strongest ally of Canadian concerns, the administration's long-standing position was clearly still intact. Indeed, badly needed support for this position, with the stamp of science on it, was in the offing, as Thomas knew well. This support was to come in the form of a long-awaited interim report out of the U.S. government's multi-year, multimillion-dollar research program into acidic deposition. Of all the non-events of 1987, and of all the possible indicators of the Reagan administration's position on acid rain, this report was to be the most revealing.

The NAPAP Interim Assessment

The National Acid Precipitation Assessment Program (NAPAP) was established by the U.S. Congress under the Energy and Security Act of 1980 (Public Law 96-294). It reflected a concern that efforts to substitute coal for offshore oil in power-generating plants might lead to increased air pollution and a growing awareness of the problem of the transport over long distances of these and other emissions. The Congress "also expressed concern over the potential impact from long-range transport on national and international policy" (NAPAP 1987: I-1).

The program was mandated to develop a ten-year plan for research and monitoring — but not pollution control — and to coordinate the efforts of the twelve federal departments and agencies involved. It was also charged to cooperate "with international, private and state organizations engaged in similar research" (NAPAP 1987: I-1). From the outset it was interagency in nature, small in staff and located in the offices of the president's Council of Environmental Quality. And from the outset the NAPAP reflected the administration's skepticism about acid rain. It also experienced organizational and perhaps political problems, despite regular increases in research funds.

With the resignation in 1985 of its executive director, the Reagan administration appointed Dr. J. Laurence Kulp, then a vice-president for research of the giant Weyerhaeuser forest products company. One immediate consequence was that the first of a series of interim assessments of the acidic precipitation problem scheduled for 1985 was further delayed.

Kulp came to Washington with strong scientific credentials and quickly established a distinct personal reputation as a hands-on, no-nonsense director. Some observers explained the problems that developed as due to Kulp's lack of understanding of, or sensitivity to, the art of working within a government bureaucracy. He was, to some, "strongly opinionated and very self-confident" (Ember 1987: 15). "He formed opinions," said one co-worker, "and was very committed to those opinions." Still others suggested "bull-headed" was a better description.[3] At any rate, Kulp soon ordered that the NAPAP interim assessment, then nearing completion, be redesigned and redrafted.

The process by which the document eventually emerged two years later is of some importance to understanding its contents. Individual chapters on specific scientific aspects of the complex problem of acidic deposition — such as meteorology, soil chemistry and aquatic biology — were written by government experts in various laboratories and agencies. They were discussed interdepartmentally with other scientists and then submitted to Kulp, who read and revised them. Each of the chapters was peer reviewed. Many then went through additional rounds of revision between the authors and the NAPAP director. The process of finalizing the chapters was seldom easy. As always in Washington, interagency disagreements were rife. But at least one participant recalled that however combative the debates between agencies, they were "nothing....NOTHING....compared to the arguments I had with Larry Kulp."

What eventually became the Executive Summary of the NAPAP interim assessment followed a strikingly different path but was no less controversial. The idea that the Executive Summary would be a compendium of the summary conclusions of the substantive chapters was discussed but vetoed by Kulp. Though argued over at the senior management level, the Executive Summary ultimately became largely the personal work of the NAPAP director. It was never submitted for an independent peer review.

The interim assessment (titled *Interim Assessment: The Causes and Effects of Acidic Deposition*) finally emerged in September 1987. Comprising over 800 pages, ten substantive chapters, and four volumes, the first of which was the Executive Summary, it was accompanied by an administration-prepared press release. In general, the Summary and the press release leave the impression that the damage from acid rain is neither serious nor extensive and is probably not getting worse. Release of the interim assessment was greeted with what one industry journal termed "a crescendo of criticism" (Ember 1987: 15).

Most of the attacks were aimed at the Executive Summary; few criticisms were directed at the contents or summaries of individual chapters. As one close observer said, "The chapters are closer to the truth than the Summary, and the Summary is closer to the truth than the press release." The basic theme of the Executive Summary, according to another participant, "is not what the individuals intended." It would be reasonable to expect, nevertheless, that the press release and the Executive Summary were more widely read — and, as probably intended, more widely reported — than the other volumes.

The Executive Summary presents remarkably sanguine conclusions about the effects of acidic deposition. "Some lakes and streams in sensitive regions," it notes, almost reluctantly, "appear to have been acidified by atmospheric deposition at some point in the last 50 years," but then adds "that most watersheds in the glaciated Northeast are at or near steady state with respect to sulfur deposition and that further significant surface water acidification is unlikely to occur rapidly at current deposition levels" (NAPAP 1984: I-8). Moreover, "lakes and streams that appear to have been acidified, at least in part, by atmospheric deposition represent a small fraction of the surface waters in the United States" (p. I-9). The Executive Summary even manages to cast the long-term twentieth-century trend of increasing emissions of sulphur dioxide in a seemingly innocuous light. It states that U.S. sulphur dioxide emissions have been "within about +/-35 percent of the 1985 value since about 1910" (p. I-10). (It could also be concluded from the same data that the trend over the 1900-70 period represented a 200 per cent increase.)

On the effect of acidic deposition on forests, buildings and human health, the NAPAP Executive Summary essentially reserves judgment. On the impact on agriculture it is much less cautious. It notes that "research results have established that acidic rain in the amounts and concentrations that currently occur in the United States has no consistent demonstrable effect on the yield of agricultural crops." But then, going beyond the careful wording here (note the terms "rain" and "consistent" in particular), it concludes "that the impact from acidic deposition on regional crop production in the United States is negligible" (p. I-25). Indeed, the authors of the Executive Summary emphasize, "there may be a net fertilizer benefit from nitrogen deposition on the order of $100 million per year" (p. I-9). And the effects on fish? "Sensitivity to acidity," the Summary suggests, "varies among fish species and their life stages" (p. I-32).

On the matter of control technologies the tone of the NAPAP Executive Summary is distinctly upbeat. "The Clean Coal Technology Program of the Department of Energy and complementary industrial efforts will accelerate the demonstration and implementation of new technology...[and] implementation of these technologies may proceed steadily based on economics alone." Thus, in the medium to long term, "technological advances in systems...may offset any potential emissions increases from increased coal use" (p. I-10). In the short term, "liming lakes or their watersheds appears to be an effective method to neutralize the acidity of surface waters" (p. I-31).

The overall thrust of the NAPAP Executive Summary is clear: the damage caused by acidic deposition is largely unproven, slight and not widespread where proven, and, at any rate, certain to be lessened by new technology made inevitable by the forces of the marketplace. The political message, in short, is that the acid rain problem is neither serious nor in need of legislated controls.

A story line of that variety was unlikely to find many sympathetic fans among American environmental groups and it did not. Nor was it likely to please the already embattled Mulroney government. Federal Environment Minister Tom McMillan reacted quickly, calling a press conference the day after the NAPAP assessment was released. He termed it "voodoo science," a phrase that was ill-suited to distinguishing the administration's politics as reflected in the Executive Summary from the generally sound science of the report itself.

More substantial criticisms of the report were numerous. First, the Executive Summary was assailed for its use of the level of pH 5.0 to define acidification. Critics pointed out that very few fish species can survive such a high level of acidity; that there is clear evidence of other aquatic system damage in the pH 6.0 to 5.0 range, including destruction of the food chains for sport fish; and that other measures of stress, especially alkalinity levels, were both more conventional and more appropriate. "We took it on the chin for that one," one NAPAP-process participant acknowledged. The aquatic effects chapter, it might be noted, as distinct from the Executive Summary, focuses on the pH 6.0 to 5.0 range. The consequence of using the pH 5.0 level as a cut-off point was to reduce drastically the number of lakes and streams counted as having already suffered ecological damage. Surveying only larger lakes and casting damage in terms of proportions of total lake surface area, rather than in numbers of lakes, further understated the seriousness of the potential threat.

Second, the Summary's assumption that aquatic systems were "at or near" a steady state and not currently in decline was disputed. In a personal letter to Kulp written prior to the release of the NAPAP report, Dr. David Schindler, a senior Canadian government scientist, termed this assumption "unproven" and noted contrary evidence (Schindler 1987). Third, the report's optimistic projections of sulphur dioxide emissions were strongly challenged by, among others, the Natural Resources Defense Council (NRDC), which pointed out that these projections were based on a set of energy supply assumptions all of which were contrary to virtually all existing evidence (NRDC 1987a).

More generally, the summary first volume of the NAPAP report was criticized for its selective biases and inattention to some of the available scientific findings. "Scientific studies inconsistent with the Administration's political line are ignored or disparaged," stated Richard Ayres of the NRDC. "Others are selectively quoted to minimize the problem" (NRDC 1987b). Canadian Ambassador Allan Gotlieb, in a letter copied to all the key U.S. agencies involved, was almost as blunt. "We believe," he said, "that the Executive Summary makes selective use of information from the main body of the report and fails to give adequate weight to scientific research undertaken in Canada, the United States and elsewhere that would lead to the opposite conclusion" (Gotlieb 1987).

NAPAP and Canadian-American Relations

These criticisms, though valid, do not place the NAPAP report as squarely in the context of Canada-U.S. environmental relations as it might be. Consider three further points. First, the report entirely ignores the impact on Canada of acidic deposition from American sources. While the chapter on emissions includes data on Canadian sources and, indeed, highlights the fact that Canadian emissions are higher per capita and per gross national product dollar than U.S. emissions, the rest of the report makes virtually no mention of aquatic or terrestrial damage in Canada, let alone provide estimates of the extent of this damage. Reference is made to eastbound emissions that end up in the Atlantic Ocean; those that head northward apparently just disappear. To be sure, foreign territory is not within the usual mandate of an American assessment program. But the result is still a little eerie. It is almost as if, for the NAPAP and the administration it represents, Canada did not exist.

Second, the Executive Summary ignores the contribution tall stacks make to the long-range transport problem by forcing more pollutants higher into the atmosphere, allowing them more time to transform chemically and thus exacerbating the acidic deposition problem. It only mentions and draws no implications from the fact that the use of such stacks has greatly increased as legislation has taken effect to force reductions in local, or ambient, air pollution. In fact, despite reductions in U.S. and Canadian emissions over the 1970s and early 1980s, the result has not necessarily been to decrease levels of transboundary flows and acidic deposition. These levels are of more consequence to Canada than bare U.S. emission statistics.

The third point to be made about the NAPAP report of relevance to Canada's environmental relationship with the United States is the manner in which the extent of damage is understated by being cast within the broad context of a U.S. national assessment. The affected lakes of the American northeast, it notes, are only a small proportion of the lakes in the United States as a whole. The forest types for which damage evidence seems to exist are only a small proportion of overall U.S. forests. And so on. The result is that the regional nature of the problem becomes, at least implicitly, a reason for not taking national action.

At the end of 1987 Canada and the United States were no closer to an agreement on long-range transport of air pollution than in 1984, when the new era of Canada-U.S. cooperation was ushered in, or for matter, in 1977, when acid rain was first declared a political issue. The long-awaited NAPAP report marked not a small step forward but a major lurch backward. What a president, a prime minister, their environment ministers and two special envoys had collectively declared at a 1986 summit meeting to be an important transboundary environmental concern had unilaterally become in 1987 a slight problem for the United States but one that still awaited a solution. And serious scientific research had become, according to a close, albeit unsympathetic observer, "nothing more than political propaganda for the Reagan Administration position on acid rain." Since assuming office, it had consistently "claimed that acid rain was not a serious problem, and the report faithfully parrots the Administration line" (NRDC 1987b). Others, both outside and inside the government, agreed. "Canada," one American official observed, "got snookered again."[4]

Reagan administration officials had promised in the spring to have, by the time of a planned bilateral meeting in November, a decision on the president's promise to consider an agreement on air quality. The meeting came and went. Another meeting in early 1988 was planned and another promise of a decision was made.

Great Lakes Water Quality

In contrast to the lack of breakthroughs on acidic deposition and the long-range transport of air pollution, Canadian-American environmental relations on the major bilateral water pollution problem seemed to witness some progress. The movement was largely illusory, however.

The cornerstone of relations in this area is the 1972 Great Lakes Water Quality Agreement, renegotiated and broadened in 1978. The essence of the 1972 agreement, maintained in the 1978 version, was a set of common general water quality objectives, certain specific regulatory standards, mutual commitments to implement national programs to achieve these objectives, and procedures for monitoring subsequent progress.[5] A key point, often misunderstood, is that while the objectives and standards were *joint* and the monitoring of progress was to be *joint*, the pollution control programs were not. The programs were to be *complementary* but developed and implemented separately in the various jurisdictions.

The 1972 agreement had been focused largely on the problem of eutrophication due to excessive nutrients, especially phosphates, in the lakes. The 1977-78 renegotiation of the agreement added a new focus — that of toxic chemicals. Officials on both sides, for example, drew up a list of hundreds of hazardous chemicals that were to be eliminated from the Great Lakes. The renegotiated document also introduced a potentially important shift in the framework within which these efforts were to be undertaken. The parties committed themselves to adopting an "ecosystem approach" rather than trying to attack each pollutant or problem individually.

Both agreements gave the International Joint Commission (IJC) responsibility for the collection and analysis of information on water quality objectives and pollution control programs, for the independent verification of data, and for the publication of reports, on at least a biennial basis, assessing progress towards these objectives. Both accords further directed the IJC to establish a Water Quality Board, to assist the commission on pollution control issues, and a Research (later termed, Science) Advisory Board, to advise specifically on scientific issues. The commission was also empowered to establish a regional office. The IJC was given the responsibility of providing "assistance in the coordination of the joint activities." Partly as a result of the latter mandate, the process of developing and implementing policies for controlling pollution in the Great Lakes that evolved in the years following the first agreement was a complex, even cumbersome, one in which the roles of governments and the role of the IJC became somewhat blurred.

The IJC reports regularly focused on what its Water Quality Board had come to call "areas of concern" — particularly polluted and degraded areas of the lakes where remedial action was most needed. One perennial area of concern, for example, is Hamilton harbour. Another is the complex of chemical industry dumps near Niagara Falls, New York. The infamous Love Canal area, now completely evacuated, its homes bull-dozed and its toxic ground water being collected for disposal, is one of the smallest of these dump sites. The highly contaminated waters of the Niagara River — into which more than 3,000 pounds of pollutants are discharged daily, 90 per cent of them from the U.S. side — are appalling evidence of the scope and severity of the problem. The cleanup of these dump sites has long been stalled by the high costs and uncertainties surrounding the optimal set of remedial actions, including who should pay for it. Under a new and separate accord concluded in early 1987, both federal governments and the governments of New York and Ontario agreed to cut these emissions in half by 1996, thus recommitting themselves to commitments already at least implied under the 1978 agreement.

The Niagara problem has long been of particular concern to Canada because of the "downstream" effects. The river and its pollution load flow over the famous falls and into Lake Ontario. Metropolitan Toronto, the largest single urban concentration in Canada, and the largest by far on the lake, receives its drinking water from those same waters. Indeed, two out of every three Canadians obtain their drinking water from the Great Lakes-St. Lawrence system.

Reviewing the Great Lakes Agreement

Under the 1978 Great Lakes Agreement, the two countries were obliged to conduct a review after the third biennial report of the IJC, but not necessarily to revise, let alone renegotiate, the agreement. As the expected date of this report approached, a number of non-governmental actors stepped in to conduct their own reviews. First off the mark were the Royal Society of Canada (RSC) and the National Research Council (NRC) of the U.S. National Academy of Sciences.

The RSC-NRC review, eventually published at the end of 1985 as *The Great Lakes Water Quality Agreement: An Evolving Instrument for Ecosystem Management*, was an experiment in binational non-governmental cooperation and the first such cooperative effort of the two countries' leading scientific bodies. The major conclusion of the report was "that we have the commitment to a basin-wide ecosystem approach, but the approach has yet to be undertaken. There has been a giant step in concept and principle but the implementation is as yet in the exploratory stage." In short, the ideas were fine but the execution was lagging.

The RSC-NRC report made a large number of recommendations concerning what were regarded by the committee as the lakes' two major environmental problems — toxic contaminants and nutrients or enrichment. It urged implementation of a new Great Lakes Surveillance Plan, development of a comprehensive toxic substances management strategy, including priority action on toxic waste treatment centres, and government clean-up action in the particularly degraded "areas of concern." It also called for more studies and more data on the biological effects of toxic contaminants, on the exposure of human beings through food consumption, on contaminant accumulations in infants and on groundwater conditions. On the nutrient problem, it recommended further study of the longitudinal process of eutrophication, regular review of ongoing monitoring programs, more research coordination with the Great Lakes Fisheries Commission, basin-wide detergent phosphate limits, new efforts to control non-point-source pollution, more emphasis on remediation of nearshore pollution problems, and a long-term commitment to improve and maintain sewage treatment systems. At the very least, the RSC-NRC said, there should be a greater effort to reach the nutrient-level targets set in the 1978 agreement and its 1983 supplement, levels that had never yet been obtained. On institutions, the general conclusion of the RSC-NRC report was that "the record of the IJC and the associated joint institutions is one of substantial success....However, these joint institutions have lagged in executing certain responsibilities...and in others, improvements could still be made." The problems generally lay in the overlapping or confusion of responsibilities between the governments on the one hand and the IJC and its boards on the other.

The RSC-NRC committee recommended that the IJC no longer be involved in the coordination of government programs and that this coordination be carried out on a direct government-to-government basis. It also recommended that the governments hold what might be termed "environmental summit meetings" on a regular basis at which their records would be publicly scrutinized. And it suggested further that the independent policy monitoring and assessment role of the commission be strengthened. The RSC-NRC review was followed by others conducted by such non-governmental advocacy organizations as Great Lakes United, a binational coalition of environmental interest groups. It remained, however, the most extensive and best informed on the toxin issues in particular, and it struck a note of realism in its recommendations that most other reviews sounded as well.

Governmental Review

Following receipt of the IJC third biennial report, the governments announced their own review process in the spring of 1987. In contrast to both 1972 and 1978, this review was a remarkably open process. A draft version of proposed amendments to the agreement was distributed to interested parties, non-governmental as well as governmental. Most of the interest groups strongly agreed with the theme of the IJC report that "the Governments should continue their commitment to [the 1978 agreement] while clarifying, strengthening and particularly providing more vigorous support to certain of its provisions" (IJC 1986). They were clearly concerned that the agreement, if opened for renegotiation, might be weakened by anti-environmental pressure from both sides.

Such pressures were never mounted. The discussions between the two sides during the fall of 1987 were low key, congenial and conducted largely at the technical level. And they were brief. No substantial gutting of the agreement's provisions occurred; indeed, no major substantive changes were attempted at all. What revisions were made consisted largely of updating technical references and modifying the detailed annexes. The emphasis was less on the substance of programs than on their implementation or "delivery." In this respect, the two sides followed one of the recommendations of the RSC-NRC review panel and provided for twice annual direct government-to-government meetings to "coordinate...work plans...and to evaluate the progress made." But there were no major new initiatives, no significant new spending programs and no substantial institutional reforms, such as a strengthening of the IJC's independence. Officials on both sides even refused, correctly so, to characterize the process as a "renegotiation" of the agreement. The modest amendments to the accord were rather quietly signed into effect at an IJC meeting in Toledo, Ohio, in mid-November by Canada's environment minister and the U.S. EPA administrator.

Conclusion

At first glance, the process of the Great Lakes Agreement review would seem to fit rather well into the model of Canadian-American relations that emphasizes the mutuality of interests, the significant role of technical experts and non-governmental organizations, and the cooperative and problem-solving spirit of bilateral discussions. It would seem to fit better, certainly, than the pursuit of an accord on acidic deposition and the long-range transport of air pollution. The fit is only superficial. This was successful problem-solving only in the sense that the "problems" dealt with consisted of dated wording and provisions in a legal document. The largely housekeeping changes made to the agreement do not themselves move the governments any closer to dealing adequately with the complex problem of pollution in the lakes. The difficult issues were largely avoided. The question of the priority to be given these efforts in terms of domestic resources was not even addressed. The solving of the most serious environmental threats to the Great Lakes basin and its inhabitants, the two governments have implicitly agreed, must await another day.

It is not surprising that the U.S. government was content with this. The Reagan administration, after all, was unlikely to change its anti-environmental stripes at this stage, especially in the midst of a fiscal crisis so severe it was wreaking havoc in the global stock markets. What may seem surprising is a Canadian government's acceptance of this unsatisfactory status quo.

The fundamental reasons for this apparent decision are not to be found, as some might argue, in philosophical liabilities or character weaknesses of the prime minister and his colleagues. This was not a willful sell-out of Canadian interests by pro-American sympathies. Nor was it a sacrifice of environmental interests on the altar of the free trade deal, though that calculation may have been made by some of those involved. Rather, the explanation here lies in precisely the same set of factors confounding pursuit of an air pollution accord. The term I have suggested for this set of factors is "environmental dependence."

The now abundant literature on dependence and *dependencia* emphasizes the extent to which a country's economy is tied to foreign purchasers of goods and suppliers of capital. The crucial factor, however, is neither mere linkage nor the concentration on a particular purchaser or supplier, but rather the extent of alternative opportunities and the costs of shifting to such new arrangements. Through most of its history, Canada has been dependent economically on a major power, first Britain and then the United States, for its markets and capital. In the same sense, albeit in a different way, Canada has become increasingly dependent on the United States with respect to the quality of its environment.

Most of the pollutants dumped into the Great Lakes originate on the American side. Most of the sulphur and nitrogen oxides that lead to acidic deposition originate in the United States — not all of them, to be sure, but enough that in both cases unilateral Canadian action to deal with the problem would be ineffective. Even drastic controls on the sources of acidic deposition in Canada, for example, would not sufficiently protect the Canadian environment. The only feasible option, therefore, is for Canada to seek American cooperation in mounting programs to reduce emissions. And therefore, on issues such as acid rain and water pollution in the Great Lakes, Canada pursues international agreements as a way of securing an American commitment to deal with the sources of what are necessarily common problems.

The other side of this relationship has its logic too. Given the large U.S. population and industrial base, the sheer amounts of both air and water pollutants in the United States are enormous. Thus, in both cases, the costs of any potential cleanup on the American side are considerable. Second, at least some, and perhaps much, of the benefit of reduced U.S. emissions accrues not to the American environment but to the Canadian. Moreover, the extent of transboundary pollution from Canada into the United States is generally so small, comparatively, that there is little potential benefit to be derived from any reductions undertaken on the Canadian side. Thus, for both reasons — high costs and limited benefits

— the U.S. political system is relatively slower to act on many transboundary pollution issues and finds bilateral agreements less attractive. But this is not always so.

The Reagan administration moved extremely quickly in late 1986 and early 1987 to conclude an international air quality agreement with Mexico. Why the contrast? The fundamental difference between the Canada-U.S. and Mexico-U.S. cases is that in the latter it is the United States that is environmentally dependent. The major air pollution problem along the Mexican-American border is a new, very large Mexican smelter; it is therefore a problem of long-range transport of air pollution *into* the United States. And it is thus a problem on which the Reagan administration, not surprisingly, found little research was needed and on which action was taken immediately.

There is a further catch. One might call it "Catch 49" in honour of the parallel comprising the largest single span of the Canadian-American boundary. Catch 49 stems from the condition of environmental dependence; that is, when Canada is negotiating these environmental issues with the United States, virtually any agreement is better than no agreement at all. When the Great Lakes Water Quality Agreement was first being negotiated, the Canadian side was trying to extract greater American commitments; it was the *demander*. When an agreement was eventually concluded, the Canadian side accepted a minimal American commitment to deal with the nutrient problem, well aware that what they had was all they could get. Similarly, in 1987, faced with the total improbability of negotiating a stronger agreement with the Reagan administration, Canadian officials opted pragmatically for modest technical changes.

The explanation for the politics of acidic deposition is essentially the same. Given environmental dependence, any Canadian government would pursue an air quality agreement. Four successive administrations in Ottawa since the late 1970s have done so. The fifth will also. Any U.S. administration would proceed cautiously and slowly. The Reagan administration is merely proceeding more slowly — and more duplicitously — than most. Its politicization, and abuse, of the science of acidic deposition is a reflection of the lengths to which it believes it must go to justify its degree of inaction. The major factor inhibiting a significant compromise by Canada has for some time been an informed and aroused domestic public opinion. But a compromise of some order seems almost inevitable.

What did not happen in the environmental area of Canadian-American relations in recent years, then, can be substantially explained by the politics of environmental dependence. The notions of interdependence and of environmental issues being common property problems may make sense in theory but fail to deal adequately with certain underlying imperatives of bilateral politics. The continuing conflicts over these issues cannot be explained by reference to common interests, to shared technical information, to a mutual problem-solving approach. The style of Canadian-American relations has changed somewhat in the mid-1980s, for a while at least. The atmospherics, as set by the summits, have changed a little more. The fundamental structural dilemmas remain. And the environmental problems remain unsolved.

PART

VI

The Year in Review

11 | 1987: Chronology and Statistical Profile

D. KEITH HEINTZMAN

For the most part of 1987, Canada's international attention continued to focus on bilateral relations with the United States, culminating in a free trade arrangement. Concurrent with this bilateral orientation, economic issues occupied the forefront with the further development and resolution of the softwood lumber trade dispute, while several similar actions by both nations were added to the economic agenda. In tandem with these and other bilateral irritants, the trade agenda was extended multilaterally, with progress made towards the inclusion of agricultural trade at the General Agreement on Tariffs and Trade (GATT) negotiations. While similar actions and events are noted in the chronology below, several other aspects of external relations are included. The first White Paper on Canadian defence since 1971 was released. Security issues were also addressed in a variety of forms, including Canadian concerns about the militarization of space, the renewal of the cruise missile testing agreement, support for and offers of assistance to resolve the conflict in Central America, the strengthening of Canada's peacekeeping function in Cyprus, and support for the U.S.-U.S.S.R. Intermediate-range Nuclear Forces Reduction Treaty. Immigration policy took a turn towards greater control over permissible entries, implemented through both administrative changes and new legislation. Environmental matters, focusing on acid rain and control over pollution of the Great Lakes' waterway, received considerable attention, as did concern over the deterioration of the ozone layer and other multilateral environmental issues. The St. Pierre-Miquelon territorial boundary and fishing dispute with France lingered throughout the year without resolution. Finally, Canada played host to both the Commonwealth and the francophone summits.

Chronology of Developments

The events that make up this chronology were chosen in part with a view to their significance for Canada's international policies. The chronology reflects developments in the international security environment, in the international political economy and in the area of international development, while also making reference to major issues in the Canada-U.S. agenda.

January 1: A December 30, 1986, letter to the U.S. lumber industry, signed by U.S. Commerce Secretary Malcolm Baldrige and U.S. Trade Representative Clayton Yeutter, is made public. Referring to the December 30 settlement by which Canada imposed a 15 per cent export tax on softwood lumber (in order to avoid a 15 per cent American countervailing duty), the letter claims that the United States will have to approve any changes in the tax, thereby contradicting the Canadian position that the Canadian law can be changed unilaterally. The letter also states that the estimated $550 million raised by the tax may not be used to benefit Canadian softwood lumber producers. In exchange for the Canadian export tax, collected as of January 8, 1987, the American lumber industry dropped its petition to have the U.S. punitive duty imposed.

January 8: Immigration Minister Benoît Bouchard announces that Canada is imposing entry visa requirements on citizens of Turkey and four African nations after a flood of refugee claims in 1986. The previous day, the North-South Institute released its annual review of Canadian foreign policy, criticizing immigration policy as being too restrictive.

January 15: The Canada-U.S. bilateral trade negotiations resume. Although the Auto Pact is not directly addressed, automotive issues are discussed with specific reference to the Canadian duty remission scheme for offshore producers. U.S. chief negotiator Peter Murphy states that the Auto Pact will be reviewed sometime during the negotiations.

January 21: U.S. Vice-President George Bush and U.S. Secretary of the Treasury James Baker arrive in Ottawa for a five-hour meeting with Prime Minister Brian Mulroney and Finance Minister Michael Wilson to discuss acid rain and the bilateral trade negotiations. No agreement is announced, but the vice-president does indicate that the prime minister's concerns over acid rain were forcefully pressed.

January 24: An interim agreement between Canada and France is signed after the two countries fail to renegotiate the 1972 treaty on fish quotas. Stipulations of the agreement include sending the dispute over the maritime boundary around the French islands of St. Pierre and Miquelon to international arbitration, and the setting of fishing quotas. The French government claims a two hundred-mile zone around its islands in the St. Lawrence. The Canadian government has accused the French fleet of over-fishing and insists on a twelve-mile boundary. The agreement provides for negotiations to begin March 15 on a further interim agreement.

January 26: The U.S. Department of Agriculture announces an offer to sell one million tonnes of subsidized wheat to the People's Republic of China (in order to counter subsidized European wheat sales), instigating an immediate protest by Ottawa. China receives approximately 17 per cent of Canada's wheat exports.

January 26: An agreement between France and Canada to license nine French trawlers to fish in the disputed waters off southern Newfoundland is announced. Newfoundland Premier Brian Peckford claims the settlement represents a Canadian sell-out.

January 26: Prime Minister Mulroney visits Italy for discussions with Prime Minister Benito Craxi. Both agree that Canada and Italy must be included in the upcoming Group of Five discussions on currency instability. From Italy, the prime minister travels to Zimbabwe and Senegal, where he states that Canada will continue to impose sanctions against South Africa.

January 27: U.S. President Ronald Reagan delivers his State of the Union Address, in which he mentions both the bilateral trade negotiations with Canada and the GATT discussions in Uruguay. In a separate briefing paper the president expresses his hope that a Canada-U.S. trade agreement will become a model for liberalizing world trade.

January 29: The United States and Mexico sign an agreement to cut sulphur dioxide emissions from smelters on the Arizona-Mexico border.

February 2: Revenue Canada cuts the feed corn duty, imposed in November 1986, on subsidized American exports to Canada from 67 to 54 per cent after reappraising American subsidies. The Canadian Import Tribunal begins hearings into whether Canadian farmers are being injured by the subsidies so that the tribunal can decide if the duty will be continued or dropped.

February 4: The United States and Canada, along with New York State and Ontario, sign an agreement to cut the flow of toxic chemicals into the Niagara River by one half by 1996 and to discuss the removal of toxic waste dumps along the river.

February 11: Officials from Canada, Japan and Western Europe meet in Washington for discussions with the U.S. Department of State on an American proposal for a space station as a multilateral effort. The primary concern for Canada is that the space station not be used for military purposes.

February 18: Finance Minister Wilson releases his third budget, which has a predicted deficit of $29.3 billion. The budget cuts $150 million from previously planned foreign aid spending and sets an aid target of 0.6 per cent of gross national product (GNP) to be reached by 1995. The budget also cancels the 1986 punitive tariff on imports of American Christmas trees, books and some computer parts.

February 19: The bilateral trade negotiations begin their eighth round in Washington after several public statements by U.S. Trade Representative Yeutter and U.S. chief negotiator Murphy that the United States wishes to discuss cultural issues.

February 19: Canadian Ambassador Noiseux returns to Syria after being recalled in 1986 in order to press Canada's position opposing state-sponsored terrorism.

February 20: Immigration Minister Bouchard announces immediate administrative changes to deter abuses of procedures for the determination of refugee status. The changes include the cancellation of the policy on non-deportation to eighteen countries and a new policy requiring refugee claimants from the United States to remain there until a Canadian immigration hearing can be held.

February 22: An accord to stabilize exchange rates around the then-current levels is reached in Paris between Canada, the United States, Britain, Japan, France and West Germany. Italy boycotts the meeting of finance ministers and central bankers. The accord includes an American pledge to reduce its federal budget deficit.

February 24: After the successful test of an American cruise missile on this day, the Department of External Affairs announces that the 1983 pact to test the cruise over Canada (which was to expire on February 28) will be renewed for another five years. On March 1, another cruise test takes place.

March 2: Secretary of State for External Affairs Joe Clark announces that Canada will build the Class 8 icebreaker (the world's largest) in order to enhance Canadian Arctic claims.

March 4: Secretary of State for External Affairs Clark announces that the Soviet Union will permit twenty-two families to emigrate to Canada. This action is partly a response to Canadian government requests during Soviet Foreign Minister Eduard Shevardnadze's visit to Ottawa in September 1986.

March 6: The Canadian Import Tribunal upholds a countervailing tariff on American subsidized feed corn.

March 7: Fisheries Minister Tom Siddon and Transport Minister John Crosbie announce that the fisheries in the disputed St. Lawrence zone and Canadian ports in the region are closed to French vessels, charging them with violating their fishing quota.

March 11: Defence Minister Perrin Beatty announces that the government has selected airfield sights at five locations in the Yukon and Northwest Territories as forward operating bases for Canadian CF-18 fighter aircraft. Other NORAD interceptors will also use the sites, and the costs of the joint Canada-U.S. project will be shared.

March 12: International Trade Minister Pat Carney announces that the Republic of Korea will increase its imports of Canadian coking coal, reduce the Korean tariff on softwood lumber imports and increase the Canadian quota on softwood lumber.

March 18: The International Joint Commission releases its third biennial report on the 1978 Great Lakes Water Quality Agreement, noting that since the signing of the original 1972 and the 1978 agreements, pollution in the Great Lakes has worsened.

April 1: The Japanese tariff on Canadian imports of spruce, pine and fir lumber is reduced from 10 to 8 per cent.

April 5-6: U.S. President Reagan visits Ottawa for the third annual summit during which Prime Minister Mulroney presses for stricter acid rain controls and proposes a treaty on both a schedule and targets for reduction. On April 6 the president addresses a joint session of Parliament and for the first time accepts American responsibility for some acid rain in Canada. Other discussions cover Canadian claims to the Arctic archipelago as internal waters and Canadian concerns about the possible militarization of space.

April 15-16: Secretary of State for External Affairs Clark attends a North Atlantic Treaty Organization (NATO) meeting in Brussels where he presents Canada's verification proposals for the U.S.-U.S.S.R. arms negotiations in Geneva. The NATO members are briefed by U.S. Secretary of State George Shultz on his tour of the Soviet Union and discussions with Soviet leaders. At the conclusion of this NATO meeting, the Group of Seven countries agree to guidelines to control the export of missile equipment and technology.

April 28: The Brundtland report by the World Commission on Environment and Development, *Our Common Future*, is released; it presses the argument that international economic development cannot be separated from issues of environmental degradation, both of which must be dealt with simultaneously and multilaterally. The report calls for sustained development for all nations in order to alleviate environmental deterioration and recommends, along these lines, a set of legal principles.

April 29: Communications Minister Flora MacDonald releases the discussion paper *Vital Links: Canadian Cultural Industries*, which states that the interests of Canadian cultural nationalists will be protected in a trade agreement with the United States.

April 30: The U.S. House of Representatives passes an omnibus trade bill that establishes a broad definition of illegal subsidies subject to countervail, requires retaliation against countries with unfair trade practices, and changes anti-dumping rules to make them more effective.

May 5: The Subsidies Committee of the GATT meets at the request of the United States, but reaches no decision on the validity of the Canadian countervailing duty against American feed corn imports.

May 10: Secretary of State for External Affairs Clark ends his eight-day visit to West Germany, Poland, East Germany and Hungary, where he expresses Canada's support for the elimination of intermediate-range nuclear missiles in Europe.

May 12: The new South African ambassador to Canada, Johannes De Kleck, presents his diplomatic credentials to Governor-General Jeanne Sauvé. At the reception, Madame Sauvé reiterates Canada's opposition to apartheid.

May 12-13: At the Paris OECD ministerial meeting, Finance Minister Wilson and International Trade Minister Carney press for agricultural trade reform. The inclusion of agriculture as an issue on the GATT agenda at the Uruguay multilateral negotiations is reaffirmed. An agreement is also reached to stop the dumping of agricultural goods at subsidized prices, which contributes to an international agricultural trade war.

May 13: The Senate Standing Committee on Foreign Affairs releases its report, *Canada, the International Financial Institutions and the Debt Problem of Developing Countries*, in the wake of the suspension of interest payments by Brazil in February. In general, the report advocates increased funding to debtor countries through international agencies and creditor governments, proposes discussions between debtor and creditor governments and recommends the creation of an international advisory group on international debt.

May 18-20: The Canada-U.S. trade talks continue at Meech Lake, and a study group on investment is established. The American negotiators raise demands that Canada loosen restrictions on foreign investment, and at the conclusion of the session both parties indicate that investment is becoming a major issue.

May 21-23: The Cairns Group of agricultural exporters meets in Ottawa for the second time since the group was formed in 1986. The group is instrumental in ensuring that agricultural trade remains on the GATT agenda. Canada is the only member of the Cairns Group that is also a member of the Group of Seven.

May 22: During a meeting in Washington between Canadian and American environmental officials, the Canadian government states that it will be flexible and not hold the United States to a specific timetable on acid rain reduction. This meeting is pursuant to the promise made by U.S. President Reagan, during his April visit to Ottawa, to consider negotiations towards a bilateral environmental agreement.

May 23: During a meeting in Quebec City of sixteen NATO countries, Norwegian officials are critical of the anticipated Canadian withdrawal from the commitment to supply troops and equipment to Norway in the event of a crisis.

May 25-29: French President François Mitterrand visits Canada and addresses Parliament, where he argues that Canada and France should present a united effort promoting aid to the Third World to alleviate the debt crisis. During his stay the president also requests that Canadian ports be reopened to French fishing vessels, a request the Canadian government subsequently rejects.

May 28: The Winegard report, by the Standing Committee on External Affairs and International Trade, *For Whose Benefit?*, is released. The report, concerning Canada's international development policies, emphasizes human-resource development and human rights.

June 1: Canada begins monitoring exports of steel in order to identify companies attempting to circumvent American Voluntary Restraint Agreements (VRAs) by transshipping steel through Canada. Exporters of steel are required to obtain an export permit citing the origin of the material. Imports of steel will also be monitored as to the final destination. This Canadian action is in response to the United States' proposed protection of steel by including Canada in a VRA (which the United States has with seventeen other countries but from which Canada is excluded). A bill which would mandate a steel VRA with Canada has been pending in the U.S. Senate since February 3.

June 3: The constitutional amendment (1987) known as the Meech Lake accord is signed in Ottawa by all first ministers, giving the provinces a greater role in Senate and Supreme Court appointments and in immigration policy, and recognizing Quebec as a distinct society.

June 5: The defence White Paper is tabled. It includes a fifteen-year budget of $200 billion, including provisions for ten nuclear-powered submarines in order to support Canada's claim to sovereignty in the Arctic. The Canadian commitment to Norway as part of NATO is officially dropped, and instead Canadian troops and equipment will be consolidated in West Germany in order to directly confront the Soviet threat.

June 8-10: The Group of Seven hold their thirteenth meeting in Venice. The Canadian call for South Africa to abandon apartheid is not included in the final communiqué. A position is taken in the statement for an end to farm subsidy trade wars. On June 11, Prime Minister Mulroney and U.S. President Reagan discuss the bilateral trade negotiations, and the president promises support in getting any agreement through Congress.

June 20: France cancels the scheduled June 24 St. Lawrence fishing dispute meeting with Canadian officials as a protest against the closing of Canadian ports to French fishermen.

June 24: Canada is the twenty-first state to ratify a United Nations convention against the use of torture or other cruel treatment.

June 30: In the House of Commons, Prime Minister Mulroney confirms that he received a letter from U.S. President Reagan rejecting a binding trade dispute settlement mechanism. Instead, the president proposed a voluntary mechanism.

July 6: After monitoring showed an increase in illegal immigration from Brazil over the past two months, Immigration Minister Bouchard announces that henceforth citizens of Brazil will be required to obtain a visa before entering Canada.

July 8: The second of the quarterly federal-provincial meetings on trade by the first ministers is held in Ottawa, where the premiers are briefed by trade negotiator Simon Reisman. Afterwards, Ontario Premier David Peterson and Manitoba Premier Howard Pawley express reservations about resolving trade disputes to their satisfaction.

July 12: During the night, 174 Asians wade ashore in Nova Scotia, claiming refugee status, and consequently precipitate a national debate on Canadian immigration policy.

July 15: Canada participates at the United Nations Conference on Trade and Development (UNCTAD) VII in Geneva, where External Relations Minister Monique Landry reaffirms Canada's commitment to constructive internationalism as the cornerstone of Canadian foreign policy.

July 16: U.S. President Reagan announces that the five-year American restrictions (through tariffs and quotas) on specialty steel imports will be extended for another twenty-six months. The Canadian government protests this action, as it affects approximately $15 million in Canadian products.

July 20: The UN Security Council unanimously adopts Resolution 598, which demands a ceasefire in the seven-year Persian Gulf War and provides for supervision by the United Nations. In his address to the General Assembly on the following day, Secretary of State for External Affairs Clark supports the resolution.

July 21: The U.S. Senate passes an omnibus trade protection bill that could affect Canadian exports of steel, potash and pork.

August 7: In Guatemala the presidents of five Central American states agree on a peace plan containing provisions for a ceasefire within ninety days. Secretary of State for External Affairs Clark sends officials to meet with Central American foreign ministers and indicates that Canada is willing to provide technical advice for the elaboration of ceasefire verification and control mechanisms.

August 14: Secretary of State for External Affairs Clark ends a four-day visit to Africa that included a ten-hour visit to South Africa. During the tour, he indicated that Canada will impose more sanctions against South Africa and may interrupt diplomatic relations with the apartheid regime.

August 21: The United States imposes a preliminary anti-dumping duty (ranging from 9.14 to 85.2 per cent) on Canadian potash.

August 24: In his speech to the UN International Conference on the Relationship between Disarmament and Development, Secretary of State for External Affairs Clark supports the position that greater economic development will enhance security for all and supports the linkage of disarmament and international development.

September 2-4: The second summit of la francophonie (the Agency for Cultural and Technological Cooperation, established in 1970) is held in Quebec City. Canada announces the cancellation of $325 million worth of debt owed by seven African nations and a $17-million aid package to African members.

September 10: Canada and the People's Socialist Republic of Albania officially establish diplomatic relations.

September 14: A meeting of the federal and provincial first ministers takes place in Ottawa (postponed from September 8) on the issue of the Canada-U.S. trade negotiations. Afterwards, Ontario Premier Peterson announces that chief American negotiator Murphy had given formal notice to include automotive trade in the talks on September 11. The premier also announces that his government will not support any agreement that removes the Canadian content performance requirements included in the Auto Pact.

September 14: Bill C-84, dealing with refugees, is passed by the House of Commons after the House was called back for an early sitting on August 11. The legislation is presented as a response for situations such as the arrival of the boatload of Asians seeking refugee status in July and will allow immigration officials to board vessels off the Canadian coast and turn them back without giving the occupants a formal immigration hearing.

September 15-16: At a conference in Montreal of forty-six nations organized by the UN Environment Program, a treaty is reached by twenty-four states (including Canada) to protect the ozone layer. The pact calls for the reduction of chlorofluorocarbons by 50 per cent over ten years.

September 16: Bill C-71, allowing the prosecution in Canada of war criminals, is given final assent.

September 17: The U.S. administration's National Acid Precipitation Assessment Program presents its research report claiming that acid rain has little damaging effect on forest and water resources. The report is criticized for its selective use of known evidence by environmental groups and Environment Minister Thomas McMillan.

September 18: As part of the campaign to prohibit illegal immigration, Immigration Minister Bouchard announces that travellers from Bolivia and Honduras must obtain visas before entering Canada.

September 18: The Canadian government agrees to send sixty more peacekeeping personnel to Cyprus at the request of the United Nations. Canada has participated in the UN Cyprus force since 1964.

September 23: Canadian trade negotiator Reisman suspends the bilateral trade negotiations over American intransigence specifically concerning Canadian demands for a binding dispute settlement mechanism. This action precipitates a period of discussions with more senior officials of both administrations.

October 1: The U.S. Department of Commerce begins to implement new domestic conservation regulations restricting the sale of certain species of fish below specific sizes. The regulations are also expanded to apply to U.S. imports in order to be more effective. The result is the restriction of some East Coast Canadian fish exports. This action is a broadening of a similar measure taken in 1983, but includes a wider range of species of fish and increases the size requirement for importation. As of January 1, 1988, similar regulations will affect approximately 20 per cent of East Coast lobster exports to the United States.

October 3: In Washington, officials from Canada and the United States initial an agreement of intent for a bilateral free trade zone shortly before the midnight deadline, but the agreement must still have the legal text formalized.

October 6: The federal and provincial first ministers meet in Ottawa to discuss the Canada-U.S. trade agreement. At the conclusion, the leaders of five provinces (British Columbia, Alberta, Saskatchewan, Quebec and New Brunswick) announce their support, while the leaders of three other provinces (Prince Edward Island, Ontario and Manitoba) express their opposition. On October 9, U.S. Trade Representative Yeutter announces in Toronto that the Congress will not pass the trade pact without provincial approval on the Canadian side.

October 9: France withdraws from the boundary and fishing negotiations concerning the French islands of St. Pierre and Miquelon.

October 13: In a speech to the New Jersey Chamber of Commerce, U.S. President Reagan refers to the Canada-U.S. trade agreement as "a new economic constitution for North America," instigating more criticism by Canadians concerned over the possible erosion of Canadian sovereignty.

October 13-17: The twenty-eighth Commonwealth Heads of Government Meeting is held in Vancouver. Forty-seven countries, including Canada, present a united front proposing renewed sanctions against

South Africa. The United Kingdom refuses to assent to the use of sanctions.

October 19: "Black Monday" — stock markets around the world drop dramatically after a selling spree began in the New York market the previous Friday.

October 19: At the UN debate on the Brundtland report on international economic development and the environment (released in April), Environment Minister McMillan expresses support for an increase in development aid and for alleviating Third World debt as measures to contribute to mitigating environmental deterioration. He also recommends an international air law, continuing the path begun with the international ozone treaty signed in September.

October 21: The House of Commons gives final reading to another refugee bill (C-55), designed to reduce the time it takes for officials to process refugee claims. The government's refugee policy has been the subject of recent criticism by church leaders and refugee aid groups concerning the trend towards a more restrictive approach to immigration.

October 30: Minister of State for Immigration Gerald Weiner announces 1988 immigration levels at a maximum of 135,000 entries, an increase of 10,000 over the 1987 level. The proposed level, if reached, would equal Canada's actual immigration in 1981, and the policy is criticized as restrictive.

November 6: Ontario Premier Peterson announces that a preliminary GATT ruling (meant to remain confidential) has gone against provincial beer, wine and liquor pricing policies. The European Community (which brought the complaint before the GATT) and Canada may reach a negotiated settlement before a final ruling is made in February 1988.

November 15: In Washington, only the governments of Quebec and British Columbia make their proposal to replace the Canadian softwood lumber export tax with equivalent provincial measures. As a part of the settlement reached on December 30, 1986, Canada agreed that the tax would be replaced by provincial charges, but the U.S. International Trade

Commission and the American lumber lobby have still to approve the provincial proposals.

November 17: International Trade Minister Carney announces that a preliminary GATT ruling has found in favour of a U.S. complaint. The ruling claims that Canada's policy of not permitting unprocessed exports of West Coast salmon and herring violates international trade practice.

November 18: Canada and the United States sign a modified version of the 1978 Great Lakes Water Quality Agreement in order to promote cleaning up the shared waterway.

November 19: Bill C-22, providing stronger patent protection for new drugs, is given royal assent after the Senate abandons its long-standing rejection of the bill. The legislation was introduced in exchange for the (primarily multinational) industry's promise to spend more on research and development in Canada, and had been linked originally to the trade agreement with the United States.

November 22-27: Secretary of State for External Affairs Clark visits Central America to express Canada's support for the Central American peace plan designed to end the civil wars in Nicaragua, Guatemala and El Salvador. While in Nicaragua, he announces a $1-million aid package for that country but is criticized by aid workers in Nicaragua for refusing to pressure the United States to withdraw its support for the Contra rebels fighting the Nicaraguan regime.

November 24: On a complaint launched by the Ford Motor Company of Canada and General Motors of Canada, the Department of National Revenue imposes a 36 per cent preliminary anti-dumping duty against Hyundai Auto Canada.

November 26-27: The annual First Ministers' Conference on the economy is held in Toronto with discussions focusing on the Canada-U.S. trade agreement. For the first time, Newfoundland Premier Peckford declares his support for free trade with the United States. Interprovincial trade barriers and regional development policies are also discussed, in part as these relate to the North American trade agreement.

December 5: The *Ottawa Citizen* releases details of a draft Canada-U.S. Arctic cooperation treaty (dated October 19), which refers to the creation of an Arctic security regime. The draft document also contains provisions that would require future voyages of American icebreakers through Canadian-claimed waters to first acquire Canadian government consent. Secretary of State for External Affairs Clark argues that such a treaty will prevent a repeat of the *Polar Sea* incident of August 1985.

December 7: The legal text of the Canada-U.S. bilateral trade agreement is completed.

December 8-10: U.S. President Reagan and Soviet General Secretary Mikhail Gorbachev hold a summit in Washington culminating in the signing of the Intermediate-range Nuclear Forces Reduction Treaty that will eliminate ground-based Soviet and American intermediate-range missiles and provides for verification procedures. Secretary of State for External Affairs Clark expresses Canada's support for the treaty, especially for the inspection regime.

December 11: The final legal text of the Canada-U.S. bilateral trade agreement is tabled in the House of Commons.

December 14: The Canadian export tax on softwood lumber sales to the United States is removed.

December 14: The House of Commons Standing Committee on External Affairs and International Trade releases its report on the Canada-U.S. trade agreement after two weeks of public hearings across the country. The report recommends accepting the agreement but also argues that acceptance should be made conditional upon Canadian exemption from American trade legislation currently before the Congress.

December 15: As a response to the agricultural trade subsidy wars between the United States and the European Community, Prime Minister Mulroney announces a farm assistance program, with most of the expected cost of $2.8 billion (by 1991) going to grain growers in the Prairie provinces.

December 17: The first ministers meet in Ottawa for two hours to discuss the Canada-U.S. trade agreement. At the conclusion of the meeting, only the premiers of Ontario, Manitoba and Prince Edward Island are explicitly opposed to the agreement. The prime minister also announces the establishment of a body to study any adjustment implications of the trade pact.

December 22: The Group of Seven (G-7) countries release a statement of agreement that the fall of the U.S. dollar will be prevented through intervention to re-establish exchange rate stability. This action, taken in the wake of the decline in the American dollar, follows several weeks of discussions, but the G-7 does not set a fixed level of exchange.

Profile

The measures chosen to depict Canada's position among nations portray past developments in economic growth, international trade, the military environment, and development assistance. The figures also capture some of the turbulence of the 1980s by presenting comparable indicators for the period from 1982 to 1986 inclusive. All countries are rank ordered according to their 1986 levels and all calculations were performed after the U.S. dollar values were deflated using appropriate price indices of $1980 = 100$.

Growth for all the countries, except France, was lower in 1986, continuing the trend begun in 1985. However, Canada suffered relatively less than most, ranking second in 1986 with 3.09 per cent growth in gross domestic product (GDP). In conjunction with slower growth, by 1986 the selected countries converged around an average GDP growth rate of 2.43 per cent. By contrast, international trade measures indicate continuing significant differences among the countries, as well as Canada's relatively high standing with a consistent surplus in trade ($16,096 million in 1986), substantial growth in exports (4.51 per cent for 1986 over 1985) and a significant increase in its share of world exports (at 4.48 per cent in 1986). This stands in marked contrast to the United States, which continued to suffer from a worsening trade deficit, to have average growth in exports and to experience a decline in its share of world exports.

In the military field, while all countries had increased spending, with the United States continuing its leading position, relative to GDP there was very little change (with the United States reflecting only a marginal decline). However, Canada increased its effort consistently with respect to both gross expenditures ($6,297 million in 1986) and relative expenditure (at 2.3 per cent of GDP for 1986).

In the field of development assistance, there was relatively little change in the position and level of the individual countries' support. The United States continued to provide in gross dollars the most, but relative to GDP the least, and to decline marginally in the latter measure, as did the United Kingdom and, since 1984, Canada. In 1986 Canada's official development assistance equalled 0.48 per cent of GDP in spite of an increase in contributions to $1,427 million.

Figure 11-1
Economic Performance of Ten OECD Countries:
Percentage Change in Gross Domestic Product
from the Previous Year, 1982-86
(percentage calculated in constant 1980 $U.S.)

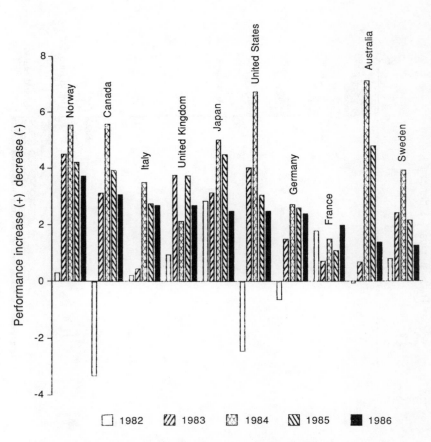

Source: OECD, *Main Economic Indicators October 1987* (Paris:OECD, 1987), 172.

Figure 11-2
Trade Balance of Ten OECD Countries, 1982-86
(billions of 1980 $U.S.)

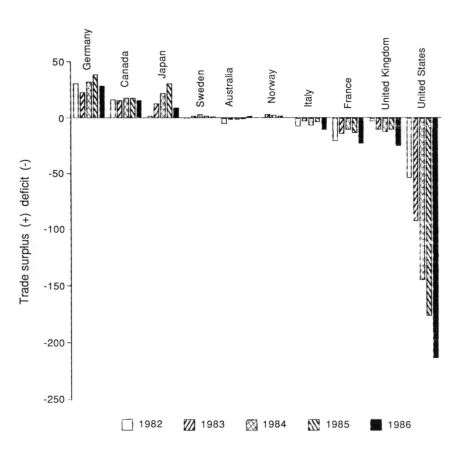

Sources: United Nations, International Monetary Fund, *International Financial Statistics December 1986* (Washington: IMF, 1987), 74-77; and Ibid (December 1987), 74-77.

Figure 11-3
Growth in Exports of Ten OECD Countries:
Percentage Change from the Previous Year, 1982-86
(percentage calculated in constant 1980 $U.S.)

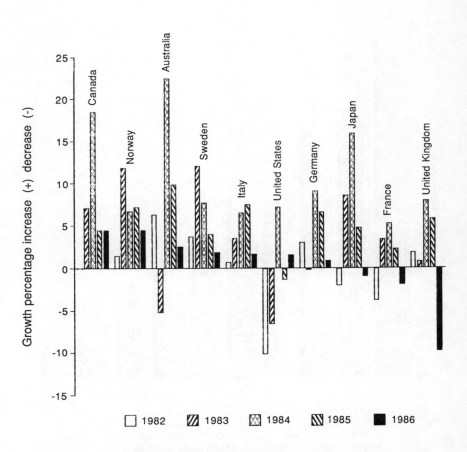

Sources: United Nations, International Monetary Fund, *International Financial Statistics December 1986* (Washington: IMF, 1987), 74-77; and Ibid (December 1987), 74-77.

Figure 11-4
Share of World Exports of Ten OECD Countries, 1982-86
(percentage)

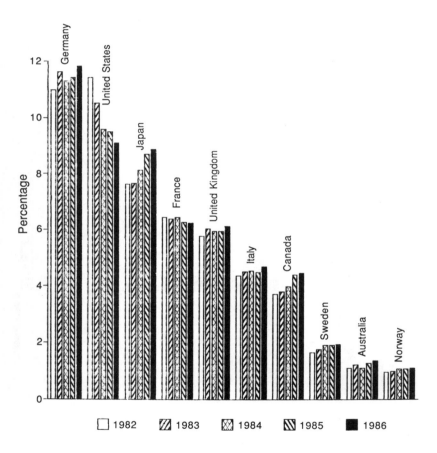

Sources: United Nations, International Monetary Fund, *International Financial Statistics December 1986* (Washington: IMF, 1987), 74-77; and Ibid (December 1987), 74-77.

Figure 11-5
Military Expenditures of Ten OECD Countries, 1982-86
(billions of 1980 $U.S.)

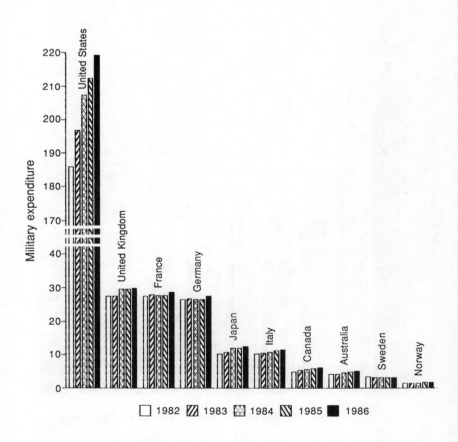

Source: SIPRI, "World Military Expenditure, in Constant Price Figures," *World Armaments and Disarmament, SIPRI Yearbook 1987* (New York: Oxford University Press, 1987), 168-72.

Figure 11-6
Relative Military Expenditures of Ten OECD Countries,
1982-86
(percentage of Gross Domestic Product)

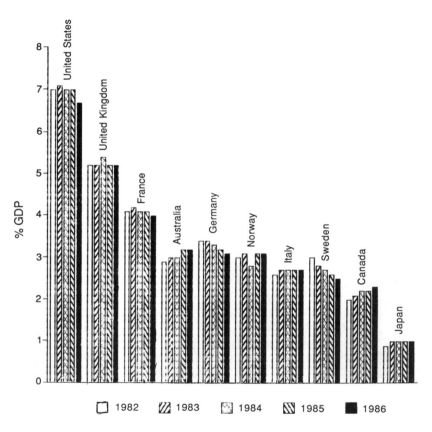

Source: SIPRI, "World Military Expenditure, in Constant Price Figures," *World Armaments and Disarmament, SIPRI Yearbook 1987* (New York: Oxford University Press, 1987), 173-77.

Figure 11-7
Public Expenditures for Development Assistance
of Ten OECD Countries, 1982-86
(billions of 1980 $U.S.)

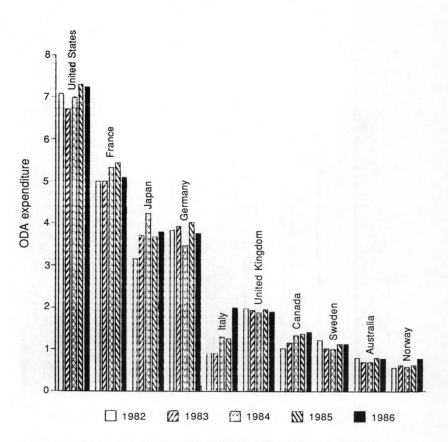

Source: OECD, Development Assistance Committee, DAC Chairman's Report for 1987,
"Development Cooperation — Draft Statistical Annex" (Paris: OECD, 1987), 76.

Figure 11-8
Relative Expenditures for Development Assistance
of Ten OECD Countries, 1982-86
(percentage of Gross Domestic Product)

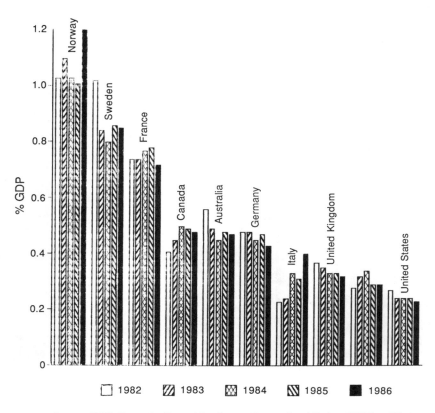

Sources: OECD, *Twenty-five Years of Development Co-operation, A Review, 1985 Report* (Paris: OECD, 1985), 335; *OECD, Development Co-operation, 1986 Report* (Paris: OECD, 1986), 52; and OECD, Development Assistance Committee, DAC Chairman's Report for 1987, "Development Co-operation — Draft" (Paris: OECD, 1987).

Notes and References

1: A World of Conflict

Notes

[1] For a more detailed review of *Competitiveness and Security: Directions for Canada's International Relations*, see Molot and Tomlin 1986.

[2] Fen Hampson discusses the White Paper andthe responses to it in chapter 3 of this volume.

[3] Statement by official of the Department of National Defence, Carleton University, June 1987.

[4] For a more detailed discussion of *Canada's International Relations*, see Tomlin and Molot 1987.

References

Government of Canada. 1985. Department of External Affairs (DEA). *Competitiveness and Security: Directions for Canada's International Relations*. Ottawa: Minister of Supply and Services.

_____ . 1986a. Special Joint Committee of the Senate and House of Commons on Canada's International Relations. *Independence and Internationalism*. Ottawa: Queen's Printer.

_____ . 1986b. DEA. *Canada's International Relations: Response of the Government of Canada to the Report of the Special Joint Committee of the Senate and House of Commons*. Ottawa: Minister of Supply and Services.

_____ . 1987a. House of Commons Standing Committee on External Affairs and International Trade. *For Whose Benefit? Canada's Official Development Assistance Policies and Programs*. Ottawa: Queen's Printer.

_____ . 1987b. Department of National Defence. *Challenge and Commitment: A Defence Policy for Canada*. Ottawa: Minister of

Supply and Services.

_____ . 1987c. Canadian International Development Agency. *Canadian International Development Assistance: To Benefit a Better World*. Ottawa: Minister of Supply and Services.

Molot, Maureen Appel, and Brian W. Tomlin. 1986. "The Conservative Agenda." In *Canada Among Nations 1985: The Conservative Agenda*, edited by Maureen Appel Molot and Brian W. Tomlin, 3-24. Toronto: James Lorimer.

Sokolsky, Joel J. 1986. "Arms Control Negotiations: Confronting the Paradoxes." In *Canada Among Nations 1985: The Conservative Agenda*, edited by Maureen Appel Molot and Brian W. Tomlin, 49-68. Toronto: James Lorimer.

Tomlin, Brian W., and Maureen Appel Molot. 1987. "Talking Trade: Perils of the North American Option." In *Canada Among Nations 1986: Talking Trade*, edited by Brian W. Tomlin and Maureen Appel Molot, 3-13. Toronto: James Lorimer.

von Riekhoff, Harald, and John Sigler. 1985. "The Trudeau Peace Initiative: The Politics of Reversing the Arms Race." In *Canada Among Nations 1984: A Time of Transition*, edited by Brian W. Tomlin and Maureen Appel Molot, 50-69. Toronto: James Lorimer.

2: Managing Global Conflict

Author's Note: The author gratefully acknowledges the assistance of Ms. Nancy E. Scott, research coordinator of the Centre for International Studies, in the preparation of this chapter.

Notes

[1] Cynics would do well to remember such summits as Munich, Camp David and Reykjavik, where vital international agreements with far-reaching consequences were created with rather little advance diplomatic preparation. While most summits, rather than creating agreements, confirm agreements reached beforehand at lower levels, the process of confirmation and hence legitimation is a vital task of international decision making, central to the focus of this article of the creation and management of international order.

[2] On the Yalta and San Francisco summits, see, respectively, Yergin 1978 and Holmes 1979.

[3] For a partial discussion, see the works on summit diplomacy by Plischke 1958 and Brams 1969.

[4] For a graphic description of the summit responses of the early 1970s by one who much preferred summitry to diplomatic instruments, see Kissinger 1979 and 1982.

References

Brams, Steven. 1969. "The Structure of Influence Relationships in the International System." In *International Politics and Foreign Policy*, edited by James Rosenau, 583-99. New York: Free Press.

de Menil, George, and Anthony Solomon. 1983. *Economic Summitry*. New York: Council on Foreign Relations.

Dewitt, David, and John Kirton. 1983. *Canada as a Principal Power*. Toronto: John Wiley.

Gotlieb, Allan. 1987. "Canada and Economic Summits: Power and Responsibility." *Bissell Paper 1*. Toronto: University of Toronto Centre for International Studies, December.

Gratton, Michel. 1987. *So, What Are the Boys Saying? An Inside Look at Brian Mulroney in Power*. Toronto: McGraw-Hill Ryerson.

Holmes, John. 1979. *The Shaping of Peace: Canada and the Search for World Order, 1943-1957*. Vol. 1, 229-95. Toronto: University of Toronto Press.

Holmes, John, and John Kirton. 1988. *Canada and the New Internationalism*. Toronto: Canadian Institute of International Affairs and Centre for International Studies.

Jockel, Joseph. 1985. "The Canada-United States Relationship after the Third Round: The Emergence of Semi-institutionized Management."*International Journal* 40 (Autumn): 689-715.

Kirton, John. 1985. "Managing Canadian Foreign Policy." In *Canada Among Nations 1984: A Time of Transition*, edited by Brian W. Tomlin and Maureen Appel Molot, 14-28. Toronto: James Lorimer.

_____ . 1987. "Shaping the Global Order: Canada and the Francophone and Commonwealth Summits of 1987." *Behind the Headlines* 44 (June).

Kissinger, Henry. 1979. *White House Years* . Toronto: Little, Brown.

_____ . 1982. *Years of Upheaval*. Toronto: Little, Brown.

Maclean's. 1987. April 13, p. 7.

Plischke, Elmer. 1958. *Summit Diplomacy: Personal Diplomacy of the*

President of the United States. College Park, Md.: Bureau of Govern
mental Research, College of Business and Public Administration
University of Maryland.

Putnam, Robert, and Nicholas Bayne. 1984. *Hanging Together: The
Seven-Power Summits*. Cambridge, Mass.: Harvard University Press

Swanson, Roger. 1975. *Canadian-American Summit Diplomacy, 1923-
1972: Selected Speeches and Documents*. Toronto: McClelland and
Stewart.

_____. 1978. "The Ford Interlude and the U.S.-Canadian Relation-
ship." *American Review of Canadian Studies* 8 (Spring): 3-17.

von Riekhoff, Harald, and John Sigler. 1985. "The Trudeau Peace
Initiative: The Politics of Reversing the Arms Race." In *Canada
Among Nations 1984: A Time of Transition*, edited by Brian W. Tomlin
and Maureen Appel Molot, 50-70. Toronto: James Lorimer.

Yergin, Daniel. 1978. *Shattered Peace: The Origins of the Cold War and
the National Security State*, 229-95. Boston: Houghton Mifflin.

3: Regional Conflict

Notes

1 The secretary-general's comprehensive blueprint for peace, first presented to the belligerents in the spring of 1985, calls for (a) an
immediate ceasefire; (b) a halt to attacks on civilians; (c) an end to the
use of chemical weapons; (d) freedom of navigation in the Persian
Gulf; (e) freedom from attack for ports, harbours and other shipping
facilities; (f) freedom of civil aviation; (g) an exchange of war
prisoners; (h) withdrawal to international boundaries; (i) a program of
reconstruction of both countries; (j) an even-handed arms embargo
against both Iran and Iraq; and (k) an ad hoc committee to consider the
causes of the war (*Christian Science Monitor* 1987a).

2 Essentially, the Arias plan called for a ceasefire in place in Nicaragua,
El Salvador and Guatemala by November 7; talks between the Sandinistas and the rebels; no foreign military aid to any Central American
insurgents; no use of one country's territory to support attacks on
another; general amnesty for political offenses throughout the region;
an end to emergency laws; the restoration of press freedoms and
political pluralism in Nicaragua; and the completion of all incumbent
governments' terms of office with maintenance of original presidential

elections schedules (*Newsweek* 1987c).
3 See also chapter 8 for a discussion of Canada's role in Central America and Southern Africa.
4 The Southern African region includes South Africa, Namibia and the nine member states of the Southern African Development Coordination Conference (SADCC) — Angola, Botswana, Lesotho, Malawi, Mozambique, Swaziland, Tanzania, Zambia and Zimbabwe.
5 The group met February 1-2, 1988, in Zambia to organize a monitoring system to ensure international compliance with the wide range of economic penalties imposed on South Africa.

References

Christian Science Monitor. 1987a. May 26.
_____. 1987b. "Mecca violence threatens to widen conflict" (Warren Richey). August 3.
_____. 1987c. "Iran set to pipe oil through Soviet Union" (Claude Van Englands). August 12.
_____. 1987d. "Iran inches toward UN negotiations to end Gulf war" (Marian Houk). August 28.
_____. 1987e. "UN Council undecided on where Iran stands" (Marian Houk). September 18.
_____. 1987f. "US lacks Gulf bases" (Warren Richey). November 10.
_____. 1987g. July 15.
_____. 1987h. June 2.
_____. 1987i. May 21.
_____. 1987j. "At deadline peace pact behind schedule but still has momentum." November 5.
_____. 1987k. "Ceasefire viewed skeptically in Salvador." November 12.
_____. 1987l. "ANC's Tambo tells blacks in South Africa to stop fighting each other" (Ned Temko). September 11.
_____. 1987m. "South Africa tightens fetters" (Ned Temko). September 11.
_____. 1987n. "Rising tensions in Angola heightens nation's reliance on Soviets" (Jill Jolliffe). May 4.
_____. 1987o. "The Case of the MIGs and Zimbabwe's new Soviet tilt" (Kurt Campbell). May 7.
Globe and Mail. 1987a. "Canada supports use of sanctions to help end

hostilities" (Martin Mittelstaedt). September 23.

_____ . 1987b. "Ottawa tight-lippped on military equipment being shipped" (Robert Matas). April 25.

_____ . 1987c. March 30.

_____ . 1987d. "Ortega says more aid vital if peace plan is to succeed." November 25.

_____ . 1987e. "PM to promote South African sanctions" (Michael Valpy). October 12.

_____ . 1987f. "Military aid to black Africa on Conference agenda" (Michael Valpy). October 13.

Mackenzie, Heather. 1987. "Britain's Assault on the Commonwealth." *Maclean's*, October 26.

Martin, Roger. 1987. "Regional Security on Southern Africa." *Survival*, September/October.

Newsweek. 1987a. "The Mines of August" (Russell Watson). August 24.

_____ . 1987b. "Settling in for a long stay" (Harry Anderson). September 28.

_____ . 1987c. "Should the Sandinistas be trusted?" (Nancy Cooper). August 31.

New York Times. 1987a. "Risky mission for UN leader" (Bernard Gwertzman). September 9.

_____ . 1987b. "Wright has talks with both parties in Nicaragua war." November 13.

_____ . 1987c. "Nicaragua accepts 4 Americans as mediators in the truce talks." November 16.

_____ . 1987d. "Contras release ceasefire plans." December 2.

_____ . 1987e. "Sandinistas and Contras open peace talks." December 4.

_____ . 1987f. "Hopes dim in talks on a Latin truce" (Lindsay Gruson). December 15.

_____ . 1987g. "Soviet is aiding Nicaragua in buildup, defector says." December 14.

_____ . 1987h. "How to prevent endless war in Central America" (William Leo Grande). December 18.

_____ . 1987i. "The Iran Contra Report." November 19.

Ottawa Citizen. 1987a. "Canadian troops could serve in Central America, Clark says." November 26.

_____ . 1987b. "Canada may open door to Contras." November 23.

Purcell, Susan Kaufman. 1987. "The Choice in Central America."

Foreign Affairs, Fall, 109-28.
South. 1988. "South Africa's commitments in Namibia and Angola are now costing it about $U.S. 1.5 million per day." January, p. 35.

4: Call to Arms

Author's Note: I would like to thank Ron Purver and John Toogood for their helpful comments on an earlier draft of this paper.

References

Arkin, William M., and Steve Shalhorn. 1987. "Subs might in fact reduce sovereignty." *Montreal Gazette*, June 22.

Bennett, Charles E. 1987. "Tough questions rise to the surface." *Globe and Mail*, October 29.

Blackburn, Derek. 1987. *Canadian Sovereignty, Security and Defence: A New Democratic Response to the Defence White Paper*. Ottawa.

Byers, R.B. 1987. "The 1987 Defence White Paper: An Analysis." *Canadian Defence Quarterly* 17 (2): 11-22 (Autumn).

Canadian Centre for Arms Control and Disarmament. 1987. *Arms Control Chronicle*, no. 21 (August).

Canadian Institute for International Peace and Security. 1987a. *A Guide to Canadian Policies on Arms Control, Disarmament, Defence and Conflict Resolution 1985-86*. Ottawa.

_____ . 1987b. Survey of International Peace and Security.

Canby, Steven L., and Jean Smith. 1987. "Canadian Defence Paper Shows Political Savy." *Armed Forces Journal International*, November, pp. 16-21.

Centre for Foreign Policy Studies, Dalhousie University. 1987. *Defence Newsletter* 6 (4).

Cox, David. 1986. *Trends in Continental Defence: A Canadian Perspective*. Occasional Papers, no. 2. Ottawa: Canadian Institute for International Peace and Security, December.

Creighton, Phyllis. 1987. "Cold War Heart." *Ploughshares Monitor* 8 (3): 4-6 (September).

Doran, Charles F. 1987. "Sovereignty Does Not Equal Security." *Peace and Security* 2 (3): 8-9 (Autumn).

Epstein, William. 1987. "Is Canada Joining the Arms Race?" *Ploughshares Monitor* 8 (3): 6-7 (September).

Financial Post. 1987. "Defence Special Report." November 16.

Frith, Douglas. 1987. "If It's a Legal Question..." *Peace Magazine* 3 (4): 24 (August/September).

Globe and Mail. 1987. "NATO chiefs to study nuclear alternatives." October 30.

Gough, Barry, and Robert Gravelle. 1987. "Canada wrong to abandon Norway." *Globe and Mail,* April 2.

Government of Canada. 1987a. Department of National Defence (DND). *Challenge and Commitment: A Defence Policy for Canada.* Ottawa.

_____. 1987b. DND. "Space Policy." Ottawa: September.

_____. 1987c. *House of Commons Debates.* Ottawa: June 5, pp. 6776-84.

Gwyn, Richard. 1987. "It's time to speak out on Arctic." *Toronto Star,* September 20.

Hunter, Iain. 1987. "Soviets ask for action on Arctic." *Ottawa Citizen,* October 7.

Johnson, Leonard. 1987. "White Paper an imitation of Pentagon publication." *Toronto Star,* July 2.

Kemp, Ian. 1987. "Challenge and Commitment: The Canadian Defence White Paper." *Armed Forces* 6 (10): 464-68 (October).

Leyton-Brown, David. 1987. "U.S. reaction to the defence White Paper." *International Perspectives,* July/August, pp. 3-5.

Macdonald, Donald S. 1971. *White Paper on Defence.* Ottawa, August.

Macdonald, Neil. 1987. "Armed Forces under fire for creaky support system, outdated thinking." *Ottawa Citizen,* October 28.

Martin, Lawrence. 1987. "Gorbachev offers deal on European troops." *Globe and Mail,* October 7.

Matas, Robert. 1987. "Tories' defence spending is lagging executives say." *Globe and Mail,* October 14.

New York Times. 1987a. December 9.

_____. 1987b. December 10.

Ottawa Citizen. 1987a. "Business council praises white paper on defence." October 14.

_____. 1987b. "The Norway Card" (editorial). February 17.

Pond, Elizabeth. 1987. "U.S. views Soviets' latest arms proposal." *Christian Science Monitor,* November 2.

Regehr, Ernie. 1987. "The White Paper, Star Wars and Nuclear Deterrence." *Ploughshares Monitor* 8 (3): 1-3 (September).

Sallot, Jeff. 1987a. "Canada ignores Arctic proposal under U.S. pressure,

Soviets say." *Globe and Mail*, October 6.

_____ . 1987b. "Fleet of A-subs likely to cost over $8 billion, study says." *Globe and Mail*, November 16.

Shalhorn, Steve. 1987. "The Subs Are Not for Arctic Sovereignty." *Peace Magazine* 3 (4): 28 (August/September).

Soviet Embassy (Ottawa). 1987. *News Release*, no. 161, December 11.

Stefanick, Tom. 1987. *Strategic Antisubmarine Warfare and Naval Strategy*. Lexington: Lexington Books.

Thatcher, Gary. 1987. "Both sides will get half a loaf at the summit." *Christian Science Monitor*, November 2.

Vancouver Sun. 1987. "Defence chief holds out jobs." June 8.

5: The World Economy

Author's Note: This chapter represents the author's views and not those of the government of Canada. The author acknowledges with special thanks the research assistance of Ian Currie.

Notes

[1] Much of this consultative activity was routine in the sense that it was scheduled: for example, the International Monetary Fund (IMF) mid-year meetings in April, the OECD ministerial meetings in May, the summit in Venice in June, and the IMF/World Bank meetings in September; others, such as the G-7 meeting leading to the Louvre Accord, were not.

[2] See, for example, the warning by the governor of the Board of Canada in his annual review, Ottawa, April 1987.

[3] Estimates suggest that productivity growth in the United States has been improving since 1982. See discussion, for example, in *OECD Economic Outlook* (Paris, December 1987).

[4] The president's State of the Union Address, January 27, 1987, was devoted almost entirely to this subject.

[5] This discussion does not take into consideration the development of the United States becoming the world's largest debtor nation in the course of the year. Policy problems arising from indebtedness continued to be focused on the developing countries; the U.S. situation will become, however, a major issue for the 1990s.

References

Bank of Canada. 1987. *Annual Review*. Ottawa.
Camps, M., and W. Diebold. 1983. *The New Multilateralism*. New York: Council on Foreign Relations.
Dornbusch, R. 1987. *Open Economy Macroeconomics: New Directions*. Cambridge, Mass.: National Bureau of Economic Research.
Financial Times (London). 1987. December 24, p. 2.
Globe and Mail. 1987. "Banks bet billions on U.S. Buck." January 13, p. B1.
Organization for Economic Cooperation and Development. 1987. *OECD Economic Outlook*. Paris.
Wall Street Journal. 1987. "Before the Fall." December 11, p. 1.

6: Weathering the Storm

Notes

[1] For a full discussion of the softwood lumber issue in Canada-U.S. relations, see Leyton-Brown 1987.
[2] Section 333(b) of H.R. 3 as passed by the House of Representatives (received in the Senate April 21, 1987) and Section 333(B) of H.R. 3 as passed by the Senate July 21, 1987.

References

Institute for Research on Public Policy (IRPP). 1987. "Roundtable on U.S. Trade Legislation." *International Economic Issues*, September.
Leyton-Brown, David. 1987. "The Political Economy of Canada-U.S. Relations." In *Canada Among Nations 1986: Talking Trade*, edited by Brian W. Tomlin and Maureen Appel Molot, 149-68. Toronto: James Lorimer.
Lipsey, R.G., and M.G. Smith. 1987. *Global Imbalances and U.S. Policy Responses: A Canadian Perspective*. Toronto: Canadian American Committee.
U.S. Congress. 1987. Trade and International Economic Policy Reform Act of 1987, Report of the Committee on Ways and Means. Washington, D.C.: U.S. Government Printing Office.
Wonnacott, Paul. 1987. "The Automotive Sector in the U.S.-Canadian

Free Trade Agreement." In *Assessing the Canada-U.S. Free Trade Agreement,* edited by M.G. Smith and F. Stone, 73-89. Halifax: Institute for Research on Public Policy.

7: The Environment and North-South Conflict

Notes

[1] The data used on energy consumption are for commercial energy. Non-commercial energy, for which little data exist, makes up a major part of developing-country energy use, especially in the poorest countries. Wood and charcoal compose two-thirds of the energy consumption in Africa and one-third in Asia. (Wood consumption is a major, multidimensional ecological problem in itself.)

References

World Bank. 1987. *World Development Report 1987.* New York: Oxford University Press.
World Commission on Environment and Development (WCED). 1987. *Our Common Future.* New York: Oxford University Press.

8: Canada and North-South Conflict

Notes

[1] See also the discussion on Canada and regional conflict in chapter 3.

References

Angus, William, and James Hathaway. 1987. "Ominous overkill in Ottawa's refugee bill." *Globe and Mail,* August 25.
Canadian International Development Agency (CIDA). 1986. *Annual Report 1985-86.* Ottawa: Supply and Services.
———. 1987. "External Affairs Minister Joe Clark and External Relations Minister Monique Landry Table Response to SCEAIT Report." Ottawa, news release, September 18.
Côté-Harper, Gisele, and John Courtney. 1987. *International Coopera-*

tion for the Development of Human Rights and Democratic Institutions. Report to the Right Honourable Joe Clark and the Honourable Monique Landry. Ottawa: External Affairs.

Culpeper, Roy. 1987. *Beyond Baker: The Maturing Debt Crisis*. North-South Institute Briefing Paper for the North-South Institute.

Environment Canada. 1987. "Canada's Perspective on Global Environment and Development." Notes for an address by the Honourable Thomas McMillan to the United Nations General Assembly, October 19. Ottawa, news release.

Ferretti, Janine. 1987a. "Submission to the Standing Committee on External Affairs and International Trade." Toronto: Pollution Probe Foundation.

_____ . 1987b. Letter to the Right Honourable Joe Clark on behalf of Pollution Probe. September 14.

Financial Post. 1987. "Aid Strategy Stresses Human Rights." November 9.

Gillies, David William. "Commerce over Conscience? Aid-Trade Links in Canada's Foreign Aid Programme." CDAS discussion paper, no. 48. Montreal: Centre of Developing Areas Studies, McGill University.

Globe and Mail. 1987a. "Power of new migrants law shocks critics." August 12; "Planned law on refugee smuggling would jail 'Samaritans,' critics say." August 12; "Churches not exempt from laws, Bouchard warns." August 13; "Tory MP breaks ranks criticizing refugee Bill." August 14; "Will change refugee bill, minister says." August 15.

_____ . 1987b. "Canada kills debts of seven countries at Quebec summit." September 3.

_____ . 1987c. "Lewis says UN must grab chance to take on environmental woes." October 19.

_____ . 1987d. "Clark wrestles with fine points of Central American politics." November 30; "Clark should condemn aggressive U.S. policy." December 5.

_____ . 1987e. "Latin Americans join forces on debt strategy." November 30.

_____ . 1987f. "Immigration changes rejected by minister." December 15.

Gordon, Sheldon. 1986. "Canada: an arms merchant for the Third World?" *Globe and Mail*, August 6.

Government of Canada. 1986. *Canada's International Relations: Re-*

sponse of the Government of Canada to the Report of the Special Committee of the Senate and the House of Commons. Ottawa: Supply and Services.

_____. 1987. *Canadian International Development Assistance: To Benefit a Better World.* Ottawa: Supply and Services.

Montreal Gazette. 1987. "Firms investing in Third World to get more aid from Ottawa." November 6.

Morrison, David R. 1985. "The Mulroney Government and the Third World." *Journal of Canadian Studies* 19 (4): 3-15.

North-South Institute. 1986. *Review '85 Outlook '86: Multilateralism Still the First Option for Canada.* Ottawa.

_____. 1987. *Review '86 Outlook '87: Canada's Foreign Policy: Testing Our Resolve.* Ottawa.

Ottawa Citizen. 1987a. "CIDA policies reflect UN concerns about world environmental issues." June 6.

_____. 1987b. "UN's swords-to-plowshares plan simplistic: Clark." August 25.

Redekop, Clarence G. 1985. "Commerce over Conscience: The Trudeau Government and South Africa, 1968-84." *Journal of Canadian Studies* 19 (4): 82-105.

Regehr, E., and E. Epps. 1987. "Silent Dealer at the Arms Bazaar." *Ploughshares Monitor* 8 (1): 21-25.

Runnalls, David. 1987. *Environment and Development: A Critical Stocktaking.* North-South Institute briefing paper. Ottawa.

SCEAIT (House of Commons of Canada. Standing Committee on External Affairs and International Trade). 1987. *For Whose Benefit?* Ottawa: Queen's Printer.

Schelew, Michael. 1987. "Misguided bills pose a threat to true refugees." *Globe and Mail*, August 13.

Schrecker, Ted. 1987. "Responding to Brundtland." Report prepared for the Canadian Environmental Advisory Council, September 1987. Peterborough.

Special Joint Committee of the Senate and the House of Commons on Canada's International Relations. 1986. *Independence and Internationalism.* Ottawa: Supply and Services.

SSCFA (Senate of Canada. Standing Senate Committee on Foreign Affairs). 1987. *Canada, the International Financial Institutions and the Debt Problem of Developing Countries.* Ottawa: Supply and Services.

Sunday Star (Toronto). 1987. "Joe Clark a hit on Latin trip." November

29.

Toronto Star. 1987a. "Tory refugee policy inspired by 'hysteria,' opposition says." August 13; "Refugee bill endangers lives, U.N. says." August 15; "Tories read public's mood on refugees." August 15.

_____. 1987b. "Finance ministers see no easy solution to Third World debt." September 29.

_____. 1987c. "South Africa on the agenda again at Commonwealth meeting in B.C." October 10.

_____. 1987d. "Now Senate set to fight new bill on refugees." November 14.

World Commission on Environment and Development (WCED). 1987. *Our Common Future*. New York: Oxford University Press.

9: Canada-U.S. Trade Disputes and the Free Trade Deal

Notes

[1] The agreement was signed by Prime Minister Mulroney and President Reagan on January 2, 1988.

References

Goar, Carol. 1987. "Ottawa's case for the disputes tribunal." *Toronto Star*, November 17.

Government of Canada. 1986. Department of External Affairs (DEA). *Canadian Trade Negotiations*. Ottawa: Minister of Supply and Services.

_____. 1987a. *House of Commons Debates*. Ottawa: Queen's Printer, March 16.

_____. 1987b. DEA. *Official Visit of President Ronald Reagan to Ottawa April 5-6, 1987: Background Papers*. Ottawa: Minister of Supply and Services.

_____. 1987c. DEA. *Canada-U.S. Free Trade Agreement: Elements of the Agreement*. Ottawa: Minister of Supply and Services.

Harrington, Denise. 1987. "Peterson sets conditions for backing trade pact." *Toronto Star*, August 11.

Laxer, James. 1987. "Free trade supporters dream in technicolour."

Toronto Star, November 3.

Leyton-Brown, David. 1987. "The Political Economy of Canada-U.S. Relations." In *Canada Among Nations 1986: Talking Trade*, edited by Brian W. Tomlin and Maureen Appel Molot, 149-68. Toronto: James Lorimer.

Rotstein, Abe. 1987. "From a business viewpoint, it's a bad deal." *Toronto Star*, November 15.

Wilkinson, Bruce. 1987. "Canada-U.S. Trade Relations and the Exercise of U.S. 'Fair Trade' Law with Respect to Canadian Potash." Paper for the Conference on Unequal Partners: A Comparison of Relations between Austria-F.R. of Germany and Canada-U.S.A., Carleton University, September 24-25.

10: Conflict over Common Property

Notes

[1] On the Canadian effort to save this particular herd's calving grounds from the possibility of U.S. oil exploration-related development, see Government of Canada 1987.

[2] On the common property theme, see, for example, Scott 1976.

[3] These and subsequently quoted comments, and much of the information in the following paragraphs, were obtained in personal interviews conducted in Washington, D.C., October 14-16, 1987.

[4] Personal interview, Washington, D.C., October 14, 1987.

[5] For the texts of the 1972 and 1978 agreements, see Canada and the United States, *Great Lakes Water Quality Agreement of 1972* (International Joint Commission, 1974), and Canada and the United States, *Great Lakes Water Quality Agreement of 1978* (International Joint Commission, 1978). For the background to the negotiations of the 1972 and 1978 agreements, see Munton 1980.

References

Ember, Lois. 1987. "Acid precipitation program head resigns." *Chemical and Engineering News*, October 12, p. 15.

Gotlieb, Allan. 1987. Letter to Honourable John Dingell, October 1.

Government of Canada. 1987. "Comments on Arctic Wildlife Refuge, Alaska, Coastal Plain Resource Assessment: Reports and Recommen-

ꓱꓥ0

dations to the Congress of the United States and Final Legislative Environmental Impact Statement." Ottawa, November.

Holsti, K.J. 1971. "Canada and the United States." In *Conflict in World Politics*, edited by K. Waltz and S. Spiegel, 375-96. Cambridge, Mass.: Winthrop.

International Joint Commission (IJC). 1986. *Third Biennial Report Under the Great Lakes Water Quality Agreement of 1978*. Ottawa and Washington.

Keating, Michael. 1987. "Environment Canada sees 25 more years of U.S. acid rain." *Globe and Mail*, January 8.

Keohane, Robert O., and Joseph S. Nye. 1977. *Power and Interdependence: World Politics in Transition*. Boston: Little, Brown.

McIntosh, Andrew. 1987. "Canada sends acid-rain expert to U.S. for analysis of Reagan's '87 program." *Globe and Mail*, January 8.

Munton, Don. 1980. "Great Lakes Water Quality: A Study in Environmental Politics and Diplomacy." In *Resources and the Environment: Policy Perspectives for Canada*, edited by O.P. Dwivedi, 153-78. Toronto: McClelland and Stewart.

————. 1980-81. "Dependence and Interdependence in Transboundary Environmental Relations." *International Journal* 36 (1): 139-84.

National Academy of Sciences (NAS), National Research Council (NRC). 1981. *Atmosphere-Biosphere Interactions: Toward a Better Understanding of the Ecological Consequences of Fossil Fuel Combustion*. Washington: National Academy Press.

National Acid Precipitation Assessment Program (NAPAP). 1987. *Interim Assessment: The Causes and Effects of Acidic Deposition*. 4 vols. Washington: U.S. Government Printing Office.

National Resources Defense Council (NRDC). 1987a. "NAPAP's Emission Reductions."

————. 1987b. "Statement of Richard E. Ayres," September 16.

Nye, Joseph. 1976. "Transnational Relations and Inter-state Conflicts: An Empirical Analysis." In *Canada and the United States: Transnational and Transgovernmental Relations*, edited by A.B. Fox et al., 367-402. New York: Columbia University Press.

O'Neill, Juliet. 1987. "EPA head opposed acid rain promise, Senate hearings told." *Globe and Mail*, April 23.

Royal Society of Canada (RSC) and National Research Council (NRC) of the United States. 1985. *The Great Lakes Water Quality Agreement: An Evolving Instrument for Ecosystem Management*. Washington:

National Academy Press.

Schindler, David W. 1987. Letter to Dr. J. Laurence Kulp, September 11.

Scott, Anthony. 1976. "Transfrontier Pollution and Institutional Choice." In *Studies in International Environmental Economics*, edited by Ingo Walter, 303-17. New York: John Wiley.

Yanarella, Ernest J., and Randal H. Ihara, eds. 1985. *The Acid Rain Debate: Scientific, Economic and Political Dimensions*. Boulder, Col.: Westview Press.

11: Chronology and Statistical Profile

References

Canadian News Facts. 1987. Toronto: Marpep Publishing.

Facts on File. 1987. New York: Facts on File.

Globe and Mail. 1987.

Government of Canada. 1987. Department of External Affairs (DEA). *Communiqué*.

_____ . 1987. DEA. "International Canada." *International Perspectives*, March/April, May/June, July/August, September/October.

_____ . 1987. Ministry of International Trade. *Communiqué*.

Organization for Economic Cooperation and Development (OECD). 1985. *Twenty-five Years of Development Cooperation, A Review, 1985 Report*. Paris: OECD.

_____ . 1986. *Development Cooperation, 1986 Report*. Paris: OECD.

_____ . 1987. *Main Economic Indicators October 1987*. Paris: OECD.

_____ . 1987. Development Assistance Committee. DAC Chairman's Report for 1987. "Development Cooperation — Draft." Paris: OECD.

SIPRI. 1987. *World Armaments and Disarmament, SIPRI Yearbook 1987*. New York: Oxford University Press.

United Nations. International Monetary Fund. *International Financial Statistics, Monthly*. Washington: IMF, various issues.